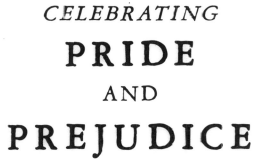

CELEBRATING

PRIDE

AND

PREJUDICE

CELEBRATING

PRIDE

AND

PREJUDICE

•

200 Years of

JANE AUSTEN'S
Masterpiece

•

Susannah Fullerton

Voyageur Press

For my daughter—
my dearest, loveliest Elinor Elizabeth

First published in 2013 by Voyageur Press, an imprint of MBI Publishing Company,
400 First Avenue North, Suite 300, Minneapolis, MN 55401 USA

© 2013 Voyageur Press
Text © 2012 Susannah Fullerton
Illustrations © as on page 240
First published in the United Kingdom in 2012 by Frances Lincoln Limited
under the title *Happily Ever After: Celebrating Jane Austen's Pride and Prejudice*

The information in this book is true and complete to the best of our knowledge. All recommendations are made without any guarantee
on the part of the author or Publisher, who also disclaims any liability incurred in connection with the use of this data or specific details.

We recognize, further, that some words, model names, and designations mentioned herein are the property of the trademark holder.
We use them for identification purposes only. This is not an official publication.

Voyageur Press titles are also available at discounts in bulk quantity for industrial or sales-promotional use. For details write to
Special Sales Manager at MBI Publishing Company, 400 First Avenue North, Suite 300, Minneapolis, MN 55401 USA.

To find out more about our books, visit us online at www.voyageurpress.com.

ISBN-13: 978-0-7603-4436-1

Library of Congress Cataloging-in-Publication Data

Fullerton, Susannah, 1960-
  [Happily ever after]
  Celebrating Pride and prejudice : 200 years of Jane Austen's masterpiece / Susannah Fullerton.
      p. cm.
  "First published in the United Kingdom in 2012 by Frances Lincoln Limited under the title Happily ever after:
celebrating Jane Austen's Pride and prejudice"--T.p. verso.
  Summary: "As Pride and Prejudice turns 200, discover all the details of its creation, groundbreaking style, and tremendous,
important legacy in this loving commemoration of Jane Austen's brilliant work"-- Provided by publisher.
  ISBN 978-0-7603-4436-1 (hardback)
  1. Austen, Jane, 1775-1817. Pride and prejudice. 2. Austen, Jane, 1775-1817--Appreciation. 3. Austen, Jane, 1775-1817--Influence. I. Title.
  PR4034.P73H37 2013
  823'.7--dc23
                        2012029595

Cover design: Connie Gabbert
Cover illustration: artplay/Shutterstock.com
Front flap: Lady Catherine and her nephews (illustration by Hugh Thomson)
Back flap: Elizabeth reads Mr Darcy's letter (illustration by Hugh Thomson)
Back cover: Portrait of Jane Austen, courtesy of the Library of Congress

Contents

Steel engraving of Jane Austen, made from the sketch by her sister Cassandra as a frontispiece to *A Memoir of Jane Austen* by James Edward Austen-Leigh.

Introduction

On 27 January 1813 a parcel was delivered to a cottage in a small Hampshire village. The woman who opened it was middle-aged, unmarried and unknown. When she removed the parcel's wrapper and took out the three books inside, she did not find her own name on the title page. Yet she still must have hugged those books with pride and delight, for the story was hers, and after seventeen years in the making it was at long last leaving the intimate family circle and was going out to make its own way in the world. The tale she had dreamed up of a young woman called Elizabeth Bennet, spirited, clever and a little prejudiced, who encounters and falls in love with a proud man called Mr Darcy, was about to face the test of readership. How would it fare? Would her story about 'pride' and 'prejudice', of mistaken first impressions, sink without a trace? Or would it be read and enjoyed? And would it endure, and be read and enjoyed for generations to come?

When Jane Austen unwrapped those first copies of her *Pride and Prejudice*, she did not know the answers to those questions; nor could she have guessed that, with the publication of her novel, the world of literature was to be changed for ever. For like Pandora's Box, that parcel released something unforgettable upon the world; but instead of the ills and problems, the real pride and real prejudice unleashed by Pandora, *Pride and Prejudice* let loose a new and lasting source of joy, a 'heart-felt delight' for the many who read it around the world.

And today, after 200 years, it has become a truth universally acknowledged that no novel is more loved. Again and again, in so many countries, it tops the polls as favourite novel of all time. It is read and studied in China; there are Jane Austen societies appreciating it around the world, even in non-English-speaking countries such as Argentina and Italy; university theses are written about it in Sweden; in India it is Bollywood-ized; in England fans take *Pride and Prejudice* coach tours; and Facebook has an International *Pride and Prejudice* Day. Brides and grooms wear Elizabeth and Darcy costumes at their weddings, cars carry 'I Love Darcy' bumper stickers and children read the novel in comic-book form. Newspapers around the world regularly use the phrases 'pride and prejudice' and 'truth universally acknowledged' to grab attention in headlines, and Jane Austen is estimated to have given 'more pleasure to more men in bed than any other woman ever', a status she has achieved mainly through the pages of *Pride and Prejudice*. It has been voted 'the most romantic novel' ever written, while Mr Darcy is considered the 'most romantic hero ever' and millions of women swooned over Colin Firth in the role.

Why does this novel have such universal appeal? Dickens's *Bleak House* is a great book, and so is Charlotte Bronte's *Jane Eyre*, yet neither novel has generated nearly the same amount of devotion, merchandise or offshoots. *Celebrating Pride and Prejudice* discusses the particular brand of magic that is *Pride and Prejudice*. Looking at its commencement, its characters, its comedy and its charm, it celebrates 200 years of this great novel.

It examines the famous first sentence and considers why it is so brilliant; it explains the novel's irony and style, its wit, its brilliant structuring, its revolutionary new techniques. It shows where *Pride and Prejudice* broke new ground and where it remains unsurpassed. How does Jane Austen make Elizabeth Bennet so utterly charming and why does she outclass every other heroine? And how has Jane Austen made Mr Darcy so devastatingly attractive even when he is behaving almost as badly as Mr Collins, a character every reader loves to hate? The book answers these questions, and discusses all the other characters in whom we delight and find a never-ending source of humour.

It tells the story of the 'birth' of *Pride and Prejudice* and how Jane Austen had to cope with rejection and discouragement when it was first written. It describes the responses of her family, friends and earliest general public, and how the twentieth century saw the novel shoot to record fame. It describes the illustrations – satisfactory and otherwise – and the covers for the many editions of the book, and shows what admirers from all walks of life have had to say about *Pride and Prejudice* and the pleasure it has given them.

It will tell the story of how the book has travelled the world in translation – and the specific difficulties it poses to anyone brave enough to try to translate it into German, Hungarian, Tamil or Hebrew – and how it has morphed into strange and interesting new forms: prequels and sequels, modernizations, 'what-if' versions, mystery novels where the crime is solved by Mr and Mrs Darcy, and even pornography. I will show how it has been used (and abused) by film directors – from the first Hollywood movie of 1940 to *Lost in Austen*, which depicted jeans-clad Lizzy Bennet talking on her mobile on a London bus, to a planned film which depicts her slaying zombies – as well as theatrical adaptations and musicals.

Manufacturers have also jumped on to the *Pride and Prejudice* bandwagon, responding to an apparently insatiable public appetite with *Pride and Prejudice* board games, *Pride and Prejudice* dating manuals and the like. From clubs and scholarly articles to twenty-first-century developments such as blogs and chat rooms, this book shows the many ways in which the world continues to express its enthusiasm for the novel.

All really good stories have a happy ending, and so does this one. On that historic day in 1813 Jane Austen opened her parcel and gave her *Pride and Prejudice* to the world. For 200 years it has lived 'happily ever after' and, fortunately, shows every sign of continuing to do so.

The table at which *First Impressions* was changed into *Pride and Prejudice*
at Chawton cottage.

'My Own Darling Child'

THE WRITING OF *PRIDE AND PREJUDICE*

'My stile of writing is very different from yours.'

Two days after receiving her copy of *Pride and Prejudice* Jane Austen wrote to her sister Cassandra. 'I want to tell you that I have got my own darling Child from London,' she announced with delight. She had always noted with sympathy and interest the difficult pregnancies and long, painful childbirths her female relations had undergone, but the 'gestation' of her 'own darling Child' went on far longer than any pregnancy and was infinitely less hopeful of a positive outcome than anything her sisters-in-law endured.

According to Cassandra Austen (who recorded these dates after her sister's death and whose memory could be faulty), Jane Austen sat down at a table in Steventon parsonage, dipped her quill in the inkpot and began to write the novel that would become *Pride and Prejudice* some time in October 1796. She had already written the hilarious stories of her juvenilia, the tale of a ruthless adulteress called Lady Susan and an epistolary novel known then as *Elinor and Marianne*. Just like her heroine Elizabeth Bennet, Jane was twenty years old, the age for attending balls at the Basingstoke Assembly rooms, the age for falling in love. Very recently she had danced and flirted with Tom Lefroy, a handsome young Irishman, and she had fallen in love with him. The excitement of her first love affair, the energy it roused in her, surged into her story. The quill flew across the pages and by August of the following year her story was complete.

It would be one of the world's great literary 'finds' if the original manuscript of her novel were to be unearthed in a trunk in a dusty attic somewhere. But such a treasure is most unlikely ever to be discovered and all we can do is speculate about that lost version. We do not even know if, like *Elinor and Marianne* (the early version of *Sense and Sensibility*), it was epistolary in style: that is, totally written in the form of letters sent between the various characters, as were Fanny Burney's *Evelina* and Samuel Richardson's *Clarissa*. Letters are certainly important in the text (forty-four are either given in full or referred to) and much vital information is conveyed via correspondence by Mr Darcy, Miss Bingley, Mr Collins, Lydia, Mrs Gardiner and others. Yet the structure and sparkling dialogue of the finished novel more closely resemble a play than an epistolary novel. Jane Austen had been discussing Fielding's *Tom Jones* with Tom Lefroy and that energetic novel was not epistolary. It seems more probable that this novel was her first attempt at writing in the more standard novel form.

She called her book *First Impressions*. It was a good title, giving an important clue to the central concerns of her story. We see Elizabeth's first mistaken impressions of Mr Darcy and Mr Wickham, so significant within the novel, as are her first correct impressions of Mr Collins and Lady Catherine, and that first vital impression of Pemberley, which goes so far in correcting her wrong first impression of its owner. Elizabeth's father succumbed to first impressions by marrying Miss Gardiner, and lived to regret it. Elizabeth has to learn about pre-judging and judging, to discriminate between initial impressions and true recognition.

Having written her book, Jane Austen was naturally keen to see it published. Her family, who were her first readers, all enjoyed it and her father decided to help. Late in 1797 he wrote to a London publisher, Thomas Cadell, bringing this new literary work to his attention. Mr Austen may have been an excellent clergyman, but he was no salesman. 'I have in my possession a Manuscript Novel, comprised in 3 Vols. About the length of Miss Burney's Evelina,' he informed Cadell. He went on to enquire about the expense of publication and offered to send the manuscript to London. Not a word about the wit and charm of his daughter's novel, no enticing hints as to its plot. It's hardly surprising that Mr Cadell scrawled across the top of the letter 'declined by Return of Post'.

But Jane Austen did not put her manuscript in a bottom drawer and forget about it. Over the following years she joked in letters about family friend Martha Lloyd wanting to learn it by heart so that she could get it published herself. A young niece recalled talk between the sisters of 'Jane and Elizabeth', accompanied by laughter over the characters. It was typical of Jane Austen to take refuge from her disappointment in laughter, but she didn't forget her book and clearly hoped that she might succeed in getting it printed. One wonders if Mr Austen tried other publishers for his daughter.

She continued to tinker with her novel. Probably in the early 1800s she changed its title. A Mrs Margaret Holford had got in before her and published her *First Impressions*, so something new had to be found. Fanny Burney's novel *Cecilia* uses the phrase 'PRIDE AND PREJUDICE' (printed in capitals and used three times in a single paragraph towards the closing pages of the book) and Jane Austen was very familiar with that novel. The phrase also occurs in Goldsmith's *History of England* (in which the pride and prejudice of Henry VIII are spoken of), in Oliver Goldsmith's poem 'Retaliation'

Thomas Cadell turned down the chance to publish *First Impressions*.

and in Dr Johnson's *The Idler* of 1758. Lord Chesterfield used the phrase in his letters to his son, and the poet Charles Churchill used it in his satire 'Independence'. The phrase that is so unutterably familiar today was also deeply familiar to Jane Austen when she took it up and employed it as her title. Probably around 1803 and 1804, she made other changes to her work, possibly very considerable ones.

And then *Pride and Prejudice* lay dormant, known only to select friends and relations. Jane Austen left Steventon, moved to Bath and then to Southampton. Her father died, family money decreased, her single status grew ever more confirmed. She started a novel called *The Watsons* but gave it up for unknown reasons. No one wanted her writing. While a publisher purchased her *Susan* (later published as *Northanger Abbey*) in 1803, he did not actually publish it. To a hopeful author, this was all most discouraging. Jane Austen could so easily have shrugged her shoulders and resigned herself to giving up writing. Posterity can be eternally grateful that she did not.

In 1809, Jane Austen, her mother and her sister moved to the village of Chawton. Back in her beloved Hampshire countryside, established in a house for which no rent was due, with more time to herself and a more settled routine, Jane Austen returned to literary composition. Perhaps Cadell's rejection of *First Impressions* still rankled, for it was not that novel she picked up. *Elinor and Marianne* had been drastically revised, probably in 1797, and was now *Sense and Sensibility*. This was sent to Thomas Egerton of Whitehall some time around late 1810 and was accepted on condition that it was published at the author's own expense. Although sure that it would cost all her very modest savings, Jane Austen was encouraged to make the attempt. In 1811, at long last, she saw one of her works in print when '*Sense and Sensibility* by a Lady' appeared in the October of that year.

Finally, there was encouragement! Her book sold well, was read and liked by the royal family, received good reviews, and brought its author a profit of £140. Had its reception been a poor one, the world would probably never have known *Pride and Prejudice*, as Jane Austen would have had no money with which to risk a second unsuccessful attempt. The comedy of Mr and Mrs John Dashwood, the passion of Marianne and the moving constancy of Elinor opened the way for the arrival of Elizabeth and Darcy, the Bennets and Mr Collins on the literary scene.

Jane Austen immediately began the 'alterations and contractions' mentioned by Cassandra Austen. In her own words, she 'lop't and crop't' *Pride and Prejudice*, fine-tuning during 1812, making whatever changes she thought necessary to her book. At the end of that November she had good news: 'P. & P. is sold. – Egerton gives £110 for it. – I would rather have had £150, but we could not both be pleased.' Egerton, who unlike Cadell had seen the potential of her book, had secured the copyright for himself, and wasted no time in publishing it.

It had been a long journey for this story of 'first impressions' and the novel had come perilously close to remaining an unknown masterpiece. Started by a young woman of twenty who was in love and full of hopes, published when its author was thirty-seven and rather more subdued by life's experiences, *Pride and Prejudice* began its journey as a published novel, making its own 'first impression' upon the world.

Most lovers of the novel would adore to own a first edition (recently a first edition of *Pride and Prejudice* sold at auction for £140,000), but it must be admitted that from a purely aesthetic point of view, it is not a particularly attractive book. The first customers found themselves in possession of three volumes, each containing about 300 pages of print and each bound in a fairly basic pasteboard. Wealthy customers could then take their copies, which looked rather like plain-covered versions of the paperbacks of today, to their own bookbinder. There the volumes could be covered in gilt and leather, perhaps with a family crest embossed on the spine (this is why grand private libraries have so many beautiful rows of matched volumes: each book was taken to the same binder and encased in colours chosen by the owner). The three volumes of *Pride and Prejudice* cost 18 shillings in total, a reasonable price for the day.

It is not known exactly how many copies resulted from that first printing – probably about 1,000 to 1,500. They were not 'perfect' copies, as there were a few misprints. Jane Austen, looking it over critically, could see that a few changes and additions were needed. The occasional 'said he' etc. would make the dialogue a little clearer, she felt, while the middle volume was shorter than those on either side of it (it was under 300 pages) and ought perhaps to be lengthened.

The *Morning Chronicle* advertised the novel's appearance on 28 January 1813, but word of mouth seems to have been more effective than the printed advertisement. Within nine months of publication, a second edition came out. This was re-set by a different firm, and apparently Jane Austen was given no opportunity to fix the mistakes of the first. In fact, new mistakes were introduced. Then in 1817 Egerton produced a third edition. Again Jane Austen was not involved with corrections, as by that time she had moved on to another publisher, John Murray of London. No new English edition came out in the next fifteen years.

The 1830s saw the first American edition, oddly titled *Elizabeth Bennet; or Pride and Prejudice*, and Richard Bentley, an English publisher, brought out a complete set of all Jane Austen's completed novels. For the rest of the 1800s there was a new edition of *Pride and Prejudice* about every two or three years. The first properly annotated and scholarly edition of the book was that produced by R.W. Chapman in 1923. Recent decades have seen *Pride and Prejudice* published in 'chick lit'-style versions, as tie-in versions to various movies, as new scholarly editions, and as cheap paperbacks and de-luxe hardback copies. Hardly a year goes by without a fresh publication and re-packaging of *Pride and Prejudice*.

Mr Collins, horrified at the idea of reading a novel (illustration by Hugh Thomson).

'A Very Superior Work'

REACTIONS TO *PRIDE AND PREJUDICE*

'Her feelings as she read were scarcely to be defined.'

There was very little to envy in the life of Miss Mary Benn. She was a poor spinster, financially dependent on her brother John, Rector of Faringdon in Hampshire, who had thirteen children to support. Miss Benn lived in a very humble abode at Chawton and was forced to rely on the charity of her neighbours. There was no health insurance to protect her when she fell ill, only the ever present fear of 'going on the parish' if help failed in other quarters. Mrs Austen and her daughters were all generous to this poor woman struggling to maintain her gentility. Mary Benn died at the age of forty-six, in 1816.

But in one respect, Miss Benn is to be envied. On the night of 29 January 1813, she was invited to Chawton cottage for supper. After the ladies had eaten, Jane Austen announced that a new three-volume novel had arrived from London that very day. *Pride and Prejudice* was duly brought out and Jane Austen began to read. Miss Benn had no idea that the woman reading her this delightful new story was its author. Jane Austen watched her listener closely for her reactions: 'we set fairly at it & read half the 1st vol. to her . . . and I believe it passed with her unsuspected. — She was amused, poor soul! *that* she could not help you know,' Jane reported to Cassandra, who was not there.

A few nights later Miss Benn visited again, and this time Mrs Austen did the reading. Jane Austen was not so pleased to pass the precious volumes to her mother, whose reading style was not all it should be: 'I beleive [*sic*] something must be attributed to my Mother's too rapid way of getting on – and tho' she perfectly understands the Characters herself, she cannot speak as they ought.' Jane Austen knew how her own characters ought to sound and it was frustrating to listen as her mother misrepresented them.

Within a few weeks Miss Benn had heard the whole wonderful story and was thus the most fortunate woman in England: the very first member of the public to read *Pride and Prejudice*. She died without ever knowing who had written it, and that she had heard it from the lips of its author.

The novel began to have its first encounters with the general public, to meet with pleasure or disdain as the case may be. Jane Austen criticized it – 'The work is rather too light & bright & sparkling; – it wants shade; – it wants to be stretched out here & there with a long Chapter – of sense if it could be had, if not of solemn specious nonsense . . . or anything that would form a contrast & bring the reader with increased delight to the playfulness & Epigrammatism of the general stile [*sic*].' – but both she and her sister knew that she did not mean it. But though she was entitled laughingly to criticize her book, no one else had that right. When one acquaintance was uncomplimentary, Jane wrote to give her sister permission to 'Kill poor Mrs Sclater if you like it.'

Her immediate family were the very first readers of the novel, but as they had been familiar with it in all its many stages of development Jane Austen did not record their opinions upon the book's publication (Cassandra's copy of her sister's novel is now at the University of Texas). But she was highly pleased when nephews and nieces loved it: 'Fanny's praise is very gratifying . . . Her liking Darcy and Elizth [*sic*] is enough. She might hate all the others, if she would.' Later, with *Mansfield Park* and *Emma* she noted down what relatives and even neighbours thought of both those novels, and it is clear from those comments that *Pride and Prejudice* was generally the family favourite. Her nephew James Edward (later his aunt's biographer) was inspired into verse on the subject of her novels:

And though Mr Collins so grateful for all
Will Lady de Burgh [*sic*] his dear patroness call,
'Tis to your ingenuity really he owed
His living, his wife, and his humble abode.

Pride and Prejudice got three reviews. The first appeared in *The British Critic* in February 1813, and must have pleased the author. The reviewer praised the story for being well told, the characters for being 'remarkably well drawn and supported', and the writing as spirited and vigorous. Altogether the book was 'far superior to almost all the publications of the kind which have lately come before us.' There was more of the same from the *Critical Review* a month later. Elizabeth Bennet was given high praise and was likened to Shakespeare's Beatrice, and it was stated that the novel did 'great credit to the sense and sensibility of the author-ess'. And a month after that the *New Review* gave a brief synopsis, included quotes from the novel and once again gave approval of the new work. With these public encomiums, the book was off to a good start.

Soon it was the season's fashionable novel. It is not known exactly when the Prince Regent read it – Jane Austen never admired him, but before long he was a devoted fan of hers, keeping all her novels in each of his residences. The aristocracy enjoyed it: the Countess of Morley, Lady Robert Kerr in Scotland and the Earl of Dudley all had words of praise for the new book. Politicians appreciated its wit and naturalness: Charles James Fox told a friend that 'nothing had come out for years to be compared with *Pride and Prejudice*', while family friend Warren Hastings 'quite delighted' Jane Austen with his admiration of her heroine.

Other writers soon realized they had been eclipsed, even if not all were prepared to admit it. Sir Walter Scott knew there was something remarkable in its pages which he could not manage himself: Jane Austen had 'a talent for describing the involvements and feelings and characters of ordinary life, which is to me the most wonderful I ever met with,' he wrote after her untimely death. He wore his copy out with rereadings and felt that the novel had 'a finishing-off in some of her scenes that is really quite above everybody'. Mary Russell Mitford was slow to admit its worth and was rare in her dislike of the heroine ('it is impossible not to feel in every line of *Pride and Prejudice*, in every word of "Elizabeth", the entire want of taste which could produce so pert, so unworldly a heroine as the beloved of such a man as Darcy'), but later called *Pride and Prejudice* 'a precious gem'. Up in Scotland, novelist Susan Ferrier complained that her ears were dinned with talk of it. Sheridan could hardly stop talking of it either and at a dinner party told his partner at table, a Miss Sheriff, to 'buy it immediately for it was one of the cleverest things he ever read'. Lord Byron's future wife, Annabella Milbanke, also loved it: 'I have finished the Novel called Pride and Prejudice, which I think a very superior work . . . I really think it is the <u>most probable</u> fiction I have ever read . . . I wish much to know who is the author.' For Miss Milbanke, whose forthcoming marriage would prove to be truly incredible, the greatest merit of the novel was its probability and believability – 'no drownings, no conflagrations, nor runaway horses, nor lapdogs and parrots'. It is tempting to speculate that her comments were passed on to Jane Austen, with the result that a lapdog (the wonderful Pug) was inserted into *Mansfield Park*, but there is no evidence for this and the women mixed in very different circles. Lady Caroline Lamb, busy writing her own novel, thought of calling it 'Principle and Passion', 'since the fashion is to call every thing in the manner of Pride and prejudice, sense and sensibility' – Jane Austen had, it seemed, become a trend-setter.

Not every reader was an admirer. Lady Davy found it merely a 'picture of vulgar minds and manners'; Madame de Staël (a popular European novelist of the day) agreed and also declared the novel '*vulgaire*'; and several clergymen were up-set by Mr Collins being such a ludicrous example of their profession. Wordsworth, never noted for his sense of humour, felt the style lacked 'the pervading light of imagination'. The Austens' neighbour Miss Augusta Bramston, of Oakley Hall, thought *Pride and Prejudice* 'downright nonsense', as Jane Austen was amused to record. But most readers were delighted, were quickly entranced by both hero and heroine, laughed at Mr Bennet and recommended the book to their friends.

Henry Austen loved to hear his sister's novel praised. The trouble was that he couldn't resist boasting of his connection with its author, and so he let out the secret. Jane Austen's own name never appeared on the front of any of her novels published during her lifetime, but before long word spread that these clever books had been written by a Miss Jane Austen, a clergyman's daughter in Hampshire. One fan, the same woman who had listened to Sheridan's recommendation of *Pride and Prejudice* at a dinner table, began to travel regularly through Chawton in

Annabella Milbanke (portrait by George Hayter) read and loved *Pride and Prejudice* before her marriage to Lord Byron.

hope of meeting the author. She even longed for a carriage breakdown near the cottage, which would increase her chances. She became the first ardent 'Janeite' – that is, one of the first readers to feel that her life had been enriched and changed by reading *Pride and Prejudice*.

Jane Austen died in 1817, with four of her novels published – *Sense and Sensibility*, *Pride and Prejudice*, *Mansfield Park* and *Emma* – and her death resulted in some articles in the newspapers and her writings receiving a little more public attention. It was the death notice in the *Courier* on 22 July 1817 that was the first written acknowledgment of Jane Austen as an author, but her gravestone in Winchester Cathedral made no mention of her works. Her books had sold only a few thousand copies (nothing in comparison with the works of Scott, Fanny Burney and Byron) and in the year of her death unsold copies of *Pride and Prejudice* were remaindered. In 1832 publisher Richard Bentley bought the copyright from Cassandra and Henry Austen, and republished it, but while it sold steadily, it was never a brilliant seller and was outsold by *Emma*.

But there was always a small band of admirers. In 1818 a critic writing for *Blackwood's* praised her 'exhaustless invention' and predicted that Jane Austen would one day be one of the most popular of all English novelists, a claim which struck many as absurd at the time. In 1821 Richard Whately, Archbishop of Dublin, wrote a laudatory piece in the *Quarterly Review*, stating that Jane Austen was brilliant at showing how women think. Another reviewer was convinced that *Pride and Prejudice* must have been written by a man, as no woman could possibly have penned anything so clever. Fanny Burney's half-sister Sarah Harriet Burney seems to have preferred *Pride and Prejudice* to anything written by her own sister, and boasted of having read it nine times. In 1843 historian and poet Thomas Babington Macaulay placed Jane Austen next to Shakespeare in greatness. Oscar Wilde rejoiced in her style, Beatrix Potter identified with her heroines, R.L. Stevenson fell deeply in love with Elizabeth Bennet, Charles Darwin's son Sir Francis Darwin longed 'for a new Miss Austen more than for a new symphony of Beethoven or a play of Shakespeare', Tennyson was a staunch fan and travelled to see places connected with the novels, and Trollope reread her novels often. Coleridge's daughter Sara thought Jane Austen 'faultless'. But these readers were the enlightened few. In the years between her death and the publication of the first proper biography in 1870 six essays were written about Jane Austen, which hardly indicates an overwhelming public interest in the woman or her books.

Throughout much of the Victorian era *Pride and Prejudice* was a neglected novel. Copyright expired in 1841 and there was no sudden rush of eager publishers. The Bentley editions were still available and trickled out of the shops, but George Henry Lewes complained that people had forgotten Jane Austen (he and George Eliot read *Pride and Prejudice* aloud to each other with delight). Most Victorian readers preferred Dickens, Thackeray, Trollope, Gaskell, or the Brontës. In the eyes of the Victorians the cool irony of the novel lacked femininity, and they disapproved of a woman who could make a clergyman a figure of fun. They found Jane Austen too restrained, and also had trouble placing her

The Story-Teller magazine, in which Kipling's story *The Janeites* first appeared.

socially – what was her class? Fanny Knight, Jane Austen's much-loved niece, grew rather ashamed of her 'ungenteel' Aunt Jane, demonstrating an unpleasant pride and prejudice very typical of Victorian society. Some readers spoke publicly of their dislike. Mark Twain announced: 'Every time I read *Pride and Prejudice* I want to dig Jane Austen up and beat her over the skull with her own shin-bone' – yet his remarks make it obvious that, in spite of his professed dislike, the great American humorist was continually drawn back to the novel. Emerson was puzzled by Jane Austen's being read at all, as he was convinced that she portrayed a 'pinched and narrow' existence in 'sterile' and conventional novels.

But in 1870 *Pride and Prejudice* emerged from its doldrums. James Edward Austen-Leigh, son of Jane Austen's eldest brother James, wrote *A Memoir of Jane Austen*. The biography, which painted a saintly, domestic, idealized portrait of his 'dear Aunt Jane', was immensely popular and sold out rapidly. Quickly Bentley reissued all the novels and in 1882 brought out a special Collector's Edition. By 1892 *Pride and Prejudice* was easy to find in the bookshops, whether in de-luxe bindings, illustrated with pretty pictures or as a cheap edition for sixpence. Fanny Knight's son, Lord Brabourne, published Jane Austen's letters in 1884, the term 'Janeite' was coined as a name for her fans,[1] and Jane Austen made it into the *Dictionary of National Biography* of 1885. By the end of the century, *Pride and Prejudice* was familiar to a huge number of readers and its author was rapidly attaining 'divine Jane' status. Readers felt she belonged to them and that Mr Collins, Lady Catherine and the Bennets were personal friends.

By the time the First World War broke out, Jane Austen had come to represent essential Englishness, the idea of England that was being fought for in the trenches. Amidst the mud and death of those trenches *Pride and Prejudice* was extremely

---

1 The term 'Janeite' was coined in 1894 by literary scholar George Saintsbury, when he wrote a preface for a new edition of *Pride and Prejudice*. Jane Austen scholar Claudia Johnson has defined the term as a 'self-consciously idolatrous enthusiasm for "Jane" and every detail relative to her'.

popular.[2] Siegfried Sassoon owned early editions which soothed him between battles, and future editor of the Oxford editions of the novels R.W. Chapman had his comforting copies with him there too. Rudyard Kipling's 1924 story 'The Janeites' depicts soldiers building solidarity and even saving each other's lives because of a shared love of Jane Austen, and clinging to her humour in a ghastly situation by naming a particularly noisy gun 'Lady Catherine de Bugg'. *Pride and Prejudice* was therapeutic for wounded soldiers and was placed on a 'Fever-Chart' for those sick in hospitals. Elizabeth Bennet and Mr Collins brought humour and comfort to those damaged by the horrors of war.

The rest of the twentieth century saw a steady rise in appreciation of *Pride and Prejudice* and Jane Austen's other works. Little books of quotations, sequels, Christmas compilations, articles in newspapers and magazines, quiz books and then films all began to appear. Of course there were also many more biographies, as people tried to discover the woman behind the books. The occasional detractor remained – D.H. Lawrence found her 'mean' and representative of all he disliked about England – but it was starting to be seen as sacrilegious to abuse such 'classic' works. Academic criticism began to appear (the first serious study of Jane Austen's fiction was published in 1939, Mary Lascelles' *Jane Austen and Her Art*) and soon a torrent of books about all aspects of Jane Austen's art was available, with *Pride and Prejudice* remaining one of the most often discussed of the six novels. Today a reader keen to know more about the novel can turn to *Teaching Pride and Prejudice, Notes on Pride and Prejudice, Understanding Pride and Prejudice, Pride and Prejudice: Notes and Analysis, Mr Collins Considered* and *In the Pride of the Moment*, or can find aspects of *Pride and Prejudice* analysed and discussed in *Jane Austen and the War of Ideas, Jane Austen: Irony as Defense and Discovery, Jane*

---

2 There is a claim that *Pride and Prejudice* was the most-read novel in the trenches in the First World War, but there seems to be no reliable proof of this claim. However, it was certainly one of the most popular war-time reads and huge numbers of copies were stained, blasted to bits, and adored on the battlegrounds.

Austen: Feminism and Fiction, Jane Austen: Women, Politics and the Novel, Jane Austen and Discourses of Feminism, Jane Austen: Real and Imagined Worlds, Jane Austen and Representations of Regency England, Jane Austen's Achievement and a host of other academic studies.

Readers invariably react to *Pride and Prejudice* by wanting to discuss its charms, its characters and its ideas. Writing a book about it is simply another way of doing just that. And today the *Pride and Prejudice* 'dialogue' seems endless – characters, professions, settings, clothing, food, crimes, the Navy, amusements, politics, finance, poetry, marriage, psychoanalysis, music and education are covered in the great range of *Jane Austen and . . .* books, connecting *Pride and Prejudice* to a fascinating range of topics (these include, among others, *Jane Austen and . . . the Clergy, the French Revolution, the Navy, the Estate, British History, Crime, Food, Marriage, Sigmund Freud, the Enlightenment, the Romantic Poets, Dancing, Mozart, Politics, Leisure, Money, Fashion, the Theatre, Her Heroines, Her Gentlemen, England, Love, Education, Religion, the Body,* and even *Jane Austen and the Masturbating Girl*).

In his novel *Changing Places* David Lodge creates a character called Professor Morris Zapp, who has named his children Elizabeth and Darcy in honour of his favourite novel. In his university career Professor Zapp aims to say 'absolutely everything that could possibly be said' about Jane Austen and her novels 'from every conceivable angle, historical, biographical, rhetorical, mythical, Freudian, Jungian, existentialist, Marxist, structuralist, Christian-allegorical, ethical, exponential, linguistic, phenomenological, archetypal' until there is nothing left to say. But as a great novel such as *Pride and Prejudice* will always be saying something new to different generations and to different cultures and nationalities, such a task is a hopeless one. The dialogue goes on, as we shall see in the last chapter.

And the number of those who delight in *Pride and Prejudice*, for its love story, its humour, its irony, its characters, continues to grow in the twenty-first century as it did in the twentieth. Katherine Mansfield knew that Jane Austen outclassed her and cherished the idea that she, along with all other readers, was 'the secret friend of the author'. Virginia Woolf loved her novels, as did her friend E.M. Forster. Henry James learned from *Pride and Prejudice*, while George Gissing recommended it for self-improvement. Authors have always been appreciative, and the list of twentieth and twenty-first century literary admirers is long: Martin Amis, W.H. Auden, John Bayley, Arnold Bennett, Elizabeth Bowen, Barbara Cartland, Bruce Chatwin, G.K. Chesterton ('The Novels of Jane Austen/Are the ones to get lost in'), Ivy Compton-Burnett, Lord David Cecil, Margaret Drabble, John Fowles, E.M. Forster, Stella Gibbons, Georgette Heyer, Reginald Hill, P.D. James, Elizabeth Jenkins, Paul Jennings, Elizabeth Jolley, F.R. Leavis, Harper Lee, W. Somerset Maugham (who placed *Pride and Prejudice* in his *The Ten Greatest Novels of the World*), Ian McEwan (who called *Atonement* his Jane Austen novel), Vladimir Nabokov, Sir Harold Nicolson, Patrick O'Brian (who described Jane Austen as his mentor and who happily exchanged one of his own manuscripts for a first edition), William Plomer, Ezra Pound, J.B. Priestley, Barbara Pym, J.K. Rowling, Dorothy L. Sayers, Freya Stark, Colm Toibin, Fay Weldon, Rebecca West, Leonard Woolf – these are just some of the writers who have loved *Pride and Prejudice*.

Winston Churchill reading *Pride and Prejudice* during the Second World War (cartoon by Martin Searle).

But there are many admirers among other professions too. Sir Winston Churchill, repeating the therapeutic uses of the novel discovered in the First World War, dealt with the stresses of the Second World War by turning to the 'calm lives' of the Bennets and Bingleys. Other political fans include Edward Heath, Mary Robinson, Harold Macmillan, Aung Sun Suu Kyi and John Major. Prince Charles, athlete Sebastian Coe, singers Dame Joan Sutherland and Olivia Newton-John, chef Gordon Ramsay, adventurer Ranulph Fiennes, cartoonist Murray Ball, comedian Terry Jones, composer Peter Sculthorpe, actors Keira Knightley and Emma Thompson – all are famous people whose lives have been enriched by *Pride and Prejudice*. (Readers who may not be famous but who love the novel are of course impossible to list or count.)

For A.A. Milne *Pride and Prejudice* was a test of character. He smuggled a copy out of his school library (which did not permit the borrowing of books) so that he could read it in the dormitory at night. For the rest of his life it remained a standard by which

A.A. Milne, who judged people by their response to *Pride and Prejudice* and who wrote a stage play, *Miss Elizabeth Bennet*.

he judged others. If you did not love *Pride and Prejudice* there was something fundamentally wrong with you, according to Milne. He is not the only person to think so. For many of us, *Pride and Prejudice* is a way of sorting the sheep from the goats. There are those excellent people who love the novel and who return to it again and again and again; and then there are the others . . . who, really, can only be pitied!

27

The famous opening sentence of Jane Austen's *Pride and Prejudice*.

'A Truth Universally Acknowledged'

THE FAMOUS FIRST SENTENCE

It is a universally acknowledged truth that 'It is a truth universally acknowledged, that a single man in possession of a good fortune, must be in want of a wife' is one of the most famous opening sentences in all of English literature. It's up there with 'It was the best of times, it was the worst of times', 'Call me Ishmael' and 'Last night I dreamed I went to Manderley again', and it is more used and abused than any of those other opening lines by the world's media and by other novelists. Why are the twenty-three words that make up this crisp sentence so famous? And what is Jane Austen telling her readers in this remarkable opening to *Pride and Prejudice*?

'It is a truth . . .', she begins, in a phrase beloved by eighteenth-century moralists. David Hume and Adam Smith often talked about 'truth' in their philosophical discourses and Dr Johnson was fond of the word too. It is a weighty word – a 'truth' is a serious matter. Yet immediately this categorical declaration, which admits of no doubt ('It *is* a *truth*' – my emphasis), invites a question. Who says it is a truth, and how can one define a truth anyway? To a believer God is a 'truth', but to an atheist he is merely a fiction. One man's conviction can be another person's lie. And so the many questions raised by this sentence start to accumulate.

Will this be a novel with great adherence to 'truth', the reader may wonder, or will truths be perpetually questioned throughout? Any reader already acquainted with Jane Austen's other novels will know that she pursues the truth of a character or a speech with accuracy and with devotion. Sir Walter Scott praised the 'truth of the description' in her writing, while in Kipling's story 'The Janeites' a character hits the nail on the head when he asserts 'Some 'ow Jane put it down all so naked it made you ashamed.' So will this novel contain page after page of 'naked truth', pure and unadorned? The word 'truth' prepares the reader for a whole vocabulary throughout the book connected with convictions, decisions, judgments and opinions. It also alerts the reader as to who is speaking of 'truth' – one character can so easily make black appear white (such as Wickham) or vice versa.

Then Jane Austen goes on to state that this 'truth' is 'universally acknowledged', and instantly the reader is put on the alert. David Hume wrote of 'truths' being 'universally allowed', but Jane Austen's phrase is hugely loaded. Is she being satirical? Is what is 'universally acknowledged' only what was universally acknowledged in 1813, or for all time? How does one decide on, or substantiate, 'universal' acknowledgment? Will the 'universal' acknowledgment in the book prove to be universal only among the inhabitants of Meryton, a small English country town (which is the case, later, when the reader is informed that Wickham is 'universally liked'); or only applicable to England; or to the early nineteenth century and no other era; or to women and not to men? In the novel that follows, there are many references to 'everyone' and 'the neighbourhood' ('neighbourhood' is used far more in this novel than in any of Jane Austen's other works), and Jane Austen reveals how inaccurate 'everyone' can often be. Everyone knows Mr Bingley will bring 'twelve ladies and seven gentlemen' to the ball, yet he actually brings two ladies and two other men; while the Bennets are 'the luckiest family *in the world*' (my emphasis) when Mr Bingley gets engaged to Jane. To what particular 'world' or 'universe' do these truths belong? And if 'universal truths' really exist (birth/ death/taxes?), who decides they are 'universal' rather than merely local?

As the sentence continues, the words 'a single man' tell us that this book will concern courtship and marriage. The 'single man' is given no name. Will there be more than one, we might wonder? Of course, in the pages of *Pride and Prejudice* we actually get several – Mr Bingley, Mr Darcy, Mr Collins and Mr Wickham – and they will all be relieved of their single status by the end of the book. Single men, in Jane Austen's England, were valuable commodities. The country was at

The sound of a carriage drew them to the window . . . (illustration by Robert Ball).

war with France (as all those red-coated regimental men in the story remind us) and war often removed young men from the social milieu, or used them up as cannon fodder. Captain Denny is safely quartered in Meryton for the purposes of the story, but he could well be sent to the Peninsula and be killed in action there; thousands of young men were. And the Empire needed men too – Australia, Canada, New Zealand and India had to be stocked with soldiers, engineers and administrators (Jane Austen's uncle, Tysoe Saul Hancock, chose to remove to India in order to make money). Such men often went out to foreign lands alone, without wives, or they simply could not afford to marry and support a wife and children in England. Statistically, more baby boys died during pregnancy and childbirth. No wonder the news that a single man had arrived sent the 'surrounding families' of a neighbourhood into spasms of excitement.

To add to the excitement, the 'single man' of the opening line is 'in possession of a good fortune'. Again, questions must arise. How good is a 'good fortune'? In *Sense and Sensibility* Marianne and Elinor discuss their idea of a 'competence' and find that what is a competence for one is riches for the other. So is a man of 'good fortune' fabulously rich (like Mr Darcy) or just scraping along (like Wickham)? Most of Jane Austen's opening sentences mention money and here the phrase about 'good fortune' stresses the power of the material world, turning men into marketable commodities like stocks and shares, and hints that any marriages made in the novel could well have economic motives. That will certainly be the case for Charlotte Lucas, who takes Mr Collins solely for his house, money and

Bingley and Jane get engaged (illustration by H.M. Brock).

financial prospects; and even Elizabeth comes to see Mr Darcy's true worth when she first sees his 'beautiful grounds' at Pemberley and realizes that to be mistress of such an estate 'would be something'.

And what exactly is 'fortune'? Its original meaning was a 'chance happening' or 'luck' (and it is this sense of luck that is intended when Elizabeth says 'We must not all expect Jane's good fortune'), but implications of financial fortune had been altering the word's original meaning up to the time when Jane Austen used the word. That the single man is 'of good fortune' is clearly more important than that he is 'of good character', or agreeable, or handsome, or simply a jolly nice chap. Has moral worth been replaced by a bank balance in the world of this opening sentence? And how much, after all, simply comes down to luck? It is very lucky that Mr Bingley happens to rent near Meryton. And how much can 'luck' be manipulated? Charlotte 'accidentally' meets Mr Collins in the lane, thus giving him the opportunity to propose, but even she had hardly dared to hope 'that so much love and eloquence awaited her there'.

The opening sentence pauses at this point, with its second comma. It's like the three acts of a play, building up to the high drama of the finale. What are we going to learn, that is so universally acknowledged, about this single man? What is going to happen to him? What is he going to need?

Of course, we are told that he 'must be in want of a wife'. But who says he must? The single man himself? Darcy certainly does not feel he must have a wife when he appears on the scene. Or the mothers of single daughters, or single women (five Bennet sisters, Charlotte, Miss King, Miss Darcy, Miss De Bourgh, etc.)? Why must he want a wife? To help him spend all that lovely money, or for sex, or to look decorative in his drawing room? Does 'must' mean 'need', as in something he can hardly live without, or does it reflect only a passing whim or thought? 'Must' is a strong word, so will the bachelor be given any choice in picking this wife he *must* have, or will she be thrust at him by society/family/ mothers who have decided he cannot be allowed to live without her? When Mrs Bennet invites Mr Bingley to go shooting on Mr Bennet's estate whenever he likes, perhaps Mr Bingley, and not a dead bird, is the game bag she really has in mind.

The words 'in want of' imply that the single man is lacking something. He has a good fortune, but still needs a wife. When he gets her, will she be another 'possession' for him? Mary Wollstonecraft in 1792 complained bitterly that men regarded women as ignorant chattels (and a stupid chattel is exactly what Lydia will be as Mrs Wickham). Men's lives were full of work, government, law and order, incomes and responsibilities, but young women were trained to net purses, not to fill them. They rarely travelled (Mrs Bennet is very hazy as to the exact location of Newcastle), and they were expected to be sweet, pretty and compliant. But is this what the single men of this novel are really in want of? Mr Bingley maybe, but Wickham and Darcy are both attracted to a girl who speaks her mind and reads books and thinks for herself, while Mr Collins is ready to take absolutely anyone who is ready to have him. Or is it that the single girls of the novel are desperately 'in want of' husbands, instead of the other way round? Single women certainly needed to be married far more than single men did – female economic survival usually depended on it. When Mr Bennet dies, his daughters will have no roof over their heads, while Charlotte Lucas will be totally dependent on the generosity (or lack thereof) of her brothers. Marriage had to be an obsession for such penurious women.

This emphatic opening sentence proves initially to be untrue: the single men are *not* 'universally' in want of wives in the early chapters of *Pride and Prejudice*. Mr Darcy is sick of being chased by desperate single women (such as Miss Bingley), while Wickham is lacking any fortune, good or otherwise, to permit him to marry. However, the opening sentence is something Mrs Bennet would agree with wholeheartedly, as would her friends Lady Lucas and Mrs Long. But does the heroine, Elizabeth, think it true and that therefore every unmarried man is fair game and her 'rightful property', or Jane, or the sensible Gardiners?

The concept of those first lines of the novel is definitely not universally true in the world of the novel, let alone anywhere else. Yet by the last sentence of the novel, which speaks of 'uniting' a single man and a single woman, the opening sentence has become true, a 'truth universally acknowledged' among most of the characters in the book (Lady Catherine still strongly disagrees that her nephew is 'in want of' Elizabeth Bennet), because all the single men have been shown, at some point or another, to be 'in want of' wives, whether their motives are sexual, financial or amorous.

By all these implications the reader is made to realize that this opening sentence cannot be taken at face value (and therefore the entire novel probably can't either). This book, it appears from its opening, will be about the difference between truths and falsehoods, between what is real and what only appears to be real. Jane Austen is making her reader puzzle, read beyond the words and think from these very first lines; she wrote not for 'dull elves'[1] but for people of perception and intelligence, and she puts those abilities in her audience instantly to work before she zooms in on the particular single men and the women they will marry. She is also showing her reader very plainly that this novel will challenge judgments and cut down to size sweeping generalizations. It will create ironies, and it will achieve multiple purposes. This is also a sentence that sparkles with zest and energy – surely it was there in the original *First Impressions* written by a bubbling young Jane Austen. It makes the reader question the 'pride' and 'prejudice' of the title (are they 'universal truths' too?); it mocks the 'universal truths' of the pompous moralists. It is a brilliant scene and mood setter, and it prepares us for the irony, comedy and sheer fun we are about to enjoy by reading *Pride and Prejudice*.

---

1 'I do not write for such dull elves/As have not a great deal of ingenuity themselves', Letter from Jane Austen to her sister Cassandra, 29 January 1813.

The first sentence has become 'universal' property. No other sentence from literature has been paid the compliment of such excessive imitation. All, or parts of it (especially the 'truth universally acknowledged' bit), have been endlessly quoted in newspapers, on radio and television, by advertisers and on the web. 'It is a truth universally acknowledged that a single woman in possession of two teenagers must be in want of a steady paycheck and employer-sponsored health insurance', or 'that an individual in possession of a humanities PhD must be want of a job', or 'that no two Goths will agree on a definition of anything even remotely connected with their subculture', or that if you are not in possession of a particular beauty product your face will wrinkle horribly and men will avoid you like the plague. Jane Austen's words crop up again and again, often in the most unlikely places. They crop up in conventional print, but are also printed on merchandise, with cushion covers, T-shirts, teapots, and even skateboards adorned with *Pride and Prejudice*'s famous first sentence.

Other novelists love it too. Writers of sequels, prequels, continuations and adaptations of *Pride and Prejudice* rarely leave it out. 'It is a truth universally acknowledged that a single girl in possession of her right mind must be in want of a decent man,' begins *Me and Mr Darcy* by Alexandra Potter, while Shannon Hale's *Austenland* opens with 'It is a truth universally acknowledged that a thirty-something woman in possession of a satisfying career and fabulous hairdo must be in want of very little.' Zombies infiltrate the opening words of *Pride and Prejudice and Zombies* with 'It is a truth universally acknowledged that a zombie in possession of brains must be in want of more brains,' and Belinda Roberts' *Prawn and Prejudice* opens with 'It is a truth, universally acknowledged, that a single man in possession of a yacht must be in want of a female crew.' Azar Nafisi's excellent *Reading Lolita in Tehran* begins with 'It is a truth universally acknowledged that a Muslim man, regardless of his fortune, must be in want of a nine-year-old virgin wife,' and in other novels it is a 'truth universally acknowledged' that 'a single girl in search of mysteries must occasionally be in want of a big damn knife' (*In the Darkness of Dreams: A Dirk and Steele Mystery*), 'a single man in possession of a good fortune must be queer' (*A Ned Rorem Reader*) and 'eventually everything turns up on the

ABOVE, OPPOSITE ABOVE AND BELOW Embroidered cushion cover, car licence plate and teapot featuring the famous opening sentence of *Pride and Prejudice*.

internet' (*Ether: Seven Stories and a Novella*).
The list goes on and on and on.

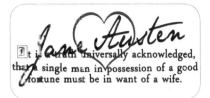

It's not only fiction writers who have hijacked the phrase. 'It is a truth universally acknowledged' 'that a single neuron in possession of a good potential must be in want of a network' (*The Neurobiology of Neural Networks*), 'that a single tract of text in possession of charms attractive to potential readers must be in want of good binding and secure lodging' (*Evolutionary Bioinformatics*) and 'that taxonomy is in a parlous state' (*The New Taxonomy*). Articles about economics, about product placement and marketing, about politics, about travel – in fact, about almost anything – have found a use for Jane Austen's famous words.

And it is seldom omitted from films that are in any way connected with *Pride and Prejudice*. 'All mothers think that any single guy with big bucks must be shopping for a wife' is what it becomes in *Bride and Prejudice*. *Bridget Jones's Diary* turns it into 'It is a truth universally acknowledged that when one part of your life starts going OK, another falls spectacularly to pieces'; *Lost in Austen* has 'It is a truth universally acknowledged that we are all longing to escape'; while the Mormon version just uses the horribly bland 'It is a truth universally acknowledged that a girl of a certain age, and in a certain situation of life, must be in want of a husband.'

A Danish author has written a whole book on the subject – *On the First Sentence of 'Pride and Prejudice': A Critical Discussion of the Theory and Practice of Literary Interpretation* (1979), which is currently out of print. *Pride and Prejudice*'s first twenty-three words have been twisted, changed, used irrelevantly and irreverently, and abused to fit the intentions of other writers who hope its glitter might rub off on them, or that using it will somehow evoke the wit, conciseness and sheer genius of one of the most famous openings ever penned.

Letters are a notable feature of Jane Austen's style in *Pride and Prejudice*. Here Elizabeth reads a letter from her aunt, Mrs Gardiner (illustration byPhilip Gough).

'Bright and Sparkling'

THE STYLE OF *PRIDE AND PREJUDICE*

'yet I think it is well expressed'

When Jane Austen began to write her novels, she did something extremely innovative in the world of English literature. She incorporated into her narration a new technique, which has become known as 'Free Indirect Discourse' (FID), and this soon became a hallmark of her writing style. She was not the very first author to use it – Goethe did so in Germany, where it was known as *'erlebte Rede'* – but she was the first English novelist to use FID consistently and extensively. Other writers followed – Flaubert, Kafka, James Joyce and Virginia Woolf were each, in their time, praised for the modernity of their styles using this narrative technique – but it was Jane Austen who led the way and showed them all how it was done.

FID (also known as 'free indirect speech') can only be used in a novel written with third-person narration. The device involves the blending of that third-person narration with first-person narrative speech. However, this is done without any speech marks, and there are no 'he saids' and 'she saids' prefacing or following the words. So while we do not actually get direct words spoken by a character, we still get the way that character thinks or speaks. FID enables us to share a character's viewpoint, join him or her emotionally and share joys and fears, prejudices and amusement. It permits us to learn things that perhaps that character would never dare to speak aloud. FID focuses on interiority of character, and provides a more intimate view. It examines inner consciousness in a way not always permitted by more standard forms of narration. It seriously alters the way in which a story is told, and is a sophisticated device that demands skill in the handling. Jane Austen loved FID because it allowed her great scope for irony: she could mingle omniscient narration with the thoughts of a character, thus highlighting any ironic contrast between the two.

Much of the FID in *Pride and Prejudice* is connected with Elizabeth Bennet. After Darcy has first proposed to her, we get an example of the technique in action:

> Her astonishment, as she reflected on what had passed, was increased by every review of it. That she should receive an offer of marriage from Mr Darcy! that he should have been in love with her for so many months! so much in love as to wish to marry her in spite of all the objections which had made him prevent his friend's marrying her sister, and which must appear at least with equal force in his own case, was almost incredible!

The first sentence is standard third-person narration. The narrator tells us that Elizabeth is astonished and thinks over what has just happened. But with the next sentence, we move inside her mind. There are no speech marks – she is not talking to herself or to anyone else – but the perspective is Elizabeth's, filtered through the third-person narration. It is not the narrator who is shocked by the proposal – everything written so far by the narrator has led up to this climax – but it is Elizabeth who is stunned by surprise. The thoughts of his being 'so much in love' are 'almost incredible' to her, but not to the narrator who created them. FID here takes us seamlessly into Lizzy's mind, before seamlessly moving back out again to allow usual narrative to continue.

Mr Collins is very often the target of ironic FID within the novel as, for example, when he speaks of Lady Catherine:

> Mr Collins was eloquent in her praise. The subject elevated him to more than usual solemnity of manner, and with a most important aspect he protested that he had never in his life witnessed such behaviour in a person of rank – such affability and condescension as he had himself experienced

from Lady Catherine. She had been graciously pleased to approve of both the discourses, which he had already had the honour of preaching before her. She had also asked him twice to dine at Rosings, and had sent for him only the Saturday before to make up her pool of quadrille in the evening. Lady Catherine was reckoned proud by many people he knew, but he had never seen anything but affability in her. She had always spoken to him as she would to any other gentlemen; she made not the smallest objection to his joining in the society of the neighbourhood, nor to his leaving his parish occasionally for a week or two to visit his relations. She had even condescended to advise him to marry as soon as he could, provided he choose with discretion.

Clearly here it is not the narrator who thinks Lady Catherine has 'such affability and condescension', or that her notice and advice is such an honour. This is Mr Collins's view only. Lady Catherine's exact degree of graciousness and condescension is therefore immediately made the subject of doubt to the reader, even if it is unquestioned by Mr Collins.

Jane Austen is especially adept at handling FID for group voices in *Pride and Prejudice*. In these cases, she does not move into the mind of just one speaker, but rather into the mind of the neighbourhood in general, or into the spiteful thoughts of old women in Meryton. When Mr Darcy, at the assembly ball, is pronounced 'above being pleased' and 'the proudest, most disagreeable man in the world', one can hear the hurt and petulant tones of snubbed gentry in a provincial town. This enables Jane Austen to provide a convincing backdrop of the Meryton milieu, without having to particularize individual characters.

Jane Austen action figure, ready with quill pen to start writing.

Throughout *Pride and Prejudice* the narration glides effortlessly between standard narrative form and the free indirect discourse of Elizabeth, Lydia, Mr Collins, the inhabitants of Meryton and several other characters in the novel. Most readers are unaware that such a technique exists or that Jane Austen is using it so extensively and cleverly, but it is a vital aspect of her style and it contributes greatly to the variety and comedy of *Pride and Prejudice*.

THE DIALOGUE OF *PRIDE AND PREJUDICE*

Lord David Cecil, who wrote a delightful biography of Jane Austen, commented that 'People who do not like Jane Austen are the kind of people who do not like sunshine.' Reading *Pride and Prejudice* does indeed feel like a burst of sunshine from a cloudy sky. What is it about the way in which it is written that communicates such sparkle, such *joie de vivre*, to its readers?

Much of this charm comes from the dialogue. Crisp, exact and witty, every speech in the novel reveals the character of the speaker and amuses the reader. No wonder film-makers are so attracted to the novel: the dialogue is a positive gift to any scriptwriter. The first chapter of the book is an excellent example. Dialogue starts after only two sentences, with 'My dear Mr Bennet . . .', and within three pages of conversation the personalities of Mr Bennet and 'his lady' are vividly before us in all their glorious absurdity. Mrs Bennet is loquacious, Mr Bennet is terse; she is silly, he is dry: 'You take delight in vexing me. You have no compassion on my poor nerves.' 'You mistake me, my dear. I have a high respect for your nerves. They are my old friends. I have heard you mention them with consideration these twenty years at least.' This dialogue in Chapter One provides a portrait of the Bennet marriage, information about their five daughters needing husbands, and brilliantly efficient character portrayal, along with the fun and comedy of the scene.

Jane Austen commented, after *Pride and Prejudice* had been published, that she ought perhaps to have added some more 'he saids' and 'she saids' to make her dialogues clearer for the reader. She was wrong! Every voice is so distinguishable from another that it is easy to know who is speaking. Who but Mr Collins would be gushing about 'her ladyship's concurrence'; who out Mary would prose on about 'the generality of female minds'; and when nerves are mentioned of course the speaker is Mrs Bennet.

Jane Austen employs exaggeration within dialogue with great skill. Foolish characters, with little sense of proportion, exaggerate, magnify and overuse language when they speak. Lydia and her 'raptures', Mrs Bennet threatening 'never to see [Elizabeth] again' if she refuses Mr Collins, Lady Catherine and her emphatic pronouncements are all good examples. Elizabeth, and the reader, should beware of Wickham when he describes Mr Darcy Senior as 'the truest friend I ever had' and speaks of being 'grieved to the soul by a thousand tender recollections', but she is seduced by his handsome face and fails to be warned by his over-the-top speeches. Elizabeth, and the reader, must constantly distinguish between gradations, nuances and extremes.

Repetition is also brilliantly used, as Jane Austen re-uses phrases that immediately bring a particular speaker to mind. She had no need to put 'Mr Collins said' in front of any speech that refers to a 'humble abode', or add 'said Sir William' after the court of St James is mentioned. Such 'speech tags' are another part of her stylistic repertoire.

Jane Austen wrote to her sister of the 'playfulness' of her novel's style. One can see her having such fun when her characters speak. They respond so wittily, or cap each other's phrases. When Darcy remarks that poetry is the '*food* of love', Elizabeth replies that if there 'be only a slight, thin sort of inclination', then 'one good sonnet will starve it entirely away'. Darcy has to smile, as she turns a well-known adage on its head. Elizabeth's ripostes to Lady Catherine, when that dowager visits Longbourn and tries to intimidate with her rank, frustrate that domineering woman exceedingly. Lady Catherine might be rich and important, but she is thoroughly beaten in that verbal duel.

The dialogue of *Pride and Prejudice* is honed to perfection, it glitters like a jewel, and from the first speech (Mrs Bennet's) to the very last (Elizabeth's), it is totally convincing, realistic, clever and economical – a dose of sunshine indeed.

They solaced their wretchedness by duets after supper.

The Bingley sisters singing duets to solace their wretchedness (illustration by C.E. Brock).

THE IRONY OF *PRIDE AND PREJUDICE*

Jane Austen's famous irony is an essential stylistic characteristic of *Pride and Prejudice*. This literary device is much used, and always with extreme skill. With irony she creates discordance between what appears to be and what actually is, and prompts her reader to question or re-evaluate a character or situation.

There is irony of 'theme'. 'Pride' and 'prejudice' are very mixed qualities, each containing good and bad aspects. In this novel 'pride' leads to 'prejudice' and 'prejudice' invites 'pride', and both become intermingled in good and bad degrees. Jane Austen handles these qualities ironically, inviting us to see their incongruities.

She uses irony of situation. The very man who thinks a young woman 'not handsome enough' to tempt him on to the dance floor will, by the end of the novel, be leading her to the altar. The militia who, by removing from Meryton, should be removing all Lydia's flirting partners will end up removing Lydia as well. Lady Catherine arrives at Longbourn to put a stop to a marriage, but ends up by promoting it instead. Elizabeth Bennet insists to Mr Collins that she is not the sort of young lady who risks her 'happiness on the chance of being asked a second time', only to be longing for a second proposal later in the story. She also finds herself at Pemberley face to face with its 'rejected' owner and is only too aware of that situational irony as she blushes with embarrassment. Many of these ironies are missed by a first-time reader, and that is one of the many reasons why *Pride and Prejudice* is always reread with increased enjoyment.

Then there is irony of character, where Jane Austen uses ironic humour to puncture pomposity, expose ill-breeding, dent self-deception and reveal stupidity. Bingley's sisters dislike the vulgarity of some of the Bennet women, but irony displays how essentially vulgar they are themselves. Irony exposes the ludicrousness of Mrs Bennet's claim that she would be ashamed to accept an entailed property if one ever came her way, when she has never been able to understand entails; it shows up Lady Catherine's vulgarity in stating that Elizabeth would be in no one's way in the servants' quarters'; it highlights the importance of money to all the characters (Mr Darcy soon draws attention in the ballroom by his height and looks, but particularly by 'the report which was in general circulation within five minutes after his entrance, of his having ten thousand a year'); it laughs at gossips ('there was much to be talked of in marrying [Lydia]; and the good-natured wishes for her well-doing, which had proceeded before, from all the spiteful old ladies in Meryton, lost but little of their spirit in this change of circumstances, because with such a husband, her misery was considered certain'); and it emphasizes a woeful lack of self-knowledge in so many of the characters.

It can occasionally be malicious, as when Elizabeth says of Miss De Bourgh, 'I like her appearance': she doesn't really like the sickly looks of the girl at all, but she thinks such a pathetic woman will serve Mr Darcy right as a wife. Very occasionally irony is self-inflicted. Mr Bennet is clever enough to know his own faults: 'Let me once in my life', he tells his daughter Elizabeth, 'feel how much I have been to blame. I am not afraid of being overpowered by the impression. It will pass away soon enough.' Irony can be truly comic: Charlotte Lucas does not do justice to 'the fire and independence of his character' when Mr Collins comes to 'throw himself at her feet', the 'fire' being from a man who is proposing to two women within a few days. There is quiet, precise irony all through the novel. Irony is directed against every character, even at times against the heroine ('Yet the misery, for which years of happiness were to offer no compensation, received soon afterwards material relief, from observing how much the beauty of her sister re-kindled the admiration of her former lover'). Irony is a tool that Jane Austen knew how to use for maximum effect. No one is safe from her ironic voice and no reader of *Pride and Prejudice* would want it to be otherwise.

LETTERS IN *PRIDE AND PREJUDICE*

'Come as soon as you can on receipt of this . . .', 'I propose myself the satisfaction of waiting on you . . .', 'Let me hear from you very soon', 'Be not alarmed, Madam, on receiving this letter . . .', 'My motive for cautioning you, is as follows . . .', 'Dear Sir, I must trouble you once more for congratulations', 'I would have thanked you before . . .', 'I do not think we shall have quite enough money to live upon' – letters of invitation, letters of thanks, begging letters and those full of explanation, letters announcing dramatic events and letters of congratulation fill many pages of *Pride and Prejudice*. The novel is packed with correspondence, with forty-four letters referred to, and eighteen of those either heavily quoted from or given in full.

Jane Austen inherited the epistolary mode of novel writing from the eighteenth-century writers. Her favourite novelist, Samuel Richardson, wrote *The History of Sir Charles Grandison* as a novel of letters. Almost certainly, *Elinor and Marianne* was written as an epistolary novel before it metamorphosed into *Sense and Sensibility* (which actually contains far fewer letters in its pages than does *Pride and Prejudice*). The scholarly debate continues as to whether or not *First Impressions* was also epistolary, but whatever its original structure, *Pride and Prejudice* is a novel in which letters play a vital role. Jane Austen took the epistolary mode and adapted it to her own more believable style of narration, weaving letters very naturally into her text, without straining reader credulity in the way that an unadulterated series of letters is apt to do.

Letter-writing was a serious business in Jane Austen's day. The world of a modern reader is filled with phones, email, texting, blogging and Facebook but what we now do so quickly with the push of a button had to be done laboriously then with paper, quill, ink bottle and considerations of cost. When Mr Collins sends a letter to Mr Bennet, it is Mr Bennet who must pay for postage, and the longer the Collins effusion, the higher the cost to Mr Bennet. Considerate correspondents wrote very small or 'crossed' their letters (writing on the page, and then rotating that page forty-five degrees and writing over what had already been written, thus saving an extra sheet of paper and more expense). Often letter-writers tried to send letters via friends who were travelling to save the recipient having to pay, or found a Member of Parliament who could 'frank' the letter (as Sir Thomas Bertram does for Fanny's letters in *Mansfield Park*), as MPs could post their letters for free. In the world of *Pride and Prejudice* letters are delivered in many ways, via servants or friends, handed over personally and sent through the post (which was remarkably efficient – Jane's letter to Elizabeth takes four days to reach her,

but that is after it has been 'missent elsewhere . . . as Jane had written the direction remarkably ill'. Normally a letter would reach its recipient within two days, carried by horse and carriage up to the north of the country). Letters in the novel convey a great deal of information and often indicate a turn of events – a newcomer arriving on the scene (Mr Collins), an illness (Jane), news of an elopement (Lydia) or an announcement of a marriage (Mr Bennet about his daughters).

Letters in *Pride and Prejudice* also reveal character. Mr Bennet is a lazy correspondent, even when his letters concern business, and this says much for his failure as a husband and father ('About a month ago I received this letter, and about a fortnight ago I answered it, for I thought it a case of some delicacy, and *requiring early attention*' – my italics). Mr Gardiner

Darcy hands Elizabeth his letter (illustration by Joan Hassall).

shoulders Mr Bennet's responsibility of keeping the Bennet women informed after Lydia's elopement, just as he takes on the task of finding Lydia, and his correspondence is punctual, sensible and to the point, like the man himself. Lydia's letters are full of trivia and show a total lack of shame – elopement, dance partners, shopping, clothes and a shotgun wedding are all jumbled together, as if each was of equal importance. When, all unconsciously, Lydia asks in a letter for 'a great slit' in her muslin gown to be repaired, it is such a meaningful line: the image symbolizes the loss of her virginity and the irreparable damage to her reputation, while also illustrating her thoughtlessness. Jane Bennet writes sweet, considerate letters and Mrs Gardiner kind, sensible ones, like her husband. Mr Darcy's long letter, placed mid-way through the novel, is a great set piece of *Pride and Prejudice*, resembling an important soliloquy on the stage. Johnsonian in its long sentences, formal in its injured feelings, yet so desperately trying to be fair, so rational and informative, it also has one of the great endings of any letter: 'I will only add, God bless you.' Such an adieu 'is charity itself', as Elizabeth later tells him.

Mr Darcy writes a superb letter, but it is Mr Collins who must surely be the most prized of all correspondents in *Pride and Prejudice*. His letters are so wonderfully comic that Mr Bennet, much as he hates the occupation, 'would not give up Mr Collins's correspondence for any consideration'. They are pompous, servile, tasteless, verbose, flowery (for example, he announces his wife's pregnancy as 'a young olive-branch'; an olive-branch appears in his very first letter as well, so he is clearly very pleased with that image), foolish, moralizing, mean of spirit and lengthy – quite simply, they are a joy to read. So memorable are they that dictionaries now include an entry for 'a Mr Collins Letter', meaning a letter of thanks for hospitality or entertainment sent by a departed guest – so named because of just such a letter sent by Mr Collins after his first stay at Longbourn.

Letters are a notable feature of Jane Austen's style in *Pride and Prejudice*. They move the plot along, reveal character, indicate arrivals and departures, make dramatic announcements, and hinder or promote courtship. Jane Austen once complimented her sister Cassandra on her epistolary style: 'The letter which I have this moment received from you has diverted me beyond moderation . . . You are indeed the finest comic writer of the age.' Cassandra's letters to Jane have not survived and we have thus no way of judging Cassandra's abilities in that respect, but surely it was Jane herself who wrote the finest comic letters of her age, when she created letters for her novel. They have successfully diverted two centuries of readers.

OTHER STYLISTIC FEATURES OF *PRIDE AND PREJUDICE*

Unlike Charles Dickens, Jane Austen is not a descriptive writer. She does not provide long passages describing houses, appearance, furniture, clothing or food. 'Things' do not play a large part in her fiction. *Pride and Prejudice* contains few concrete nouns (carriages, gowns, dishes on the table, etc.), but it has plenty of abstract ones (pride, prejudice, hope, sense, astonishment, respect, happiness, consideration, comprehension, reputation, regret – the list goes on). However, when description really matters, and can tell the reader something more than simply about appearances, it is there. We do not need to know whether Longbourn is built of brick or stone, is two-storeyed or three, because such detail would tell us nothing of Elizabeth herself. But with Pemberley, it is a different case altogether. Mr Darcy needs to be revealed – to Elizabeth and to the reader – without prejudice. He needs to be placed in his proper context, not standing diffidently in a Meryton ballroom, nor awkwardly next to Miss Bingley, but in his natural element, 'at home' as master, brother, landlord and employer. What better way of achieving this than by describing Pemberley as a well-run estate, a place where servants are happy, a loving home for Georgiana and a place where 'natural beauty' is to the fore, where taste is evident and where everything is well regulated. And so Jane Austen describes the setting of 'rising ground' for this man rapidly rising in Elizabeth's esteem, rooms that are 'lofty and handsome' (just like their owner), furniture 'neither gaudy nor uselessly fine' (reflecting Darcy's taste) and a picture gallery with its generations of Darcys (showing so clearly why he has a reason to be proud). Economical as ever in her style, Jane Austen describes Pemberley and Mr Darcy at the same time.

'Oh,' said Lydia, stoutly, 'I am not afraid; for though I *am* the youngest, I'm the tallest.'

Contrast is an important part of Jane Austen's style – even contrast of height is used to reveal character (illustration by Hugh Thomson).

Contrast is another important feature of *Pride and Prejudice*. There is the contrasting of letters and of speech (both discussed earlier in this chapter), and there is contrast of character. The reader is continually forced to compare Darcy with his friend Bingley, and both those gentlemen with Mr Wickham. We must contrast each Bennet sister with her siblings. Elizabeth refuses Mr Collins, but Charlotte Lucas accepts him, and this tells us much about the differences between the two women. Mr Bennet in his role as father must be compared with Sir William Lucas in the same role, and sensible Aunt Gardiner is a contrast to vulgar Aunt Philips.

There is contrast of action too. Elizabeth receives two unwelcome proposals and both her suitors essentially tell her the same thing: that a girl with as small a dowry as hers and with such a family should be grateful to be asked, and should immediately say 'Yes'. Yet each unsuccessful proposal is handled very differently. Jane Austen cleverly allows Mr Collins to speak for himself: 'To fortune I am perfectly indifferent and shall make no demand . . .', and he assures her, 'in the most animated language of the violence of [his] affection'. As he speaks, Mr Collins reveals himself to be a fool with every word. 'Violence of affection' from a man who has changed that 'affection' from Jane to Elizabeth while Mrs Bennet was 'stirring the fire'! But the last thing Jane Austen wants is for readers to think the hero of her novel is also a fool or so arrogant that we want no more of him. Mr Darcy opens his proposal by speaking of his 'ardent' feelings, but after that Jane Austen does not permit her hero to speak directly. His proposal is given as reported speech. 'He spoke well, but there were feelings besides those of the heart to be detailed, and he was not more eloquent on the subject of tenderness than of pride.' Jane Austen lets Mr Collins make a pompous ass of himself, but she won't allow her hero to upset or alienate the reader with his direct utterances. Later, though, when Darcy has learned how to propose properly, she gives him direct speech: 'But your *family* owe me nothing. Much as I respect them, I believe, I thought only of you . . . *My* affections and wishes are unchanged, but one word from you will silence me on this subject for ever.' By using different narrative techniques, permitting or blocking dialogue, Jane Austen ensures that two men who confidently propose in completely the wrong way are properly differentiated as buffoon and hero in the minds of her readers.

Pride and Prejudice is a beautifully shaped novel. The first half leads up to the climax in the centre of the book: Darcy's first proposal and his letter of explanation. After that important moment, his pride and Elizabeth's prejudice both start to disappear. The novel then develops her growing 'pride' in him and his generosity of spirit, and his 'prejudice' against his aunt and all she stands for. It's like a piece of music rising in a crescendo to a climax, and then diminishing, working through all its themes and motifs until it reaches a happy, peaceful conclusion. It has beautiful symmetry: pride and humility are both there, as are reason and passion, energy and decorum. It is not only Elizabeth and Darcy who are 'united' in the very last sentence but so many intangibles as well.

Pride and Prejudice is a novel of manners, told politely – there is nothing ill bred or boisterous in its style. Civilization is both discussed in its pages and reflected in every one of those pages. This is a novel that involves the reader, inviting evaluation, intellectual discernment and intelligent response. Its shape, clarity, sparkle, harmonies and contrasts together form a whole which achieves what David Cecil so aptly described as 'Mozartian perfection'.

ELIZABETH.

Elizabeth Bennet (illustration by Robert Ball).

'As Charming a Creature'

THE HEROINE, ELIZABETH BENNET

'Dearest, loveliest Elizabeth'

When Jane Austen's grandparents picked up that very new object called a 'novel' (something that originated in England only in their lifetimes), the chances were that the book would tell of the adventures and love affairs of a young man. Robinson Crusoe alone on his island, Tom Jones wandering the highways and byways of England, Tristram Shandy recounting the problems of his conception, or the intrigues and upsets encountered by Roderick Random, Humphry Clinker, Gulliver and Joseph Andrews – these were the fictional accounts available to Jane's Austen and Leigh grandparents. There is no 'Woman Friday' for Crusoe, no Mrs Shandy for Tristram, while Gulliver does his best to escape his wife by setting off on long ocean voyages. Women play small roles in these early novels.

When a book did centre around a female, as is the case with Samuel Richardson's *Pamela* (1741) and *Clarissa* (1747), and with Frances Burney's *Evelina* (1778), *Cecilia* (1782) and *Camilla* (1796), the heroines try terribly hard to be good and to please everyone. Circumstances are sometimes against them – Mr B. tries to deprive Pamela of her virtue, the dastardly Lovelace rapes Clarissa, and Evelina gets into some hopeless muddles – but this is largely through no fault of their own. These heroines are models of deportment and decorum. They are women who respond, rather than provoke; who want to obey society's rules instead of flout them; who are deferential to people of rank; and who are interesting more for what happens to them than for who they are. Richardson marries his Pamela off to Mr B. and she becomes a preaching prig, while his Clarissa decides that the only suitable response

Elizabeth Garvie as a superb Elizabeth Bennet in the 1980 BBC adaptation of the novel.

to being raped is to die (and she then takes hundreds of pages to do so), while Burney's Evelina, Cecilia and Camilla all look up to the men they marry as near-perfect beings infinitely above themselves.

The conduct books of the day, which taught young ladies how to behave, all recommended female reserve, modesty, silence, meekness and even lack of physical energy. Fordyce's *Sermons*, for instance (the book Mr Collins reads for the edification of his Bennet cousins), insist that any young lady hoping for a husband should sit quietly, repress her wit (should she be so unfortunate as to have any) and always obey her parents and betters.

It is into this literary scene of pattern young women that Jane Austen introduces Elizabeth Bennet. This remarkable heroine is mentioned in the first chapter of *Pride and Prejudice* when Mr Bennet says to his wife: 'I dare say Mr Bingley will be very glad to see you; and I will send a few lines by you to assure him of my hearty consent to his marrying which ever he chuses of the girls; though I must throw in a good word for my little Lizzy.' She is 'Lizzy', not 'Elizabeth', when we first hear of her, and she is clearly her father's favourite. 'Lizzy is not a bit better than the others; and I am sure she is not half so handsome as Jane, nor half so good humoured as Lydia,' retorts Mrs Bennet, putting down her second daughter and making it clear that Lizzy is no favourite of hers. This is hardly an auspicious beginning for a heroine; she is not the beauty of her family, as a heroine ought to be, and she is not always good humoured. A heroine who can get cross – what new creature was this? Mr Bennet informs us that Elizabeth has 'something more of quickness than her sisters'; then she is not mentioned again in the opening chapter.

She makes her physical appearance in Chapter Two, and gets to speak: '"But you forget, mama," said Elizabeth, "that we shall meet him at the assemblies, and that Mrs Long has promised to introduce him."' Elizabeth Bennet first opens her mouth in *Pride and Prejudice* in order to contradict her mother! She does it politely, but she does it all the same. Readers used to well-behaved young ladies who were invariably polite to their mamas must have raised their eyebrows at this. Elizabeth has one more brief speech in the second chapter, and then is not encountered again until the middle of the third.

By this point she seems destined for Mr Bingley (as her name has been linked with his), and has been portrayed as the favourite of her father and no favourite of her mother, but we still know little of her character. Then she appears at the Meryton assembly ball: 'Elizabeth Bennet had been obliged, by the scarcity of gentlemen, to sit down for two dances . . .' Worse and worse! A heroine no man wants to dance with when she should, by the standards of any eighteenth-century novel, be drawing the interested gaze of every gentleman in the room. And then Darcy calls her 'tolerable; but not handsome enough' to be tempting. She is merely a young lady 'slighted by other men'.

Gemma Arterton as a modern-day Elizabeth Bennet in *Lost in Austen*.

How does this apparently 'ordinary' heroine react? Does she imitate conduct-book heroines and swoon, blush or go into a decline? No, she laughs. She tells the story of Darcy's scorn 'with great spirit' among her friends, she promises her mother she will never dance with Darcy if he ever does ask her, and she jokes with her best friend about her own mortified pride. By the end of Chapter Five the reader knows that Elizabeth Bennet is not in the common mould of heroines. She has a sense of humour, she can look a man who has insulted her in the eye, and she is witty and clever. She has emerged as a heroine who could well turn out to be 'as delightful a creature as ever appeared in print', someone new and memorable in the world of fiction.

Inevitably, some contemporary readers found her too 'novel' a creation. Writer Mary Russell Mitford thought Elizabeth pert and forward and far from worthy for such a man as Darcy. She was a highly unconventional, new sort of heroine, and it is easy for modern readers to underestimate just how astonishing she was for readers of the time. But most readers were entranced. In 200 years there have been few who have not fallen in love with Elizabeth Bennet while reading *Pride and Prejudice*. Robert Louis Stevenson even asserted that on every rereading he wanted to fall to his knees and worship her. Her popularity has proved that she is, without doubt, one of the most outstanding heroines in all literature.

Elizabeth Bennet is twenty years old, is the second of five daughters, can expect no fortune and has had little formal education. Her figure is 'light and pleasing', she is of average height, and she has 'tolerable' teeth and beautiful dark eyes. Dark blue, or dark brown? We are never told; nor do we know what colour her hair is, what her taste in clothes is, or whether she physically resembles her sisters or parents. She is moderately accomplished and can play and sing pleasantly and without parade; she cannot draw, and she is reasonably well read. Physical exercise is important to her. She performs no memorable or heroic action. How has Jane Austen made out of this rather unpromising material such a wonderful heroine?

There are many reasons to love Elizabeth Bennet. First, she is clever, as her father recognizes. Mary might quote deep philosophical extracts, but it is Elizabeth who is the 'brainy' one of her family. Her intelligence shines from her eyes; she is observant, skilled with language, and generally excellent at judging other people (note how quickly she correctly evaluates Miss Bingley and Mr Collins). Mr Gardiner, a sensible and intelligent man, relies on her judgment; Mr Bennet respects her opinions. But being her father's favourite and the brightest of her family has made Elizabeth just a little too confident in her own intellectual prowess. 'I beg your pardon; one knows exactly what to think,' she asserts, yet in the course of the novel she comes to wish that such assertions had been more reasonable, more accurately based on facts rather than on self-confidence. For her judgment, in the cases of Wickham and Darcy, proves to be 'too quick', formed on insufficient evidence. At the beginning of the novel Elizabeth displays both 'pride' and 'prejudice', and she must learn to eliminate both and judge more clearly. It is a joy to watch Elizabeth undergo this learning process, to see her realize her mistakes, amend her judgments, improve in her knowledge of human nature. A crucial moment is Darcy's letter. She has already judged Miss Bingley on her letters and Mr Collins on his, and she was right both times. Now, though, she must read Darcy's side of the story she has heard from Wickham and compare it with Wickham's account – 'On both sides it was only assertion' – and she must admit that in her judgment of Wickham she was wrong. This important letter-reading scene, placed exactly halfway through *Pride and Prejudice*, is when Elizabeth starts her real education. 'Until this moment I never knew myself,' she ruefully admits. Elizabeth recognizes that unless one truly knows oneself, one does not know the world. In confronting her own mistake of accusing Darcy of being 'blinded by prejudice' when she was equally blinded herself, she learns and changes. How different from a conduct-book heroine who is so perfect that she has nothing to learn; and how much more interesting for the reader!

Elizabeth is the only female character in the book to learn and grow. Her mother, her sisters, her friend, her aunt, Lady Catherine and the Bingley women are all exactly the same at the end of the novel as they were at the beginning. But not Elizabeth. As a daughter, sister, as a woman proposed to three times and as a discriminating reader of letters, Elizabeth is constantly being educated, challenged and changed. As her perspective is largely imposed on the story, the reader is challenged and changed along with her. Every rereading of *Pride and Prejudice* is a learning experience. With Elizabeth, we too learn to judge true worth, to recognize hypocrisy and to laugh wisely.

Elizabeth is also admired for her strength. She has physical strength, a rare quality in the novels of Jane Austen's day. On long country walks she crosses 'field after field at a quick pace, jumping over stiles and springing over puddles with impatient activity', and she doesn't care that her petticoats get muddied as she does so. She runs faster than Jane, she dances without any sign of exhaustion, and she delights in regular exercise. Modern readers are soon impatient with *Mansfield Park*'s Fanny Price, who is shattered by one sunny afternoon out of doors. Fanny needs iron tablets, but Elizabeth would be the last heroine for whom you would prescribe such medication. Her physical stamina is far more attractive than Fanny's conventional frailty. Yet, unlike her sister Lydia, she knows how to control her physical energy. Lydia romps and laughs too loudly, her spirits are 'animal' ones – unrestrained, imprudent and unthinking – but Elizabeth knows where and when to draw the line.

And Elizabeth has strength of mind as well as body. Unlike Marianne Dashwood of *Sense and Sensibility*, she doesn't give in to despair. Even in the poignant moment of recognition that she has lost 'exactly the man, who, in disposition and talents, would most suit her' and who 'would have answered all her wishes', she does not shriek and sob, like Marianne. Nor does she decide to die, like Clarissa. No: Elizabeth rallies her spirits, supports her family through their troubles, and forces herself into a better humour. Unlike Fanny Price, she copes well with change. Unlike Anne Elliot, she can find causes for laughter even when pining for the man she loves.

She also has strength when coping with adversity. If insulted, she uses humour as a weapon, and she does it brilliantly. There's a wonderful moment on the path at Netherfield when Miss Bingley and Mrs Hurst (out walking with Mr Darcy) are rude to her. Elizabeth responds so cleverly: 'You are charmingly group'd, and appear to uncommon advantage. The picturesque would be spoiled by admitting a fourth,' she tells them. Her reference to the picturesque is a subtle but devastating one. To be truly picturesque (according to the great exponent of the picturesque movement, William Gilpin), a scene needed a group of cattle, preferably one bull and two cows. By telling them that they are picturesquely grouped, Elizabeth is implying that Darcy is a bull, and that the Bingley women are cows (how apt!). Little wonder that she 'runs gaily off, rejoicing' at having had such verbal revenge. When Elizabeth is challenged, she challenges back: 'if I do not begin by being impertinent, I shall soon grow afraid of him.' Sturdy, resilient and strong, Elizabeth

Lady Catherine and Elizabeth in the wilderness (illustration by Joan Hassall).

brings energy and elasticity of mind to *Pride and Prejudice*; she is the reason it is a 'light and bright and sparkling' novel.

Jane Bennet would make an entirely appropriate heroine for an eighteenth-century novel. Jane is sweet, kind, modest, pliant. When Bingley leaves her, she loses strength and grieves. Her behaviour is invariably respectful and considerate. She is a lovely character, and every reader is moved by her 'I do not deserve it. Oh! why is not every body as happy?' when she is finally engaged to Bingley. But Jane Bennet has no depth. She is no competition to Elizabeth as heroine, in the way that Marianne is to Elinor in *Sense and Sensibility*. She never surprises the reader. Elizabeth, however, has depths that need many rereadings to fully comprehend. She flouts conventions – walking alone to Netherfield, refusing to bow down when Lady Catherine pulls rank. She can be unexpected – Darcy proposes, she refuses to play the role of obliged and grateful female: 'In such cases as this, it is, I believe the established mode . . . But I cannot . . .' She teases Darcy, needling him, probing his character and revealing more of her own in the process. As she tells him during their engagement, 'You were disgusted with the women who were always speaking and looking, and thinking for *your* approbation alone. I roused, and interested you, because I was so unlike *them*.' She makes him smile, and prods him into re-evaluating his assumptions, just as she makes herself question her own preconceptions. They puzzle each other in a way that Bingley and Jane would never think of doing, and her lack of conventionality and her depth of character soon bewitch him. In the process, the reader too is roused, interested and, ultimately, bewitched.

The essence of Elizabeth's character is charm. Charm is an extremely difficult quality to portray on the pages of a book. Fanny Burney might insist that her Evelina is charming, but readers are not actually charmed by Evelina. Jane Austen never tells us that Elizabeth is charming and when the word is used in *Pride and Prejudice* it is usually insincere or ironic ('Wickham has every charm', Mrs Bennet will be a 'charming mother-in-law', Lady Catherine has a 'charming daughter'). But Elizabeth is the only one of Jane Austen's heroines who is totally charming ('charm – to enchant, to delight, to allure', according to Chambers

Dictionary). Anne Elliot is loving, warm and incredibly good (too good to be really true?), Emma has verve, intelligence and is so wonderfully human in her ability to say and do the wrong thing, Elinor and Fanny are moral and worthy, Marianne is passionate, and Catherine Morland is sweet and naive, but these heroines do

LEFT Elizabeth at the door of her parents' home (illustration by Philip Gough); OPPOSITE Elizabeth and Darcy in an illustration by Joseph Miralles from the 1997 children's adaptation of *Pride and Prejudice* by Fern Michaels.

not charm the other characters and the reader on every page. Elizabeth Bennet does, and in this Jane Austen has done something unique. Literature is full of heroines who are beautiful, brave, loyal, feisty, intelligent and fascinating, but the reader searching for a heroine who personifies charm will come up with a very short list indeed. There is no recipe for this magic ingredient. Elizabeth's charm is a mixture of her sense of fun, her loving and loyal personality, her spirit and *joie de vivre*, her independence and self-sufficiency, and her love of playing with words.

Just once in the novel Mr Collins gets it right, and that is when he tells Elizabeth, 'You are uniformly charming.' Jane Austen was charmed by her own creation, Mr Darcy succumbs rapidly to her charm, and Elizabeth charms the socks off the reader again and again. One publisher of *Pride and Prejudice*, George Saintsbury, was so charmed by her that he said he wanted to 'live with and marry Elizabeth Bennet', while A.C. Bradley, Professor of Poetry at Oxford, confessed, 'I was meant to fall in love with her, and I do.' It is Elizabeth's extraordinary charm that has so much to do with the appeal of *Pride and Prejudice*.

In her juvenilia Jane Austen loved creating heroines who broke the rules, because she felt it made them more interesting and because she wished to shatter the ideal 'perfect' heroine. In these early writings, young women steal, elope, tell lies, embark on man hunts, escape from prison, have children and then promptly forget them, and confidently rampage through life with bravado, having plenty of fun in the process. These women are extremes, as their youthful creator well knew, but then so are the incredibly virtuous Pamelas, Evelinas and Camillas of eighteenth-century fiction. With Elizabeth Bennet, Jane Austen found the middle ground by creating a heroine who is admirable but not faultless, fun but not un-restrained, accomplished but not a paragon, courageous but not absurdly heroic. Elizabeth is an extraordinarily believable and convincing character and, as she tells Mr Collins, 'a rational creature speaking the truth from her heart'. As such, she has spoken to generations of readers and found her place as the world's most popular heroine.

— OPINIONS OF ELIZABETH BENNET —

'Elizabeth is, as Jane intended her to be, my favourite. I've always had a weakness for a girl with a bit of a mouth on her and, by Regency standards, she definitely qualifies. She's witty, bright, sensible and seems to have very little in the way of vanity.'

Terrence N. Hill, co-author (with Steve Chandler) of *Two Guys Read Jane Austen*

'By her behaviour [Elizabeth] fashions him into a fitting companion for herself, for Darcy has the discrimination and responsiveness to rise to the challenge.'

John Hardy, author of *Jane Austen's Heroines*

'Elizabeth Bennet is not my favourite heroine – that must be Anne Elliot – but I love her only a little less than Anne. Indeed, we would have to sacrifice Jane Austen's good opinion were we *not* to see Elizabeth's merits ('how I will be able to tolerate those who do not like *her*, at least, I do not know') which is unthinkable. Elizabeth's predominant characteristics are wit, liveliness and spirit, but like every Austen heroine she is concerned to identify and live up to the highest moral standards, and it is this combination of the serious and the playful which makes her so appealing. I just wish she did not use that vulgar expression about keeping her breath to cool her porridge!'

Maggie Lane, author of *Understanding Austen*, *Jane Austen's Family*, *Jane Austen's England*, *Jane Austen and Food*, *Jane Austen and Names* and *Jane Austen's World*

'When Elizabeth finally realizes Darcy is right about her dysfunctional family, she stands by them anyway, fully realizing the enormous social, economic and psychological cost of doing so. That sacrifice is the source of her moral integrity. It is what makes her a great heroine.'

Michael Giffin, author of *Jane Austen and Religion*

'Elizabeth Bennet loves life and lives it to the full. For me, more than any other Jane Austen heroine, Lizzy Bennet is a feel-good character, a go-getter, a unique blend of intelligence and passion; as she says of herself, "a rational woman speaking from the heart." Who could ever be tired of this irrepressibly light, bright and sparkling heroine?'

Hazel Jones, author of *Jane Austen and Marriage*

'Elizabeth has many qualities that we know were Jane [Austen]'s – her ready wit, her sharpness of eye and occasionally of tongue, her salty taste for human folly, coupled with her enjoyment of a good flirtation.'

Sheila Kaye-Smith, co-author (with G.B. Stern) of *More About Jane Austen*

Mr DARCY.

Fitzwilliam Darcy (illustration by Robert Ball).

'Mr Darcy . . . is the Man!'

THE HERO, FITZWILLIAM DARCY

'Such a charming man! – so handsome! – so tall!'

In the wonderful world of literature, there are many fabulous heroes. Handsome, brooding, passionate, strong, daring, adventurous and enigmatic, they stride through novels, conquering all difficulties and winning a lady love at the end. Literature provides such a variety – the Prince Charmings of fairytales, naughty but charming Tom Jones, terse and plain Mr Rochester, mysterious Heathcliff, confused David Copperfield, determined John Thornton, murderous Maxim de Winter, right through to modern 'crusader' Mikael Blomquist in Stieg Larsson's popular trilogy. These, and other heroes, find careers and find themselves, run businesses and estates, and also fall in love, but when it comes to a true 'romantic hero', there is one literary creation who towers over them all, an archetype, the progenitor of a million Mills and Boon lovers, the supreme bourgeois female fantasy and the most desirable man in fiction (and film): Mr Fitzwilliam Darcy.

The fairy godmothers turned out en masse at baby Fitzwilliam's christening and loaded him with all the good things of life. But the bad fairy was present as well, bestowing a fault that would later give him problems, ensuring that his carriage ride through life would include jolts and overturnings. So while the reader is presented with the embodiment of female dreams (tall, handsome, rich, clever, passionate), this paragon is not perfect: he has lessons to learn and trials to bear, and there will be great interest in watching him do so.

At the Netherfield ball, Elizabeth interrogates Mr Darcy: 'May I ask to what these questions tend?' he asks her. 'Merely to the illustration of your character . . . I am trying to make it out,' she replies. Jane Austen often refers to 'pictures' and 'portraits' in *Pride and Prejudice*. Elizabeth, and the reader, must find the real Mr Darcy among the various pictures presented. We too must 'sketch his character' and 'make him out'. Who is this enigmatic hero?

His physical appearance is all that could be desired in a hero. On first entering a country ballroom, he 'soon drew the attention of the room by his fine, tall person, handsome features, noble mien'. Even other men pronounce him 'to be a fine figure of a man', while the ladies consider him 'handsomer' than his friend. No film director has ever selected a 'blond' Darcy, and although his hair colour is never described, we all assume that if he is tall and handsome, he must also be 'dark'. It is important that he is tall, as he must tower both literally and metaphorically over every other man in the novel. Mr Knightley in *Emma* is also very tall, whereas Henry Crawford of *Mansfield Park* might be attractive to women, but he is 'undersized', just like his morals. Darcy is twenty-eight years old, Cambridge educated, has one sister, and has lost both his parents. There is little other information to help any reader form a 'first impression'.

The most generous of Darcy's fairy godmothers was the one who gave him Pemberley. At the age of twenty-three he found himself owner of a splendid and beautiful house, which has been in his family for generations, with a park 10 miles around, fine furniture, works of art and a library. Deirdre Le Faye in *Jane Austen: The World of her Novels* speculates that as Pemberley is in Derbyshire 'it may be that some part at least of Mr Darcy's wealth comes from mineral resources rather than agriculture. The hills of the Peak District in this part of Derbyshire provided not only limestone for buildings, but also marble and alabaster for architectural decorations or other works of sculpture and art, as well as lead, iron and coal for manufacturing purposes.' Marble, iron and alabaster are all hard substances, and it is tempting to further speculate that they play a role in forming the determined characters of Mr Darcy Senior and his son, as well as filling their pockets. Darcy will need to be 'softened' in the course of the story. Whatever the source of their wealth, it is undoubtedly large – Darcy is worth £10,000 per year. He is not the richest man in Jane Austen's fictional world (that is Mr Rushworth of *Mansfield Park*, who has £12,000 per year), but he is a millionaire by today's standards, and his fortune makes him a prize matrimonial catch.

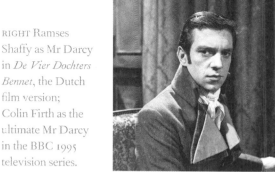

But Pemberley, while a glorious gift, also brings responsibilities. Darcy has time for holidays in Hertfordshire and Kent, but that is only because he has the right people in charge back home – Mrs Reynolds indoors, Mrs Annesley to care for Georgiana, and a good steward and gardeners outdoors. Darcy has had to learn how to best handle his responsibilities and to choose his staff, and he learns from mistakes such as his poor choice of Mrs Younge to chaperone his sister. He must consider the happiness and welfare of so many who are 'in his guardianship', and he fulfils these responsibilities admirably.

Only a young man of intelligence could do all this so well, and it is made very clear that Darcy is clever. Clever in his use of words – there are no abuses of language in any of Darcy's speeches, and he uses words precisely and fluently. Darcy is a reading man too and has clearly added to 'the improvement of [his] mind by extensive reading'. He is 'always buying books', he enjoys reading when at Netherfield, and he even wants to 'talk books' in a ballroom (how could Elizabeth resist that?). Jane Austen despises any of her characters who despise books (such as John Thorpe of *Northanger Abbey*), but Mr Darcy properly appreciates books and learns from his collection. His intelligence is also visible in his long letter to Elizabeth: although written in great perturbation of mind, it is still well structured, rational and clear. His mind is active, questioning, ready for challenges – this is a hero who thinks.

Darcy has also been given honesty at his christening. 'Disguise of any sort is my abhorrence,' he claims emphatically. He feels forced to be honest in his first proposal (though he is shooting himself in the foot by speaking so frankly). His honesty prevents him from easily enduring fools and bores; he cannot arrange his face with a false smile and please everyone in the process. His honesty leads him to confess his own faults to Bingley and to Elizabeth, to examine his own character and resolve to amend what is wrong in it.

Many a movie hero has appeared sexy and desirable simply by being the 'strong and silent' type. If a hero says nothing, women will find him inscrutable – that, at least, is the theory. Jane Austen knew that the more an author gives a character to say, the greater the chance he can alienate the reader by *what* he says (see discussion on page 51 about Darcy's first proposal and Jane Austen's limiting of his direct speech there). Darcy is not a 'chatty' man (as is his friend Bingley). Only 128 speeches in all of *Pride and Prejudice* are uttered by Darcy, and many of them are less than one line long. His 100th speech starts off his second proposal and he grows more loquacious once Elizabeth has accepted him. Apart from those direct speeches, there are of course, general references to him talking ('He spoke well', he 'assured her that whatever she wished him to say should be said', he 'apologised for his intrusion', etc.), but more often Darcy is silent ('He made no answer', 'he listened without attempting to interrupt', 'he said nothing'). Darcy is a man who speaks only when he has something to say. Is he reticent? Is he shy (as Matthew Macfadyen portrays him in the 2005 movie version), or is he simply unwilling to 'give himself the trouble' to 'recommend himself to strangers'? In *So Odd a Mixture: Along the Autistic Spectrum in 'Pride and Prejudice'* Phyllis Ferguson Bottomer speculates that Darcy is slightly autistic, that it is 'not pride but subtle autism that is the major reason for Darcy's frequent silences, awkward behaviour at social events'. She suggests that, because of his mild autism, Darcy is stressed by the noise and socializing of the Meryton assembly, even frightened of being dragged into a situation of dancing with a strange girl, and that this makes him vulnerable and rude. According to Phyllis Ferguson Bottomer, Darcy does not really register Elizabeth's presence and is unable to properly connect with those around him, except for Bingley and his sister, whom he already knows. He struggles with polite chit-chat, lacks flexibility, can be too controlling, is awkward in conveying his message and finds it hard to be companionable – all signs of autism. But although well argued, it is a controversial theory, for what reader wants to think the hero has a language or personality disorder?

When Elizabeth stands before Darcy's portrait at Pemberley, she notices 'such a smile over the face, as she remembered to have sometimes seen when he looked at her'. Darcy has a sense of humour – he smiles at Elizabeth's witty responses, he smiles sardonically at others. Look at the way he handles Miss Bingley, finding amusement in taunting her and reducing her to silence. But Darcy needs to learn to laugh as well as smile, to laugh at himself and at the world. He needs a woman who can match him in intelligence, who can bring spontaneity and laughter into his life. And all this his chosen Mrs Darcy will teach him.

Fitzwilliam Darcy is more capable of change than any other character in *Pride and Prejudice*. Elizabeth shocks him when she turns him down, but he resolutely begins to analyse himself, to probe his own character painfully, and to improve. Even at the end of the novel, he is still developing and learning (Elizabeth 'remembered that he had yet to learn to be laught at, and it was rather too early to begin'). He is an intricate character, who must build a new portrait' of himself after his self-image has been shattered by her emphatic rejection. Elizabeth also learns and changes, correcting her self-image too, but Darcy's transition is longer and more challenging than hers. He must cross social distances (there is an important scene where he and Elizabeth discuss relative distances, during which he moves his chair closer to her and then pulls it back), he must financially assist and negotiate with a man he loathes, he must search London for a fallen woman. No wonder that Elizabeth is 'proud of him. Proud that in a cause of compassion and honour, he had been able to get the better of himself.'

When Elizabeth angrily refuses Darcy's proposal, she accuses him of not behaving in 'a more gentleman-like manner'. Darcy is shocked by the accusation. *Pride and Prejudice* examines the concept of gentlemanliness, questioning the preconception that all that is needed to make a gentleman is inherited money, a large property and nothing to do. It was a question that interested Jane Austen and she explored it further in *Emma*, where Mr Knightley, her most perfect gentleman, loves working on his land, prefers walking to riding in his carriage, and has no airs and graces at all. In *Pride and Prejudice* there are various candidates for the role of 'true gentleman'. Mr Bingley, sociable and amiable, always considerate of others,

is a gentleman (although one generation removed from 'trade'), but he is too easily led; a gentleman should know his own mind and not be swayed this way and that
by others. Bingley's brother-in-law Mr Hurst 'merely looked the gentleman', Mr
Philips, 'breathing port wine', is no gentleman, Mr Bennet is too selfish to qualify,
but Mr Gardiner, intelligent, practical, polite and helpful, is a true gentleman, even
if he does live in Gracechurch Street and earn his own living.

So how accurate is Elizabeth's accusation against Mr Darcy? Where does Darcy
go wrong and fail to be gentleman-like? On the shelves of the Pemberley library,
there is certain to be a book by Lord Chesterfield. The Earl of Chesterfield (from a
Derbyshire family) wrote *Letters to his Son, Or the Fine Art of Becoming a Man of the
World and a Gentleman* and it was published in 1774. It was a best-seller and became
a sort of Bible of good manners to several generations. Mr Darcy Senior and his
wife, Lady Anne, obviously never gave this invaluable guide to their son to read.
Had they done so, Darcy would have made less of a mess of his entrance into *Pride
and Prejudice* and of his first proposal. Darcy arrives at the Meryton ball and within
thirty minutes has offended all the locals. He 'declined being introduced to any other
lady, and spent the rest of the evening in walking about the room'. Although there
is 'a scarcity of gentlemen' he dances with no local girls, yet insultingly 'advertises'

his presence as a potential dance partner by stroll-
ing through the room (much as Mr Elton struts
in front of Harriet Smith in *Emma*). Charlotte
Lucas tries to excuse this behaviour: 'One
cannot wonder that so very fine a young
man, with family, fortune, every thing in
his favour, should think highly of himself. If I may so express it, he has a *right*

Elizabeth and Darcy (illustration by Helen
Sewell) as they appear in the Heritage Press
edition of *Pride and Prejudice*.

to be proud.' Elizabeth agrees, but remarks, 'I could easily forgive *his* pride, if he had not mortified *mine*.' By not dancing with the young ladies of Meryton, Darcy has dented their self-esteem, and offended their anxious mamas, and so given a bad impression of his character. Such behaviour was not uncommon among the aristocrats of the Regency era, but Lord Chesterfield would have told him never to appear above his company, even if socially and financially he is far beyond them.

In the ensuing chapters of the book Darcy continues to give poor first impressions to those who meet him. He turns away from Wickham without greeting him, he is haughty with Mr Collins, and he barely speaks to Mrs Bennet and Mrs Long. He seems stiff, overly formal, fastidious and arrogant. a man who can't take a joke against himself, and who speaks in abstractions about pride and resentment when he speaks at all. Nor does it do him any service to be seen near Lady Catherine. As her nephew and guest, he cannot contradict her; he can only look 'a little ashamed' of her ill-breeding, and say nothing.

He then comes to Hunsford parsonage to offer marriage to Elizabeth. His speeches and actions on that occasion would have shocked Lord Chesterfield. It is an unfortunate irony of situation that he chooses the worst possible moment: Elizabeth has been rereading Jane's letters and brooding over the injury Darcy has done her sister by separating her from Bingley. Darcy enters the room and 'out-Collinses' Mr Collins when it comes to a seriously bad proposal. He informs Elizabeth that he has tried hard to conquer his love for her ('In vain have I struggled'), insults her family ('a degradation'), and exudes confidence that she will accept his hand. He is tactless, he is wrong about Jane and he shows jealousy of Wickham. Even his body language is all wrong. Lord Chesterfield insisted that a gentleman should be in complete control of his limbs and never make an awkward gesture, but Darcy walks about the room 'in an agitated manner', leans casually against the mantelpiece, walks 'with quick steps', stops, starts again, and rushes from the room. It is almost a textbook example of how to get it wrong.

Jane Austen liked creating difficult and complex characters – it challenged her as an author. She refused to depict a romantic 'paragon' as her hero. Fanny Burney produced in her *Evelina* the excellent Lord Orville, who is a perfectly behaved

~ SEXY PHEROMONES ~

In 2012 scientists at the University of Liverpool identified a pheromone in the urine of male mice that makes them irresistibly attractive to female mice. It is an unusual protein and is responsible for female preference to specific males. It is also a vital part of the mouse's messaging system, advertising location, territory ownership and dominance.

The sexy pheromone has been named 'Darcin', after the irresistible hero of Jane Austen's *Pride and Prejudice*.

hero from beginning to end and terribly boring, in consequence. Jane Austen had no interest in creating such puppets. She wanted to explore complexity in a man, to show why he is what he is and how he can change. She herself was reserved with strangers. Jon Spence in *Becoming Jane Austen* argues persuasively that she put herself into Mr Darcy. Lord Chesterfield would argue that a true gentleman, shy or not, should be equal to every social occasion, but Darcy has been taught all his life to rank his own importance high. 'I have been a selfish being all my life, in practice, though not in principle. As a child I was taught what was *right*, but I was not taught to correct my temper. I was given good principles, but left to follow them in pride and conceit . . . allowed, encouraged . . . to be selfish and over-bearing, to care for none beyond my own family circle, to think meanly of all the rest of the world.' But love is a civilizing force. In order to win her, Darcy shows Elizabeth, and the reader, that he *can* learn and change, eliminate his faults, correct the 'pride' that an evil fairy godmother (and his parents) gave him, yet keep the good pride that makes him a worthy master and landlord. Jane Austen shows, in Darcy, how easily qualities can cross the borderline between good and unaccept-able: fastidiousness can veer into pride, reserve grow into coldness, reticence turn to haughtiness. But such problems can be reversed. Darcy, taught by his parents and aunt to be selfish, is then taught by Elizabeth to be more humble: 'What do I not owe you! You taught me a lesson, hard indeed at first, but most advantageous. By you, I was properly humbled.' This 'confession' to his 'dearest, loveliest Elizabeth' is a deeply moving moment in *Pride and Prejudice*. When Darcy has learned to deserve her and is changed, not in essentials but in his public persona, he removes her to 'all the comfort and elegance of their family party at Pemberley', where we know they will be blissfully happy with each other.

Darcy has always been Jane Austen's most popular hero. Miss Sheriff, Sheridan's dinner companion in 1813 to whom he recommended *Pride and Prejudice*, was one of the first Darcy fans. There have been legions more since. Not all devotees wear 'Team Darcy' or 'Mrs Darcy' T-shirts, not all sigh lustfully over Colin Firth acting Mr Darcy (though most of us do), but all recognize that Darcy set a new standard for romantic heroes and that he outdoes them all. His appeal transcends literature and film. Pets have been named for him (cats, dogs, birds, horses, chinchillas); there is even a bathroom tap named 'The Mr Darcy model' (a sleek chrome design); there are hundreds of objects adorned with his words, his face and his house. It is scary to think how much further it might be taken – 'Darcy Viagra pills' perhaps? – but currently 'Brand Darcy' is alive and flourishing.

P.D. James once described *Pride and Prejudice* as 'Mills and Boon, written by a genius'. Thousands of Mills and Boon and Harlequin Romance writers have modelled their heroes on Mr Darcy. Strong and silent, tall and handsome, rich and clever, these men confidently and assertively sweep women into their arms and plant bruising kisses on their trembling lips. They masterfully run their estates or businesses, deal ruthlessly with fools or villains, yet they always have something to learn from the heroines. Georgette Heyer, supreme mistress of the Regency romance, adored Jane Austen's novels and many of her heroes owe a great debt to Mr Darcy. No writer of Regency romance can escape having her tight-pantalooned and hessian-shod hero compared with Darcy. He out-dukes every duke, out-shines every earl. Darcy is the archetype, the model that other romance writers have imitated or had in mind as the ultimate romantic hero.

There are no online fan clubs for Mr Rochester or Heathcliff, but Darcy has fan sites where his admirers can 'share, discover and connect with other fans' (www.oh-darcy.livejournal.com and www.fanpop.com/spots/mr-darcy) and there is even a 'Jane Austen Fight Club' on the web where fans of 'Fitzwilliam "King of Hearts" Darcy' can battle it out in his defence. Whereas there are no 'Mrs de Winter' mugs for sale, nor sequels depicting the married life of Mr and Mrs David Copperfield, or badges proclaiming 'Gilbert Blythe is MINE', Darcy has mugs, badges and sequels galore. In his fictional life, and his afterlife, in his influence and his sex appeal, Fitzwilliam Darcy is unique. After 200 years he is still going strong, and is still hot!

— OPINIONS OF MR DARCY —

'He is the hero in whom sexual desire is most overt and overpowering. For what is he doing when he makes his first proposal to Elizabeth but telling her that he is so desperate to get her into bed that he will marry her even though it will be a degradation to him? The sexual charge is stronger in *Pride and Prejudice* than in any of the other novels, and that is a proper part of its character and appeal. But Darcy has also made a good fantasy figure for his admirers because he is something of a mystery.'

Richard Jenkyns in *A Fine Brush on Ivory:*
An Appreciation of Jane Austen

'The scene in which Elizabeth tells Mr Darcy of Lydia's elopement is one of the most romantic in all of Austen's writings, particularly upon rereading, when we know he is leaving the room full of purpose. In that moment, he emerges as a true hero. Having demonstrated, through glimpses into his private life,

that he is self-aware enough to admit his flaws and work to improve himself, he now shows his other side: that he is a man of honour and of the world, able and willing to use his knowledge and resources to set someone else's world to rights. Mr Darcy protects those who are dependent upon him – that's what a hero does. And with Elizabeth, that's what he continues to do in my novels: obtain justice for those who cannot seek it themselves.'

Carrie Bebris, author of the Mr & Mrs Darcy Mystery series

'Is there anything sexier in a Jane Austen novel than Mr Darcy reading a book?'
Karen Doornebos, author of *Definitely Not Mr Darcy*, quoted in *Jane Austen's Regency World* magazine

'The celebrated Regency author, Georgette Heyer, described *Pride & Prejudice* as a "masterpiece" and Jane Austen as her favourite author. Austenesque humour abounds in Heyer's Regency novels and Mr Darcy is the inspiration for her much-loved heroes: Mr Beaumaris (in *Arabella*), Sylvester, Duke of Salford (in *Sylvester*) and the Marquis of Alverstoke (in *Frederica*).'
Jennifer Kloester, author of *Georgette Heyer's Regency World* and *Georgette Heyer: Biography of a Best Seller*

'When I was introduced to the novel at the age of fourteen, I read twenty pages and then besieged my stepmother's study until she told me what I needed to know. I needed to know that Darcy married Elizabeth . . . . I needed this information as badly as I had ever needed anything. *Pride and Prejudice* suckers you. Amazingly – and I believe, uniquely – it *goes on* suckering you. Even now, as I open the book, I feel the same panic of unsatisfied expectation, despite five or six rereadings. How can this be, when the genre itself guarantees consummation? The simple answer is that the lovers really are made for each other by their creator. They are *constructed* for each other: interlocked for wedlock.'
Martin Amis, quoted in *The Friendly Jane Austen*

Mr Bennet makes an announcement (illustration by Chris Hammond).

The Female Line

HER RELATIONS

'Whatever my connections may be . . .'

Jane Austen was essentially a family novelist. She came from a large family herself, and well knew the dynamics of family life and sibling rivalry. She knew the importance of producing sons who could inherit the family home or take on family livings, and she realized the difficulty of marrying off daughters with small dowries. She recognized how parents could have their favourites among their children (her mother's favourite was her eldest son, James), and how genetics carried some qualities into the next generation but not others: 'How soon, the difference of temper in Children appears!' she wrote once to her niece. She studied neighbouring families at balls or when she stayed with friends, she observed and noted and, when she began to write, she decided that 'two or three families in a country village' was the 'very thing to work on'.

What she saw and experienced of family life went into *Pride and Prejudice*. She knew that older siblings are traditionally cautious, conservative and well behaved, that middle children tend to be ignored, and younger ones more inclined to take risks or rebel. She knew how siblings often form pairs within families, finding an ally in their most like-minded brother or sister. In her own family one brother was selected for fortune and position. There is no record of how this affected Edward Austen's brothers and whether it made them jealous, but she was certainly aware of how the luck of one benefited all the others indirectly in the Darwinian struggle for survival. Her own family had its share of trouble – a mentally defective child (George Austen), the death of Cassandra's fiancé Tom Fowle, the collapse of Henry Austen's bank, to name just a few of their problems. But the Austens also experienced joys and companionship, and were generally a happy family. Family experience, happy and unhappy, went into her creation of the Bennets, one of the greatest comic families in all of fiction.

MRS BENNET

'She was a woman of mean understanding, little information, and uncertain temper. When she was discontented, she fancied herself nervous. The business of her life was to get her daughters married; its solace was visiting and news.'

It is Mrs Bennet who gives us the first spoken words of *Pride and Prejudice*, so it is appropriate that she should be the first discussed in this chapter.

G.B. Stern, in her *More About Jane Austen*, categorically awards Mrs Bennet the prize of 'the Worst Mother in Jane Austen's novels'. She is given this title because she dislikes Elizabeth, foolishly dotes on Lydia and is like the madam of a brothel in the way she foists her daughters on to available men. But is Mrs Bennet really worse than cold Mrs Ferrars, who regularly disowns her children in *Sense and Sensibility*, or *Persuasion*'s Mary Musgrove, who does nothing but whine about her offspring and goes gaily out for dinner when her son is injured? Mrs Bennet is vulgar, stupid, obsessed with her nerves, possesses no tact and can't recognize humour even when it hits her in the face, but as a mother, she does at least try to care for her five girls and their futures.

Mrs Bennet was Miss Gardiner before she married. She grew up in Meryton, the daughter of an attorney, with one sister and one brother. Both sisters love company, gossip and pretty clothes. One married her father's clerk and stayed in town, the other married a country gentleman attracted by her 'youth and beauty' and went to live at his home, Longbourn. Both Miss Gardiners came from a respectable family, but are not the daughters of a gentleman. Mr Gardiner Senior was able to give each of his girls a dowry of £4,000. Obviously she was expected to marry and this she did young; Mrs Bennet is probably in her mid-forties when *Pride and Prejudice* opens. She has lived in a small town, never travelled, and has been exposed to very little variety or excitement in her life, one exception being the arrival of Colonel Millar's regiment in town when she was of an age to appreciate all the charms of a red coat. Her education would have been very rudimentary and she has never been a reader, so has done little to increase her knowledge of the world. Like most girls of the era, she was ignorant. She brought to the marriage her prettiness, the 'sparkling eyes' which her daughter Elizabeth inherits, her good humour, a dowry and fertility, but very little else. In many ways, Mrs Bennet is still a child, seeing things in black and white, of 'uncertain temper', self-absorbed and difficult to handle. However, considering the education of most girls of that era, Mr Bennet is unreasonable in expecting a great deal more.

Mrs Bennet married the wrong man; Mr Bennet married the wrong woman. They are an ill-matched pair who today would have long since managed to divorce but who, as a Regency couple, are stuck with each other. While both are busy feeling sorry for themselves, their children suffer. He does nothing to curb his wife, educate her or soften her vulgarities. Instead, he sits back and laughs at her, making her at the same time a figure of fun to her more intelligent daughters. He often refuses to escort his wife and daughters to balls, he is lazy and selfish, and he thinks little of the running of the household (for two weeks he holds on to a letter announcing Mr Collins's arrival and only thinks to tell his wife on the day of the expected arrival that there will be an extra person for dinner and an extra bed to be made ready).

Mr Bennet, disappointed in his marriage, finds bitter consolation in laughing at his wife and, of course, we laugh with him – it is so easy to laugh at Mrs Bennet. Her boasts ('I know we dine with four and twenty families'), her faux pas ('Good Lord! Sir William, how can you tell such a story? – Do you not know that Mr Collins wants to marry Lizzy?'), her nerves ('such tremblings, such flutterings, all over me, such spasms in my side, and pains in my head, and such beatings at heart, that I can get no rest by night, nor by day'), and her triviality ('I dare say the lace upon Mrs Hurst's gown . . .') – all combine to make her memorably comic every time she appears.

One particularly enjoyable aspect of Mrs Bennet's discourse is Mrs Long. Rather like Mrs Gamp's imaginary friend Mrs Harris in Charles Dickens's *Martin Chuzzlewit*, Mrs Long is a barometer for Mrs Bennet's feelings. Mrs Long never actually appears or speaks within the novel but, as a woman with nieces to be married off, she is both rival and fellow-sufferer to Mrs Bennet. It is Mrs Long who

~ MRS BENNET: DOMESTIC GODDESS? ~

The recipe book *Tea with the Bennets* by Margaret Vaughan is based on the idea that Mrs Bennet keeps 'a very good table' at Longbourn. Its recipes include 'Surly Curd Tart' for Mary Bennet, a 'Sharp Apple and Honey Tart' for Lizzy, 'Indelicate Pudding' for Mr Wickham and a suet pudding for Mr Collins, along with other delicacies Mrs Bennet is likely to have ordered her cook to produce for the tea table at Longbourn. For, as she reminds Mr Collins, she is 'very well able to keep a good cook for her family'.

Mrs Bennet doesn't have many good qualities, but she is a competent domestic manager. She provides for the physical comfort of her husband and never defies him or goes behind his back, much as she must have been tempted to do so. Her home is always ready to welcome (and feed) visitors – 'The venison was roasted to a turn – and everybody said, they never saw so fat a haunch. The soup was fifty times better than what we had at the Lucas's last week; and even Mr Darcy acknowledged, that the partridges were remarkably well done; and I suppose he has two or three French cooks at least.' She is well aware of domestic provisioning for her home ('how unlucky! There is not a bit of fish to be got today . . . ring the bell. I must speak to Hill, this moment'). Her girls are well dressed and know the rules of social etiquette (Lydia breaks those rules, but the others know how to behave, and they have not learned all that from their father), and the servants are controlled and seem to have stayed loyally with the family for years. There is none of the penny-pinching of the Norris home, or the disorder and dirt

Tea with the Bennets
of Jane Austen's Pride and Prejudice

An Anthology of Recipes by
Margaret Vaughan

of the Price establishment in Portsmouth. Mrs Bennet invites, and is invited out, and need have no shame of her home or the 'very fine dinner[s]' on her table. As Margaret Drabble asks: 'We may wince from her pushiness and ignorance on first reading, but on the tenth are we not a little more impressed by the evidence that she runs a generous household, keeps a good table, is a good hostess?' While it might be rather hard to think of Mrs Bennet as a 'domestic goddess', she runs an orderly, comfortable home and *Tea with the Bennets* is a tribute to those housewife y skills.

---

gives the first news of Mr Bingley's arrival in the neighbourhood. When Elizabeth suggests that Mrs Long could introduce them all to Bingley (since it appears that Mr Bennet will not), Mrs Bennet crossly replies: 'I do not believe Mrs Long will do any such thing. She has two nieces of her own. She is a selfish, hypocritical woman, and I have no opinion of her.' Later, however, when Jane is sure of Mr Bingley, Mrs Long becomes 'as good a creature as ever lived – and her nieces are very pretty behaved girls, and not at all handsome: I like them prodigiously.'

While Mrs Bennet does try to find husbands for her daughters, aware of their financial plight if they are left unmarried, of course she goes about it in the wrong way. Her vulgarity disgusts Mr Darcy, making him even more determined to separate Bingley from Jane Bennet. The Bingley women find her 'intolerable'. She embarrasses Elizabeth and Jane at public and private dances (Elizabeth 'blushed and blushed again with shame and vexation'), she is unable to control Lydia (or even see that Lydia needs control), and she is unaware of her own favouritism. She could so easily blight the futures of all her girls, with her tactlessness and vulgar manoeuvrings. Yet, though Elizabeth cringes at things her mother says and does, she and Jane have not lost all respect or fondness for their mother. When Jane becomes engaged to Bingley, she thinks first of telling her mother: 'I would not on any account trifle with her affectionate solicitude.' Elizabeth too wastes little time in carrying the news of her engagement to a stunned Mrs Bennet. Both girls recognize that their father has been at fault in his treatment of his wife, and that their mother has cared for their interests in a practical way. To embarrass one's children is a fault, but surely to neglect them totally is worse. There are far worse mothers than Mrs Bennet.

However, at the end of *Pride and Prejudice* Jane Austen gives her hero and heroine a wedding present: she makes their married home a long way away from Mrs Bennet!

MR BENNET

'In his library he had been always sure of leisure and tranquillity; and though prepared . . . to meet with folly and conceit in every other room in the house, he was used to be free from them there.'

A highly comic moment in *Pride and Prejudice* is when Mrs Bennet fears her husband will challenge Mr Wickham to a duel. 'Above all things', she begs her brother, 'keep Mr Bennet from fighting.' It's funny because it reveals how little Mrs Bennet knows of the man whose home and bed she has shared for twenty-three years: indolent, selfish Mr Bennet is the very last man in the novel likely to get involved in a duel. It's made even more amusing by her knowledge that were he to fight, he'd be hopeless at it: 'and then he will be killed, and what is to become of us all?'

Jane Austen introduces her readers to Mr Bennet in the first chapter. Another writer might have provided a lengthy description of his character, his parentage and how he came to inherit Longbourn early in life, how he mistakenly came to marry and the way in which that marriage disillusioned him. Trollope would certainly have done so, and so would Dickens and George Eliot. But not Jane Austen. She launches her Mr Bennet straight into conversation with his wife and by the end of a dozen speeches, there's hardly a need for the brief summary the narrator gives of him at the end: 'Mr Bennet was so odd a mixture of quick parts, sarcastic humour, reserve, and caprice, that the experience of three and twenty years had been insufficient to make his wife understand his character.' Mrs Bennet does not understand him and never will, but the reader already has a shrewd idea of his personality and is delighting in his sardonic humour and dry wit.

Mr Bennet probably married in his early twenties. He saw pretty, sexy Miss Gardiner and was strongly attracted physically. In order to get her into his bed, he married her. This sounds like the behaviour of a young man, not a more mature one. His 'first impressions' won the day. Because of his lust (which makes it easy to see that Lydia is his daughter as well as her mother's), he found himself the husband of a very silly woman. Instead of trying to improve her, he retreats into the world of

Mr and Mrs Bennet at home (illustration by Hugh Thomson).

books, finding his emotional satisfactions there, except in his relationship with his favourite daughter, Elizabeth. He is ironic at the expense of his wife and children, which is 'not the sort of happiness which a man would in general wish to owe to his wife', and he is inadequate as a husband and father. Mr Bennet's bitter mockery tells us all we need to know of the sad story of his marriage. His view of society is a bleak one: 'For what do we live but to make sport for our neighbours, and laugh at them in our turn?' he asks. Mr Bennet has a 'room of [his] own' and he hates to have it invaded, but when he shuts the library door, he shuts out the world and all its joys, its loving and its human interaction. He also tries to shut out his responsibilities. He pays a high price for his detachment.

A woman who once met Jane Austen likened her to Mr Bennet: 'her keen sense of humour I quite remember, it oozed out very much in Mr Bennett's [*sic*] style'. Certainly Jane Austen is at her ironic best with Mr Bennet and it's easy to picture her delight as she created his witty speeches. Look at these examples: 'If any young men come for Mary or Kitty, send them in, for I am quite at leisure'; 'Let us hope for better things. Let us flatter ourselves that I may be the survivor'; 'From this moment you must be a stranger to one of your parents. – Your mother will never see you again if you do *not* marry Mr Collins, and I will never see you again if you

Mr Bennet (illustration by Isabel Bishop).

do'; and 'If you are a good girl for the next ten years, I will take you to a review at the end of them.' Such lines add enormously to the comedy of *Pride and Prejudice*. But is Mr Bennet's wit the same wit as Jane Austen's? In the early chapters of the novel we admire his intelligence and share his wry view of the world, as does Elizabeth (in the main). But gradually some distance appears between Elizabeth and her father: she acknowledges that he is wrong in his treatment of her mother, wrong to permit Lydia to go to Brighton, and she grows all too aware that her father can 'cruelly' mortify her with his ill-timed pleasantries. As readers, we too start to find Mr Bennet's sarcasm destructive and unkind. Elizabeth's humour is social – she delights in the 'follies and nonsense, whims and inconsistences' of her fellow human beings; but Mr Bennet's humour is anti-social. His cynical wit is never tempered by distress; he gains enjoyment from the discomfiture of others. Like Mr Bennet, Jane Austen played with words and delighted in her power of skewering an acquaintance in one sentence, but she did so privately in letters to her sister; there is no record that she offended family or friends with cruel humour (perhaps because she was able to get revenge on neighbourhood fools and bores through the mouths of such characters as Mr Bennet). And as she created his funniest lines, she remained aware that her Mr Bennet was a deeply flawed man. Because he is funny, we don't condemn him as perhaps we ought, or blame him as we should – Jane Austen wickedly makes us laugh *with* Mr Bennet. But rereadings of *Pride and Prejudice* reveal the emotional aridity, indolence and selfishness of this fascinating man.

Unlike most other characters in the novel, Mr Bennet has self-knowledge. It is not very comfortable for him to have this, and he tries to ignore it much of the time, but it is there. For example, on his return from London he admits how much he has 'been to blame' for Lydia's elopement. When he thinks his beloved Lizzy might be repeating his own great mistake in life, he begs her: 'My child, let me not have the grief of seeing *you* unable to respect your partner in life' (that one italicized *you* speaks eloquently of his twenty-three unhappy years – it's a powerfully emotional moment). But Mr Bennet bounces back, knowing that even an unhappily married Lizzy would not long prevent him from seeking his usual consolations. His emotional doors open briefly to depict his unhappiness and then he shuts them again.

Lizzy is his favourite child, and the one who most resembles her father. At times she resembles him too much. 'I am going to-morrow where I shall find a man who has not one agreeable quality, who has neither manner nor sense to recommend him. Stupid men are the only ones worth knowing, after all,' she exclaims, when disillusioned by Wickham and Bingley and disgusted by Mr Collins. It could be Mr Bennet saying those words. Had Darcy never reappeared to propose to her again and give *Pride and Prejudice* a happy ending, there is every reason to expect that Lizzy would utter more such bitter speeches. Mr Darcy saves her from becoming too much like her father. We can see Mr Bennet's genes in his other daughters too: Mary resembles Mr Bennet in her emotional coldness, while Lydia and Kitty have inherited his financial carelessness (every year Mr Bennet has spent 'his whole income' and has no turn for saving). Only Jane seems to have no genetic inheritance from her father.

In such a patriarchal society, a neglectful father sends a message to the Wickhams of the world. Mr Bennet does not chaperone his girls to public balls (though he does attend the private Netherfield ball), he allows Lydia to set off for Brighton with friends he hardly knows, and he even lets his brother-in-law take over the search for Lydia in London. To sexual predators, this was a clear message of neglect, as Elizabeth recognizes: 'Lydia has no brothers to step forward; and [Wickham] might imagine, from my father's behaviour, from his indolence and the little attention he has ever seemed to give to what was going forward in his family, that *he* would do as little, and think as little about it, as any father could do, in such a matter.' Yet this is the man his wife imagines will endanger his own safety in a duel!

Mr Bennet does not change. When last heard of in the novel, he is paying surprise visits to Pemberley, inconsiderate to the end. He is a character who must be viewed in tandem with his wife; his wit is a foil to her folly. We'd never enjoy him half so much without her. He could have been a tragic figure, embittered by his mistaken first impression. He could have turned to drink or gambled away his house and income, or slit his throat. Dostoevsky would probably have depicted him doing all those things. But Jane Austen was no tragic Russian – she kept Mr Bennet alive so she could have fun with him, ensuring that we watch Mr Bennet making sport of his neighbours and his wife, and can laugh at him in our turn.

JANE BENNET

'She is the most beautiful creature I ever beheld!'

All of Jane Austen's heroines have sisters. Some of those sisters are ghastly, such as Elizabeth Elliot, or foolish, like Emma's sister Isabella Knightley, or cause worry, as Marianne Dashwood does for Elinor. But no sister brings such pleasurable companionship, such happy sharing of news and opinions or such sympathetic understanding as does Jane Bennet. Jane Austen is known to have been extremely close to her sister Cassandra. Probably much of Jane and Elizabeth's sisterly affection is based on Jane and Cassandra's warm attachment to each other. Jane and Elizabeth share a bedroom, and so much else besides. Theirs is a strong and enduring intimacy.

Jane Bennet is almost a paragon. She would fit well into those eighteenth-century novels where heroines are good, loyal, obedient, sweet, virtuous and ever considerate of the feelings and needs of others. Reverend James Fordyce (whose sermons Mr Collins admires) would approve of Jane. So would the authors of conduct books for young ladies. Jane is modest, polite, generous and always ready to think the best of everyone.

Ironically, it is Jane's very virtues that cause her problems. Always wanting to believe others charming, she is taken in by Miss Bingley. 'Miss Bennet's pleasing manners grew on the good will of Mrs Hurst and Miss Bingley . . . By Jane this attention was received with the greatest pleasure; but Elizabeth still saw superciliousness in their treatment of everybody, hardly excepting even her sister, and could not like them.' Elizabeth is later pleased when Jane learns to see the two women for what they are and is no longer 'the dupe of Miss Bingley's pretended regard'. 'Dupe' is a strong word (and is only used in *Pride and Prejudice* in connection with Jane) and it indicates that, for all Jane's virtues, penetration is not one of them. It pleases Elizabeth when Jane grows 'unforgiving' and sees the Bingley women for what they are.

'Perfect propriety' in a female meant that she could not show a man when she was really keen on him. Jane's 'composure of temper and a uniform cheerfulness of manner' hide her true feelings and are deceptive, with the result that Mr Bingley and Mr Darcy are left unaware of the strength of her love for Bingley. Regency women had to manoeuvre delicately in courtship: show too much interest and you lost your respectability, show too little and you lost your man. Charlotte Lucas discusses this problem with Elizabeth: 'If a woman conceals her affection with the same skill from the object of it, she may lose the opportunity of fixing him; and it will then be but poor consolation to believe the world equally in the dark . . . In nine cases out of ten, a woman had better show *more* affection than she feels.' But how was a woman to recognize that tenth case and restrain her feelings? Jane, of course, almost loses Mr Bingley because she is too composed, too generally smiling to all and sundry. Mrs Bennet refers to a man in London besotted with Jane when she was only fifteen who seemed sure to 'make her an offer', and Elizabeth mentions in passing that Jane has 'liked many a stupider person' than Bingley. Jane Bennet is twenty-two and beautiful; has she been attracting, but losing, young men since she was fifteen, because of her lady-like reserve?

Jane also has no sense of humour (Fordyce disapproved of 'wit' in a female). She misses Lizzy's jokes and subtleties, she smiles rather than laughs. Throughout *Pride and Prejudice* Elizabeth and Jane share twelve private conversations. These give the reader the chance to know Jane well. We see all her many virtues, appreciate her 'super-excellent disposition' (no other character in Jane Austen's fiction is described as 'super-excellent'). But Jane's greatest virtue in the novel lies not in herself but in the contrast she provides with others. She is contrasted with Lydia – in courtship one sister displays too much passion and the other too little. She is contrasted with

Mary – Jane is practically caring and sympathetic, while Mary quotes empty phrases. Jane's generosity of spirit shows up Miss Bingley's essential meanness. But most of all, we compare her with Elizabeth. Jane is simply not as intelligent, not as witty, not as sparkling, not as charming as Elizabeth. Readers always like Jane Bennet, but they do not fall in love with her. She's like the girl in the nursery rhyme who is made of 'sugar and spice and all things nice', except that the 'spice' is missing. There's too much 'sugar' in Jane; as Mr Darcy points out, 'she smiles too much'. But the tartness, the 'spice', is there in Elizabeth, and what a difference it makes! It's like the contrast between an overly sweet dessert wine and a bottle of chilled Dom Pérignon champagne. While sweet wine cloys and one glass can be too much, the other sparkles and fizzes, and one glass is certainly not enough.

Jane Bennet epitomizes the correct young woman of the day, she is a pattern of all the expected virtues, but she is not the reason we read and reread *Pride and Prejudice*.

MARY BENNET

'Mary had neither genius nor taste; and though vanity had given her
application, it had given her likewise a pedantic air and conceited manner, which
would have injured a higher degree of excellence than she had reached.'

Being a middle child can be hard. The classic 'middle child' is neglected through receiving less attention than the oldest and the youngest of a family. A middle child tends to have low self-esteem, is often lonely and can be introverted. Anne Elliot of *Persuasion* suffers the problems of her middle position in a family of three girls, and feels isolated and unloved. Mary Bennet is one of five girls, and her position among so many, born so close together, is very much that of the middle child. She is a classic case of 'middle-child syndrome'. She is isolated, an outsider, and she lacks any form of emotional support from parents or siblings. It does not help that Mary is 'the only plain one in the family', so cannot compete with any of her sisters when it comes to looks and attracting men. She is probably nineteen years old at the opening of *Pride and Prejudice*, but as readers we forget that Mary is still a teenager because she sounds more like a woman of fifty.

Mary's first appearance comes in the second chapter, when her father pokes fun

Greer Garson as Elizabeth, Ann Rutherford as Lydia, Maureen O'Sullivan as Jane, Heather Angel as Kitty and Marsha Hunt as Mary, in the 1940 film.

at her: '"What say you, Mary? for you are a young lady of deep reflection I know, and read great books, and make extracts." Mary wished to say something very sensible, but knew not how. "While Mary is adjusting her ideas . . ."' Mr Bennet is merciless, and the picture of Mary needs few further words from Jane Austen. Mary is not clever, yet tries hard to be; she is not wise, yet likes to think that she is. Probably she has tried to attract notice or affection from her father by reading 'great books', but this strategy hasn't worked. Mr Bennet knows that the ideas are simply not there, rather than in need of 'arranging', within Mary's head.

The next glimpse the reader has of Mary is no more complimentary. At the Lucases, Mary is eager to display her prowess at the piano, 'always impatient for display'. She plays a long and difficult concerto and she plays better than does Elizabeth, but her air is pedantic and she makes her audience feel uncomfortable. The Netherfield ball gives her another 'such an opportunity of exhibiting', and this time Mary sings. 'Her voice was weak, and her manner affected', but she hastens from one song to the next until Mr Bennet puts a stop to the agonizing performance: 'That will do extremely well, child. You have delighted us long enough.' Again it is cruel, yet we laugh along with Mr Bennet at poor silly Mary. For Mary is comic – a bore, given to spouting ridiculous moral clichés, and self-complacent.

Unable to compete intellectually with Jane and Elizabeth, unable to enjoy the flirtations and gossip of her younger sisters, Mary lives in her own space where she does not have to compete with anyone. It's hardly surprising that she distrusts emotion – when Lydia elopes, Mary remains serene and unmoved by the disaster; when her sisters ignore her, she appears unruffled. However, there are occasional glimpses of Mary's feelings; they cannot be entirely suppressed. She admires Mr Collins and would have accepted him if he had proposed to her. She is 'disconcerted' when her father abruptly ends her musical performance, and at the end of the novel, when her sisters' marriages oblige 'her to mix more with the world', she submits 'to the change without much reluctance' because she is no longer 'mortified by comparisons between her sisters' beauty and her own'. When a space is finally made for her within the Bennet family, Mary adapts to fill it with relief. Jane Austen even provided Mary with a husband after *Pride and Prejudice* (in comments she made after it had been published) – one of Mr Philips' clerks – and thus Mary ends like her Aunt Philips, a resident of Meryton, married to a legal clerk on a small income.

Probably Mary Bennet is more to be pitied than scorned, but nevertheless Jane Austen makes us laugh at her. Mary is always so inappropriate in what she says, her attempts at profundity are so shallow, her solemnity is so ill timed and out of place. She parrots phrases from books without properly understanding them; her ideas are all second-hand rather than original. She pads out her speeches because once she has grabbed an opportunity to speak, she is reluctant to relinquish it, and she goes on about emotions that she can neither feel nor comprehend. 'But we must stem the tide of malice, and pour into the wounded bosoms of each other, the balm of sisterly consolation' is a typical 'Mary Bennet phrase' – meaningless, trite and of no sisterly consolation whatsoever. Mary tries to parade her knowledge, but instead continually parades her lack of knowledge, and this is always funny.

Mary, as one of only two Bennet girls left unmarried when the novel ends, has inspired sequel writers who want to provide her with adventures and a lover. Most such writers have removed her from her milieu, reinforcing the view that Mary is an outsider at Longbourn. Colleen McCullough in *The Independence of Miss Mary Bennet* sends Mary off to investigate the plight of the poor in Derbyshire,

Mary Bennet's Chance by Virginia Aitken sends her to Cambridgeshire, while *Mary Bennet* by Jennifer Paynter depicts her ending up in Australia. Often sequel writers regard her as an 'ugly duckling', ready and waiting to be turned into a swan. However, Mary Bennet was clearly never of great interest to Jane Austen, and she never plays a major role in the novel, so it is hardly surprising that Mary has failed to interest readers of sequels hugely either. And in movies Mary has usually been parodied, turned into an absurd caricature, with piano playing and singing so ghastly that everyone must laugh as they watch her. Mary herself comments that 'exertion should always be in proportion to what is required': little exertion needs to be expended on Mary Bennet by any reader of *Pride and Prejudice*.

KITTY BENNET

> *'By the middle of June Kitty was so much recovered as to be able to enter Meryton without tears; an event of such happy promise as to make Elizabeth hope, that by the following Christmas she might be so tolerably reasonable as not to mention an officer above once a day.'*

Catherine Bennet, or Kitty as she is usually called, is the least interesting and the least individualized of the Bennet girls. She is seventeen when the novel opens, is closest to Lydia in age and personality, and is also obsessed with officers and balls.

Kitty is characterized mainly by negatives: she is not as tall as Lydia, not as wild, 'not of so ungovernable a temper', nor so assertive. Although older, she is in Lydia's shadow and is 'less irritable, less ignorant, less insipid' than the sister she follows. She is pretty, and she never lacks partners at the Meryton assemblies, but there is no energy or sparkle about Kitty. 'Peevish', 'mortification', 'cross', 'fretful' are the words Jane Austen connects with Kitty.

Perhaps Kitty's peevishness has a medical cause. She coughs. 'Don't keep coughing so, Kitty, for heaven's sake,' her mother scolds. 'I do not cough for my own amusement.' Kitty replies. Could she be in the early stages of TB? If so, her parents show no concern at all.

Kitty, according to Austen family memory, finally marries a clergyman. Holidays with the Darcys and Bingleys improve her, as does being 'removed from the influence of Lydia's example'. So there is hope that, one day, Kitty will make a respectable wife and mother.

LYDIA BENNET

'Lydia was Lydia still; untamed, unabashed, wild, noisy, and fearless.'
A schoolteacher in today's classrooms would pick out Lydia Bennet as a 'problem' child. Probably she'd be diagnosed as ADHD and sedated with Ritalin into a calmer condition.

In *Pride and Prejudice* Lydia is introduced to the reader as 'a stout, well-grown girl of fifteen, with a fine complexion and good-humoured countenance'. In other words, she's a strapping lass who smiles and laughs a lot. As her mother's favourite (and she is surely a younger copy of her mother) Lydia has been brought 'into public' much earlier than she should have been. The excitements of ballgowns and officers, dancing and flirting have filled her 'vacant mind' and addled what little brain she ever had. Lydia is an over-sexed teenager with raging hormones, 'absolutely uncontrolled', determined to have her fun and go her own way.

Like many teenagers, Lydia is careless with her own life and future. She runs off with Wickham without a thought for her own security. How easily she could end up like young Eliza in *Sense and Sensibility*, who is left pregnant and penniless by Willoughby; how easily could she end up like Maria Rushworth of *Mansfield Park*, shut away from the world for her sexual disgrace! But Lydia is wild and heedless. In announcing her elopement by letter to Mrs Forster, she suggests that her parents need not even be informed of her disappearance. Marriage, the most important event in a young woman's life, was a family concern, involving parental advice and consent, yet Lydia can write 'You need not

Lydia Bennet shows off her new bonnet to her sisters Jane, Elizabeth and Kitty (illustration by Joan Hassall).

send them word at Longbourn, if you do not like it,' and thinks her escapade a hilarious joke. She flouts legal and moral laws with impunity, just as modern teenagers carelessly experiment with drink-driving, drugs and unprotected sex.

The disorder of Lydia's mind is reflected in her language. In letters she underlines half the words and ignores the rules of grammar. In speech, she is 'a most determined talker', loudly interrupting Sir William, Mr Collins, her sisters and her parents. She blasphemes, uses slang, and disregards the feelings of her listeners (as when she makes Kitty cry even more by boasting of the fun she will have in Brighton).

Lydia is a spoiled child and nothing ever seems to dent her bouncing high spirits. Her mother (perhaps clinging to this reminder of her own youth) has over-indulged her; her father has ignored her. But with Lydia, there is no growth of character, no learning from her mistakes. Her visit to Longbourn as a married woman reveals her as loud and boastful as ever, never for one moment feeling embarrassed by the shame she has brought on her family. Just as flippant, still exaggerating, still fearless, 'Lydia was Lydia still'.

Ghastly as Lydia Bennet is, she and Elizabeth make credible sisters; Jane Austen has taken genetics into account. Both are attracted by Wickham, both break society's rules (Elizabeth walks alone through the countryside), both have high energy levels (Elizabeth arrives 'almost wild' at Netherfield after jumping over stiles and puddles) and they share the same thoughts about Miss King ('nasty little freckled thing'). Both sisters have inherited from their mother a tendency to judge too hastily, to form strong first impressions based on little evidence.

Lydia Bennet becomes Mrs Wickham at the age of sixteen and sets off with her husband to be an army wife in the north of England. Many a sequel writer has speculated as to her fate there, but Jane Austen gives no reason to hope that it will be a prosperous one: 'Their manner of living, even when the restoration of peace dismissed them to a home, was unsettled in the extreme. They were always moving from place to place in quest of a cheap situation, and always spending more than they ought. His affection for her soon sunk into indifference; hers lasted a little longer.' This picture of Lydia Wickham's emotional, domestic and financial

'HERE COMES THE BRIDE': LYDIA'S WEDDING

'We were married, you know, at St Clement's, because Wickham's lodgings were in that parish,' Lydia tells Elizabeth. This statement leaves the reader of *Pride and Prejudice* rather confused, as there are two churches bearing that name. How typical of Lydia to be inexact in her information!

The Church of St Clement Danes is situated in the Strand and is probably the church which gave its name to the 'Oranges and Lemons, the Bells of St Clements' nursery rhyme (though the other St Clement's disputes this claim). After the Great Fire of London, it was rebuilt by Sir Christopher Wren. It cared for a large parish, filled with cheap lodgings and some rather insalubrious dwellings – the sort of cheap accommodation Wickham needed on his arrival in London.

The other possibility is St Clement Eastcheap Church, close to London Bridge and right in the heart of the City of London. (Jane Austen's favourite novelist, Samuel Richardson, married his second wife there, and is buried there.) It is therefore very near the Gardiners' home in Gracechurch Street. Although built on an ancient church site, St Clement Eastcheap was destroyed in the Great Fire and had to be rebuilt. It had an extremely small parish and would have been uncomfortably close to the Gardiners for Wickham and Lydia when they first arrived in London, which is what makes the other St Clement's a more probable wedding venue. Wickham had to have been resident in that parish for fifteen days before the marriage.

The wedding takes place at 11.00 a.m. on a Monday. Such events were required to take place during canonical hours, according to parish laws. Lydia worries that Wickham might be late, causing the ceremony to be postponed. Her Uncle Gardiner gives her away and there are no guests, no party, no bridesmaids, no fuss. Wickham wears a blue coat, not his red militia uniform. Mrs Bennet worries about Lydia not knowing which warehouses to visit to purchase her wedding finery, but Lydia had no money to spend in those warehouses anyway. She would probably have worn a white dress. As Hazel Jones explains in *Jane Austen and Marriage*, 'White dresses were commonly chosen by brides from the middle of the eighteenth century, but coloured gowns retained their popularity until white became an acceptable colour for day wear — acceptable as in washable.' (Jane Austen's mother wore a red dress when she married George Austen.) Bonnets with veils attached were popular for brides.

The Church of St Clement Danes, probably where Lydia and Wickham get married.

What is very certain is that, white dress or no, Lydia is no virgin bride. When Mr Darcy finds her in London, she is actually living with Wickham (Aunt Gardiner writes to Elizabeth of Lydia's 'present disgraceful situation'). Indeed, it is highly likely that the couple broke an English law while en route to London. In 1698 an act passed by Parliament specifically prohibited 'unlawful commerce [i.e. sex] between men and women in hackney coaches'. So often was this law broken that commissioners of coaches seriously considered removing the blinds from the coach windows and stripping cushions from the seats. Lydia and Wickham are not noted for restraint or prudence, and as an eloping couple they are extremely likely to have had sex in the hackney coach that transports them into London.

Lydia's family can be grateful that, thanks to Mr Darcy, the wedding takes place at all. But, for once, Lady Catherine de Bourgh gets it right: she describes Lydia's wedding as 'a patched-up business'.

insecurity is not a pretty one. And surely children must be added to it: 'stout' Lydia at sixteen would in all likelihood be very fertile. Jane Austen knew a woman who gave birth to twenty-two babies. If twenty-two little Wickhams appeared before Lydia reached her mid-forties, Elizabeth and Jane would be persecuted by the sort of begging letters that Lydia sends in the final chapter of *Pride and Prejudice*. One shudders to think of Lydia as wife and mother when there is no money to pay the bills. While it is hard to see the essential Lydia ever really changing, surely the 'good-humour' would be wiped from her countenance with such a fate.

MR COLLINS

'Can he be a sensible man, Sir?'

In 1987 a book was published that was all about Mr Collins. *Mr Collins Considered* by Ivor Morris begins with the statement, 'There is no one quite like Mr Collins.' Imagine how such a comment would have delighted him! With what self-important pride he would have taken an autographed copy up to Rosings and presented it to his esteemed patroness. He'd have made sure, too, that a copy was sent to Longbourn, so that Elizabeth Bennet would realize what she had missed out on by turning him down.

Ivor Morris's book continues less positively: 'His name has become a byword for a silliness all of his own – a felicitous blend of complacent self-approval and ceremonious servility . . . If Mr Darcy and Elizabeth Bennet are a pair of literature's classic lovers, Mr Collins is surely one of its prize idiots.' That is not something he'd have wanted Lady Catherine to read after all.

But Ivor Morris is right: there is no one like the inimitable Mr Collins. As readers we do not go inside his head (what a weird and wonderful place that would be!); we watch him from the outside and view him publicly. He is a flat character, who is exactly the same at the end of the novel as he was at the beginning. He never changes or develops, but who would want him to? We'd never want to meet Mr Collins in real life, but he is a total delight in the pages of *Pride and Prejudice*.

William Collins is 'a tall, heavy looking young man of five and twenty'. He is a clergyman who says he is 'ever ready to perform those rites and ceremonies which are instituted by the Church of England', yet who does nothing to protect his poor parishioners from the nosey interference of Lady Catherine de Bourgh. She is happy with him as a clergyman because her needs are secular, not religious. But what sort of clergyman, we must ask, writes to an afflicted father whose daughter has brought scandal and misery to the family and says 'the death of your daughter would have been a blessing in comparison'?

Mr Collins comes to Longbourn in search of a wife, settles on Jane, proposes to Elizabeth and ends up with Charlotte Lucas. Such inconstancy makes us question the depth of his emotions. He speaks continually in clichés, and that makes us question his feelings even more.

Jane Austen is merciless in depicting Mr Collins. Her heroine describes him as 'a conceited, pompous, narrow minded, silly man'; her Mr Bennet delights in his absurdities and fatuousness; while Jane Austen as narrator condemns 'the stupidity with which he was favoured by nature'. But the joy of reading about Mr Collins comes from his complete ignorance of his own stupidity. Mr Bennet's irony sails over his head, unnoticed. Never once is he taken aback; indeed, setbacks only make him more fluent and pompous. Emotionally Mr Collins is a shallow man (we learn that he made no friends at university, and he doesn't seem to care which woman he marries so long as he gets a wife); nothing hurts his feelings or dents his self-esteem. In fact, he is a remarkably utroubled character. The reader never sees Mr Collins mortified or distressed or ashamed. He is mercenary, without seeing that he is so (even introducing £1,000 and the interest it earns into his proposal). He prearranges compliments and thinks there is nothing wrong

Mr Collins and Charlotte (illustration by Hugh Thomson).

97

in so doing. He is poorly co-ordinated physically (to dance with him is sheer misery) but he doesn't realize his faults in that area either, and he has no idea how to suit his conversation to his audience (he talks of parish duties in the ballroom).

Mr Collins is at his dreadful best when it comes to his correspondence. 'The promised letter of thanks from Mr Collins arrived on Tuesday, addressed to their father, and written with all the solemnity of gratitude which a twelvemonth's abode in the family might have prompted.' His letters are given in full, or mentioned in passing, but they arrive regularly and always entertain the reader (and Mr Bennet, who greatly values this correspondence). As Anthony Trollope remarked, 'the letters of Mr Collins would move laughter in a low-church archbishop'.

Mr Collins would not be enjoyed half so much on his own. He must be seen in partnership with Lady Catherine de Bourgh. It is his grovelling to her yet his pride in holding her living, his fawning and flattery so amusingly mixed with his own vanity, that make him such a superbly comic character. Mr Collins has been very lucky to get his church living, as only a 'chance recommendation' brought him to Lady Catherine's notice. Usually such appointments came from personal connections and influence. There were many clergymen without livings during the Regency era, as there was an oversupply of rectors, so he has been most fortunate to encounter such a patroness. However, surely no benefactress ever before had

— MR COLLINS'S PREFERRED READING —

When Mr Collins is invited to read aloud to his cousins, he is offered a choice of novels. Almost shuddering at the sight of them, he 'protested that he never read novels' and turns instead to Fordyce's *Sermons*, probably left handy by Mary, for it is hard to imagine any other member of the Bennet family reading such a book.

Sermons to Young Women, a two-volume book by Reverend James Fordyce, was published in 1766. It was a very popular work. By the time in which *Pride and Prejudice* is set, it was fifty years old. The sermons advocate female docility and passivity, a pliable temper and meekness at all times in young women, and an insistence that areas of thought, activity, politics and action must always be left to men. Fordyce argues that 'men of the best sense have usually been averse to the thought of marrying a witty female'. His sermons are sentimental in tone, pompous in their masculine superiority, and dreadfully boring to read.

Fordyce was a Scot, a Presbyterian, a poet and an excellent orator. In Glasgow he delivered a fiery sermon on the 'folly, infamy, and misery of unlawful pleasures', and published this sermon in 1760. Soon there was a demand for more of the same. He then moved to London, where he preached only on Sunday afternoons and proved extremely popular.

Mary Wollstonecraft railed against Fordyce's writings as extremely demeaning to young women. She was not alone. In Sheridan's play *The Rivals* (acted out by the Austen family in 1784), the heroine Lydia Languish uses pages from Fordyce's *Sermons* to curl her hair. So it is hardly surprising that, in *Pride and Prejudice*, Lydia Bennet 'gapes' as Mr Collins opens the volume and within three pages rudely interrupts him, bringing his reading to a close. 'I have often observed', he stiffly announces, 'how little young ladies are interested by books of a serious stamp, though written solely for their benefit . . . But I will no longer importune my young cousin.' Lydia ought to have listened, for she may then have learned to avoid the 'infamy and misery' that would be created by her unlawful pleasures with Wickham, but readers are left in no doubt that Jane Austen condemns Mr Collins's dislike of novels (her father was a clergyman and he loved novels) and his choice of reading material.

Elizabeth with Mr and Mrs Gardiner
(illustration by Philip Gough).

at her disposal such a marvellous blend of 'servility and self-importance', florid pomposity and eagerness to please, as is found in Mr Collins. He condemns himself and Lady Catherine with every speech he utters.

A psychiatrist could find rich pickings in Mr Collins, of whom we are told that 'the greatest part of his life [was] spent under the guidance of an illiterate and miserly father', who raised him in 'subjection'. Nothing is said of his mother; he is an only child, so perhaps she died in childbirth. His upbringing has turned him into a Uriah Heep and made him ''umble', but 'a fortunate chance had recommended him to Lady Catherine de Bourgh when the living of Hunsford was vacant' and she, being a woman who can swallow any amount of flattery, has given him a living. This has made him vain. Whatever its consequences to his psychology, it has proved a rich mixture for literature. His thanks ('he had never met with such attention in the whole course of his life'), his apologies ('but he continued to apologize for about a quarter of an hour'), his compliments ('Miss De Bourgh is far superior to the handsomest of her sex') and his proposal ('Allow me, by the way, to observe, my fair cousin, that I do not reckon the notice and kindness of Lady Catherine de Bourgh as among the least of the advantages in my power to offer. You will find her manners beyond any thing I can describe; and your wit and vivacity I think must be acceptable to her, especially when tempered with the silence and respect which her rank will inevitably excite') – all these fabulous conjunctions of Mr Collins with his esteemed patroness show him at his unique best as a character. Mr Collins is, for all the wrong reasons, one of the most memorable men in fiction. Anthony Trollope, with justification, called both Mr Collins and Mr Bennet 'the immortal heroes of *Pride and Prejudice*'.

MR AND MRS GARDINER

'Mrs Bennet had the pleasure of receiving her brother and his wife, who came as usual to spend Christmas at Longbourn'

In a family with more than its fair share of embarrassing relatives – 'Mother' Bennet, 'sister' Lydia, 'cousin' Collins and 'Aunt' Philips – it's a relief that Elizabeth has 'some relations for whom there was no need to blush'. The Gardiners are sensible, practical, intelligent and amiable.

Edward Gardiner is Mrs Bennet's brother, possibly younger than she is, as he has married and started a family much later than his sister. He is in trade and lives in the smoky, noisy commercial part of London in Gracechurch Street, 'within view of his own warehouses'. Jane Austen does not state the nature of his business, but the Cambridge University Press edition of *Pride and Prejudice* notes that at that time 'the street housed exchange [stock] brokers, cheese-mongers, linen-drapers, fire insurance companies, booksellers, druggists, jewellers, hardware manufacturers and much else'. It's hard to imagine Mr Gardiner as a seller of cheeses (imagine the jokes Miss Bingley could make about that), but, whatever his line of trade, he is prospering. He supports a large family, can afford a holiday up north, regularly invites his nieces to be guests in his home, and he and his wife can be generous with Christmas gifts when they visit Longbourn.

Mr Gardiner is one of the few married men in *Pride and Prejudice* who has chosen a sensible wife. 'M.' Gardiner (she could be Mary, Margaret, Maria, Marianne?) is from Derbyshire and she makes him an affectionate wife; they are a well-matched couple. They have four children – girls of eight and six and 'two younger boys'.

The Gardiners play an important practical role in the novel. They invite Jane to London, where she learns to see Miss Bingley for the false friend that she is. They take Elizabeth to Derbyshire, where she has her memorable encounter with Mr Darcy at Pemberley (made even more memorable on film by one wet shirt!), and Lydia is married from their home. Mrs Gardiner gives her nieces good advice, Mr Gardiner pledges money on their account, and together they offer all their nieces a positive example of a happy marriage. Uncle and Aunt Philips encourage

Lydia and spread gossip about the Bennet family, but Uncle and Aunt Gardiner try to restrain Lydia and prevent further disgrace to the family.

Jane Austen pays this admirable couple the compliment of 'honourable mention' at the end of her novel: 'With the Gardiners, they were always on the most intimate terms. Darcy, as well as Elizabeth, really loved them; and they were both ever sensible of the warmest gratitude towards the persons who, by bringing her into Derbyshire, had been the means of uniting them.'

THE GARDINERS' CHILDLESS CHRISTMAS

The Gardiners come to spend Christmas at Longbourn 'as usual' (my italics), but they do not bring their children with them. They are presumably left in the charge of London servants. To a modern reader this seems heartless behaviour. But England was not yet celebrating the family-oriented festive Christmas of the Victorian era. Jane Austen wrote letters on Christmas Day without noting anything special or different about the day at all. In 1812 her niece Fanny wrote to a friend describing the Christmas holidays at Godmersham Park, and while there were games, gifts and good food on offer, Godmersham festivities were spread over many days and Christmas Day itself got no special mention from Fanny. Mrs Gardiner hands out her Christmas presents as soon as she arrives and doesn't wait for Christmas Day to do so. Probably the Bennets and Gardiners would all have gone to church on 25 December, but otherwise the day would have passed unmarked by special celebrations. So the Gardiners, in leaving their offspring at home, are not depriving them of a festive family day. Their childless Christmas would not have been regarded as out of the ordinary by any Georgian.

MR AND MRS PHILIPS

'a sister married to a Mr Philips, who had been a clerk to their father, and
succeeded him in the business'

Mr and Mrs Philips are a hospitable couple. They regularly entertain their Bennet nieces, and offer open house to other inhabitants of Meryton. Mrs Philips has never lost her girlish partiality for officers – she spends an hour peering out her window at Wickham the day he first arrives in town, and she often invites officers to dine. She is a cheery, relaxed hostess, providing noisy entertainment, with 'hot supper' to follow. As a hostess, she is watchful of her guests' comfort, plying Mr Collins with 'coffee and muffin'.

Her home seems to be the centre of all gossip in Meryton. Mrs Philips has nothing else to do but pick up and then pass on the latest news. She hears from the apothecary's boy that Jane and Elizabeth have left Netherfield, she first brings the news of Mr Bingley's return to his rented home, and she rapidly passes the news of Jane and Bingley's engagement to 'all her neighbours in Meryton'. Thanks to Mrs Philips, readers are made aware of what a small and nosey community it is. Like Mrs Bennet, she is a foolish and embarrassing woman – 'whenever she *did* speak, she must be vulgar'.

Mr Philips probably has a drinking problem. Even before all his guests arrive, he is 'breathing port wine'. The Georgians were a hard-drinking lot and port wine (a strong red wine from Portugal) was a popular drink. Perhaps, like Dr Grant of *Mansfield Park*, he is so hospitable because company gives him an excuse to open another bottle.

The Philipses have no children of their own. They are not fashionable (hot suppers were not the 'in' thing), they are not cultured (their home has no piano), and their manners are not cultivated (Mrs Philips throws up a window and yells her invitations into the street). When Miss Bingley looks down her nose at them, she has some justification for doing so.

Lady Catherine and her nephews (illustration by Hugh Thomson).

'The Same Noble Line'

HIS RELATIONS

'the voice of every member of their respective houses'

LADY CATHERINE DE BOURGH

'The party then gathered round the fire to hear Lady Catherine determine what weather they were to have on the morrow.'

It is always a shock to meet rudeness and Lady Catherine de Bourgh is outrageously rude. She shocked the first readers of *Pride and Prejudice* and she continues to shock us today. One of Jane Austen's monsters, she is a highly believable ogre. Anyone who has suffered a dictatorial employer, a bossy neighbour or an insolent relation will recognize Lady Catherine as an all too credible creation.

Lady Catherine is spoken about well before the reader comes face to face with her. According to Mr Collins, she is 'all affability and condescension', a 'charming' woman, who 'likes to have the distinction of rank observed'. Yet Elizabeth suspects that 'in spite of being his patroness, she is an arrogant, conceited woman', and Wickham confirms these suspicions by telling her that Lady Catherine is 'dictatorial and insolent'.

Before introducing us to this formidable woman, Jane Austen shows us her house. Rosings Park is 'a handsome, modern building, well situated on rising ground'. It has an impressive display of windows in its front (Georgian window tax does not force Lady Catherine to block up or remove windows; she 'advertises' to the world that she can easily afford to pay any tax at all), it has a grand entrance hall of 'fine proportion', lots of showy ornaments (including a chimney piece worth £800), and there's a host of servants to run round after the mistress. There is even an 'antichamber' [sic] so that those approaching through this series of rooms are made to feel like commoners coming to bow down to royalty. Every-thing is designed to remind those who enter of 'their inferior rank'.

Lady Catherine is 'a tall, large woman, with strongly-marked features, which might once have been handsome' (how condemning is that 'might'!). She was sister to Lady Anne Darcy, and is widow to Sir Lewis de Bourgh, knight, but no information is given concerning the length of her widowhood. Films often por-tray her as a woman in her sixties or seventies, but this is inaccurate. Her daughter is about the same age as her cousin, Fitzwilliam Darcy (he is twenty-eight), as they were 'in their cradles' at the same time, so Lady Catherine is probably in her mid-to late forties and is most unlikely to be over sixty.

The award for 'Jane Austen's Worst Talker' must go to Miss Bates of *Emma*, but Lady Catherine can probably claim second place. 'She was not rendered formidable by silence.' In the Rosings' drawing room 'there was little to be done but to hear Lady Catherine talk, which she did without any intermission till coffee came in'. She intrusively interrogates Elizabeth about her family and the Bennet finances, she endlessly instructs Charlotte on domestic matters, and she rudely interrupts the conversations of others. Even during card games she keeps talking – 'Lady Catherine was generally speaking – stating the mistakes of the three others, or relating some anecdote of herself.' Her talk is all personal; she is self-centred and vain. No amount of flattery seems too much for her; she laps it up without question. Praise of *her* house, *her* daughter, the dishes on *her* table, the view from *her* window – she complacently swallows all. And when others fail to provide commendations enough, she supplies them herself: 'There are few people in England, I suppose, who have more true enjoyment of music than myself, or a better natural taste. If I had ever learnt, I should have been a great proficient,' she boasts.

Lady Catherine has various functions within the novel. She illustrates 'pride' in its worst excesses (she feels no real affection for her nephew, only pride in his wealth and estate): her pride is damaging to herself and others. It is of the ri-diculous variety – we laugh at Lady Catherine's absurd pronouncements. 'Are the shades of Pemberley to be thus polluted?' she demands to know. Readers must compare her obnoxious pride with that of her nephew: he too has worried that marriage to Elizabeth might be 'a degradation' to his name and lineage, and has to be taught to banish such mistaken pride. But his aunt will never learn to correct hers: 'she sent him language so very abusive, especially of Elizabeth, that for some time all intercourse was at an end'. To the last, she thinks Pemberley a 'polluted' place. In Lady Catherine Jane Austen shows that pride, where there is no 'superiority of mind', can be a serious fault, whereas Darcy has the superiority and 'regulation' to, eventually, soften his pride into a virtue.

Like the monster in a fairy tale, Lady Catherine is an obstacle to the path of true love. She tries to foist her own daughter upon Darcy as a wife. 'This match . . . can never take place.' she insists, 'Mr Darcy is engaged to *my daughter*.' With her sister, Lady Anne, she planned that it should be so. 'While in their cradles, we planned the union,' she states (this grammatically incorrect sentence conjures up an absurd image of Lady Catherine and Lady Anne climbing into the cradles of their babies to do this planning). She comes to Longbourn to prevent Elizabeth from accepting Darcy – she fails. She rushes off to Darcy to stop him from marrying Elizabeth – and fails in that too. 'Unluckily for her ladyship, its effect had been exactly contrariwise.' Her words give Darcy hope ('Lady Catherine's unjustifiable endeavours to separate us, were the means of removing all my doubts') and he hurries away to propose successfully to Elizabeth. Lady Catherine has achieved the opposite of all she intended and is of great assistance to the novel's romantic plot.

Lady Catherine also brings balance to *Pride and Prejudice*. Elizabeth is over-burdened with awful relations; Darcy needs some on his side so that he cannot grow too complacent. His aunt and cousin Anne amply redress that imbalance. Darcy is shamed by his aunt's 'ill breeding' and has to occasionally pretend not to hear her, just as Elizabeth must blush for, or ignore, Mrs Bennet's vulgarities.

Jane Austen must have met Lady Catherines: women who exerted petty power in their little spheres of life, women who rudely dominated in conversation, dictated the behaviour of others and used their rank to intimidate and control. Lady Catherine is the only titled person in the novel, and is a bad example of the worst traits of the English aristocracy. But she is wonderful to read about, a pleasure to dislike, and she plays a vitally important role in *Pride and Prejudice*. As Elizabeth says, 'Lady Catherine has been of infinite use, which ought to make her happy, for she loves to be of use.'

— IS THERE A REAL ROSINGS PARK? —

Fans of *Pride and Prejudice* have made something of a game out of trying to identify the 'originals' of Jane Austen's houses. She was proud of her ability to conjure both her characters and their homes from her imagination. However, she was always extremely accurate with topography, and readers have not been able to resist searching out grand houses in the correct geographical locations that might at least bear a resemblance to the places she describes.

Rosings is situated near the village of Westerham in Kent, four hours' carriage ride from London. Jane Austen often travelled via Westerham when going from Steventon to visit at Godmersham or Goodnestone, and on the way she would have seen Chevening House. Her Uncle Francis owned property near Chevening and she could well have gone to visit the stately home at some time in her life. After she had written *Pride and Prejudice* one of her relatives became Rector at Chevening. Chevening House was built in the second half of the eighteenth century and became seat to the Earls Stanhope. It was possibly designed by Inigo Jones. Today it is used as a country residence by the Foreign Secretary and the Deputy Prime Minister. The Chevening entry on *Wikipedia* mentions the connection with Rosings as a 'suggestion'.

It is certainly grand enough to be a possible candidate for the original of Rosings. The Chevening parsonage no longer exists but historical records indicate that it did resemble, in location, view and geographical features, Mr Collins's 'humble abode'. One of Jane Austen biographers, John Halperin, suggests in *Inside 'Pride and Prejudice'* that Lady Catherine is based on Dowager Lady Stanhope, wife of the 2nd Earl, a woman who dominated her husband and was determined and assertive. Interestingly, Lady Stanhope's mother-in-law was named Catherine Burghll.

Perhaps Jane Austen did take aspects of Chevening when she created her fictional house and estate, but it does not really matter. What is important is how she uses Rosings to reveal character. Readers of *Pride and Prejudice* see it through the eyes of Mr Collins, Sir William Lucas and his daughter Maria, and they see Lady Catherine boasting of its glories. Then it is shown through the eyes of Elizabeth Bennet and, like Elizabeth, we refuse to be as impressed as Mr Collins thinks we should be.

View of Chevening Place, engraved by S. Lacy (after Thomas Mann Baynes), 1830.

ANNE DE BOURGH

'It is the greatest of favours when Miss De Bourgh comes in.'

Anne de Bourgh is of absolutely no use to anyone. In her, Jane Austen has created one of the most successful 'nonentities' in fiction. Mr Collins praises Anne as 'a most charming young lady' who is 'far superior to the handsomest of her sex', but in reality she is 'thin and small', 'sickly and cross'. Her features are insignificant, she seems barely able to speak and she is stupefyingly dull. She is passive, inert, withdrawn and pathetic. She has been named for Lady Catherine's sister, Lady Anne Darcy, though she is such a shadow that she seems lucky to have even been distinguished with a first name by her creator. She is destined in marriage for her cousin Fitzwilliam, which perhaps explains why her mother has not 'presented her' at court or taken her out into society. One wonders if, when Darcy is no longer available, Anne's mother will shove her in Colonel Fitzwilliam's direction instead. Anne is twenty-eight, the same age as Darcy (perhaps very slightly older – it is indicated that she was born first of the two), so she is virtually 'on the shelf' as far as suitors are concerned.

A doctor could find an interesting challenge in diagnosing the medical condition of this young woman. Does she have a nutritional deficiency, which could be fixed by vitamins or iron tablets? Is she an abused child, cowed by her assertive mother into a state of near imbecility (yet she appears to change little when her mother is out of

Her ladyship, with great condescension, arose to receive them.

Lady Catherine, Anne de Bourgh and Mrs Jenkinson (illustration by C.E. Brock).

the room)? Phyllis Bottomer suggests, with considerable justification, that Anne de Bourgh is well advanced on the autistic spectrum ('[she] is extremely passive and withdrawn, with limited facial affect or ability to initiate conversation'). She certainly has 'indifferent' health and is surprisingly feeble for such a young woman – just to curtsey and hold out her hand seems to exhaust her. Mrs Jenkinson is more like a nurse aide to her than a companion. Or perhaps she is just a serious hypochondriac.

Anne's only attraction is her fortune: she is 'heiress of Rosings, and of very extensive property'. Such prospects would inevitably attract plenty of Wickhams did her mother not keep her too closely guarded for her to become prey to any fortune hunter. Jane Austen uses Anne de Bourgh to comment on the uselessness of arranged marriages: it's all very well for her mother to plan the union of the Pemberley and Rosings estates, but human nature being what it is, those plans go awry. And surely no red-blooded male would ever wish to be saddled with Anne de Bourgh!

Anne's life is extremely dull. She takes a daily drive in the carriage, and she eats her meals, but she neither plays nor paints, embroiders or sings, and nor does she have any of the traditional female accomplishments. Conversation is beyond her – she 'said not a word to [Elizabeth] all dinner time'. Is this because she is painfully shy, or cowed, or because she has nothing at all to say? As she is a thinly sketched character, whose main purpose is to be a possible mate for Mr Darcy, we are not informed.

Sequel writers have tried hard to give poor Anne some excitement in an afterlife to *Pride and Prejudice*. In *Miss de Bourgh's Adventure* she is taken to Bath and finds love and duplicity there (while her mother is recuperating from being run down by a reckless coachman); in *Darcy and Anne* she finds excitement en route to Pemberley; while in Jane Gillespie's *Deborah* Anne plans suicide but instead starts a new life as Deborah Smith. Mr Collins considers her 'born to be a Duchess', but even the most imaginative of sequel writers cannot see Anne in that elevated role. It is more believable that she will quietly fade from life, unmissed by anyone except Mr Collins.

GEORGIANA DARCY

'Georgiana's reception of them was very civil; but attended with all
that embarrassment which, though proceeding from shyness and the fear of
doing wrong, would easily give to those who felt themselves inferior, the
belief of her being proud and reserved.'

Much is said about Miss Darcy before she finally enters the plot in Volume III of *Pride and Prejudice*. Miss Bingley gushes over her accomplishments and praises her as an excellent pianist. Darcy confides to Elizabeth that Georgiana planned an elopement when she was only fifteen, so clearly his little sister is romantic and impressionable. However, loyalty to her brother prevented this intended journey to Gretna Green, so she must have strong family feeling too. Wickham calls her 'very, very proud' and the people of Lambton say she is 'exceedingly proud'. She is intended by Darcy and Miss Bingley to be the future Mrs Charles Bingley.

So the reader grows as curious as Elizabeth to meet Darcy's sister. Georgiana is sixteen years old, tall like her brother, with a 'womanly and graceful figure' and 'good humour in her face'. She is 'less handsome than her brother', but with a huge fortune of £30,000 is a great prize in the marriage market. It is this money, plus the desire to be revenged on Darcy, that tempted Wickham to try to entice her to Scotland for a hasty marriage. Left to the guardianship of her brother (who is twelve years her senior) and her cousin Colonel Fitzwilliam, for most of the novel Georgiana lives with Mrs Annesley in London, being turned into a truly accomplished young lady.

Contrary to expectations, Elizabeth finds Miss Darcy's manners to be 'perfectly unassuming and gentle' and soon perceives that the girl is half crippled by shyness. She can barely manage 'a word . . . beyond a monosyllable', and ventures 'a short sentence' only when 'there was the least danger of its being heard'. Once Wickham's name is mentioned by Miss Bingley, poor Georgiana is so 'overcome with confusion' she reverts to total silence.

Some critics have wondered why, if he is so eager for her to marry his friend, Darcy did not bring her with him to Netherfield. But this would have interfered with her education, for she is not yet 'out' (girls were usually presented at the age of seventeen or eighteen). It would also have seriously disrupted Jane Austen's plot. Had Darcy been early depicted in company with his sister, his more affectionate and amiable traits would have been revealed much sooner, thereby undercutting Elizabeth's prejudice against him. Georgiana's presence would also have made it easier for Wickham's lies to be earlier detected by everyone.

She is also kept at a distance so that she can stand as a near-perfect rival to Jane Bennet. Miss Bingley writes, 'I really do not think that Georgiana Darcy has her equal for beauty, elegance and accomplishments . . . My brother admires her greatly already.' So it is only in Volume III that the reader is shown Bingley's perfect indifference to Miss Darcy. Miss Bingley's friendship with her is also shown to be imaginary and just one of her stratagems for attracting Darcy, for the only time they are all shown together in a room, Miss Bingley takes no notice of Georgiana at all.

Orphaned at the age of ten or eleven, moved around from Derbyshire to Kent to London, placed in the charge of Mrs Younge and then Mrs Annesley (both older women), Georgiana has probably been lonely. Her shyness, even when with people she knows well such as the Bingleys, is evidence that she has been little in company and lacks friends her own age. Girlfriends are extremely important to teenage girls and she appears to have none at all. She is anxious to get acquainted with Elizabeth, but uncertain how to go about it. Her brother's marriage to Elizabeth brings Georgiana a sister, a friend and a return to living permanently at Pemberley – no wonder 'four sides of paper were

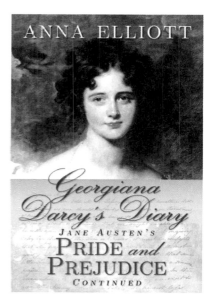

Georgiana Darcy's Diary, a novel by Anna Elliott with illustrations by Laura Masselos, inspired by Darcy's sister.

Elizabeth plays the Rosings piano at the request of Colonel Fitzwilliam (illustration by Philip Gough).

insufficient to contain all her delight' at this prospect of a more settled, and a more social, life.

Georgiana Darcy has proved more popular with sequel writers than her cousin Anne because she is a more attractive character, and because they can believably create romance for her, with dastardly fortune hunters thrown in for good measure. In various novels, she is married off to a tutor to the Darcy children, to a widowed Willoughby from *Sense and Sensibility*, to Captain William Price from *Mansfield Park*, to Colonel Fitzwilliam, or she is totally ruined by finally managing to successfully elope with Wickham. In the pages of *Pride and Prejudice*, however, Georgiana Darcy is a pleasing young woman who has been a great responsibility for her brother (she can certainly be blamed for some of the gravity of Darcy's demeanour), a temptation to Wickham and an imaginary rival for Jane Bennet. Though she is a woman with little to say, she has many functions within the novel.

COLONEL FITZWILLIAM

> *'Colonel Fitzwilliam, who led the way, was about thirty, not handsome,*
> *but in person and address most truly the gentleman.'*

Darcy's maternal grandfather was an earl, one of the highest ranked noblemen of England. This earl had at least three children including Lord —, who inherits his title, Lady Catherine Fitzwilliam and Lady Anne Fitzwilliam. The Earl's eldest son has had sons of his own, and one of those younger boys is Darcy's cousin, the

Honourable — Fitzwilliam, who chooses rather to be known by his earned title of Colonel. Colonel Fitzwilliam is 'about thirty'; abilities and connections have enabled him to reach a high military rank quickly at a relatively young age. He has grown up in luxury and developed 'habits of expence [*sic*]', but can expect no estate or large financial inheritance to come his way. If he wants to be rich, he must marry an heiress.

Colonel Fitzwilliam is very attracted to Elizabeth – talks to her, walks with her and even sits waiting a whole hour to say goodbye to her. Does Darcy consider his cousin a rival? He certainly moves their way when he sees the Colonel monopolizing Elizabeth's attention. While the Colonel is 'not handsome', he does have pleasing manners and address, and Elizabeth obviously enjoys his company. But he does not fall enough in love to forget money or be prepared to endure greater 'self-denial and dependence' for the sake of a pretty wife. 'Younger sons cannot marry where they like,' he warns Elizabeth. There are so many single women in *Pride and Prejudice* who cannot marry where they like and here Jane Austen redresses the balance a little, showing that the single men in her novel are not all in possession of good fortunes.

Rivals or no, Colonel Fitzwilliam and his cousin Darcy are friends. Darcy refers to their 'constant intimacy'; they share Georgiana's guardianship; and the Colonel is an executor of Mr Darcy Senior's estate. Together they travel every year on a duty visit to their Aunt Catherine. On army leave, Colonel Fitzwilliam is probably often at Pemberley. Although older than Darcy, he is at his cousin's 'disposal', probably because the younger man pays the costs and provides their means of transport.

Colonel Fitzwilliam is a likeable character, but a forgettable one. Elizabeth soon puts him out of her mind ('Colonel Fitzwilliam was no longer an object'). As a contrast to his cousin, he makes Darcy's finer qualities stand out more sharply. Elizabeth has three suitors – a stupid one, an arrogant one and a half-hearted one. Today the Colonel would be called a man with a 'commitment problem', but he hardly stirs Elizabeth's emotions – her passion must all be reserved for Mr Darcy.

Wickham is introduced (illustration by H.M. Brock).

'Delighting in the Ridiculous'

OTHER CHARACTERS

'the prospect of constant society, and good society'

The characters of *Pride and Prejudice* are solid and substantial. The vast number of sequels is testament to how very real Jane Austen made her fictional creations. Readers feel they know these imaginary people as well as, or better than, actual people in their own lives. 'What do you mean Mr Darcy isn't real?' reads one T-shirt slogan – with justification. As George Henry Lewes stated of her characters, 'You know the people as if you had lived with them.' They seem to be living, breathing human beings, a part of our world. As Virginia Woolf said of them, they 'are so rounded and substantial that they have the power to move out of the scenes in which she placed them into other moods and circumstances.' Nor are they static characters. E.M. Forster analysed this aspect of their appeal in his *Aspects of the Novel*:

> Why do the characters in Jane Austen give us a slightly new pleasure each time they come in, as opposed to the merely repetitive pleasure that is caused by a character in Dickens? . . . the best reply is that her characters, though smaller than his, are more highly organized. They function all round, and even if her plot made greater demands on them than it does they would still be adequate . . . All the Jane Austen characters are ready for an extended life which the scheme of the book requires them to lead, and that is why they lead their actual lives so satisfactorily.

Having enjoyed their company, we want more of these characters; we want to know their fates, we want to laugh at them or with them again.

At least seventy-two[1] people are mentioned by name in its pages (four of these are dead – Sir Lewis de Bourgh, Mr Darcy Senior, Lady Anne Darcy and Mr Wickham Senior). Apart from the major characters (hero, heroine, their families and close friends – those who form the plot of the novel), there's a gallery of those who play small roles – governesses, neighbours and the like. Then there are those who do not have 'walk-on' parts or ever get to say a word (distant friends, servants, etc.) but who are simply referred to in passing. They too breathe life into the novel and flesh out its sense of a real community.

MR BINGLEY AND HIS FAMILY

'Mr Bingley was good looking and gentlemanlike; he had a pleasant countenance, and easy, unaffected manners. His sisters were fine women, with an air of decided fashion.' Everyone likes Mr Bingley. He's so amiable and easy-going. He could be 'Charlie-the-guy-next-door', happy to care for your dog or water the houseplants when you go on holiday. But cheerful, sweet-natured, generous and gregarious as that 'boy next door' might be, is he ever seriously considered a heart-throb? Mr Bingley is good enough for Jane Bennet, but he could never be the true hero of *Pride and Prejudice*, a worthy partner for clever, witty Elizabeth.

Charles Bingley has inherited 'property to the amount of nearly a hundred thousand pounds from his father'; this brings in four or five thousand per year, so he's very well off. He rents Netherfield Park and thinks of buying an estate of his own, as did his father, but lacks the resolution actually to do so. He is susceptible to pretty girls and falls rapidly for lovely Jane Bennet.

A true hero needs resolve and determination, and these are qualities Bingley lacks. The 'ductility of his temper' means he is too easily swayed by others, and Jane Austen uses strong language to show what she (as narrator) and her heroine think of such persuadability. Bingley is 'the *slave* of his designing friends', and 'in

---

1 It is hard to be exact about this figure – it depends how many people are comprised in 'all the Miss Webbs' that Lady Catherine knows. There could be three, or more.

the *custody* of his friend' (my italics) – these images of imprisonment condemn Bingley's weakness. Of course, he is younger than Darcy, and very modest, but a hero needs to rely more on his own judgment and less on that of others if he wants to really be heroic. Bingley is impulsive (he decides in less than thirty minutes to rent Netherfield and decides just as quickly to leave for London), he lacks steadiness (choosing one county as his future residence one day, another county the next), and he fails to see other people clearly. Bingley lacks penetration. As Mr Bennet observes, he and Jane Bennet are well suited.

In spite of these faults, which serve to throw Darcy's strengths into better light, Charles Bingley makes a delightful secondary hero of the novel. His engagement to Jane is a prelude to the climax of his friend's engagement, and it's a moving moment when he claims Elizabeth's sisterly affection and makes Jane a 'very happy woman'. Bingley is not sexy, he does not sweep any female reader off her feet, but he is an awfully nice fellow, and admirably fills his 'guy next door' role first at Netherfield and later up in the north when he buys an estate near Pemberley.

Miss Bingley is one of *Pride and Prejudice*'s most influential characters. Thousands of Mills and Boon/Harlequin Romance writers have imitated Jane Austen by putting into their novels a Miss Bingley-like female who does her best to thwart the heroine and grab the handsome hero for herself. Miss Bingley is the original 'bitch' figure of romance fiction. Cold, snooty, richer than the heroine and often malicious, she manipulates, professes false friendships and insults from the first page to the last.

Caroline Bingley comes to live with her brother Charles at Netherfield to 'keep his house' and 'preside at his table'. She has a fortune of £20,000, like her sister Louisa, and the two women are 'very fine ladies', 'proud and conceited' through 'associating with people of rank'. Both choose to forget that they are only a generation removed from the trade that made the Bingley money up in the north of England. Wealth makes them feel 'entitled to think well of themselves, and meanly of others'. Caroline is 'rather handsome', has a town education and dresses very smartly.

She desperately wants to marry Mr Darcy, and her attempts to snare him form wonderful comedy in *Pride and Prejudice*. She flatters him ('You write uncommonly fast') and flatters all his family ('I am quite in raptures with [Georgiana's] beautiful little design for a table'), and she insults Elizabeth in an effort to undercut her rival ('I never could see any beauty in her. Her face is too thin; her complexion has no brilliancy; and her features are not at all handsome. Her nose wants character; there is nothing marked in its lines. Her teeth are tolerable, but not out of the common way; and as for her eyes, which have sometimes been called so fine, I never could perceive any thing extraordinary in them. They have a sharp, shrewish look.') She makes great sport of Elizabeth's relations ('You will have a charming mother-in-law, indeed'), foolishly thinking that this will put Darcy off.

None of her tricks work. Darcy politely puts her down again and again ('there is a meanness in *all* the arts which ladies sometimes condescend to employ for captivation') and her manoeuvres only serve to make him think more highly and more often of Elizabeth. The more frustrated she grows, the more unwise her tactics become, and we laugh at her throughout and enjoy her discomfiture. Again and again, Miss Bingley's nastiness and shallowness are revealed. The sisters solace their 'wretchedness' over Jane's illness by 'singing duets', Miss Bingley's letters to Jane reek of insincerity, and her manners are revealed to be anything but ladylike.

Miss Bingley is yet another in the tally of single women within the novel. Unless she catches Mr Darcy, she could spend the rest of her life living with her brother. While she at least has a fortune to help her attract that all-important husband, Caroline Bingley must clearly lower her expectations after she misses out on Darcy. Although 'very deeply mortified' by Darcy's marriage (readers delight in imagining an off-stage scene in which she is informed of his engagement to

Mr Bingley (illustration by Robert Ball).

Elizabeth), she is not willing to cut off any chance of meeting more single men of good fortune at Pemberley. She pays off 'every arrear of civility to Elizabeth' so as to 'retain the right of visiting' there. Miss Bingley might have lost the battle, but she will do her best to ensure that she does not lose the war as well.

Her sister Louisa has caught her husband with the bait of her £20,000. But what a husband! Mr Hurst is indolent, stupid, a parasite on his brother-in-law and 'a man of more fashion than fortune'. He thinks only of his dinners and card games and he never reads a book. Jane Austen, through Mr Hurst, shows that while marriage was the aim of every single woman, it did not necessarily bring happiness or companionship. While Mr Bennet escapes his marital miseries by going to his library, Mr Hurst deals with his by falling asleep. *Pride and Prejudice* provides so many fascinating examples of the married state.

CHARLOTTE LUCAS

'I am not romantic you know. I never was. I ask only a comfortable home . . .
I am convinced that my chance of happiness with him is as fair, as most people
can boast on entering the marriage state.'

'Just lie back and think of England!' If ever a bride needed such advice on her wedding night, that bride is Charlotte Collins. For 200 years readers and critics have debated Charlotte's decision to share the home and bed of Mr Collins. 'How *could* she?' the romantics wail. 'How could she *not*?' the pragmatists reply. Modern readers shudder at the thought of Mr Collins clumsily claiming his marital rights. As Ruth Perry writes in *Sleeping with Mr Collins*, 'In our day, the intimacies of marriage with a repellent man would be an insupportable form of prostitution.' But Charlotte shows no sexual disgust, and never appears to feel like a prostitute. She wants children and a home, she tries to be a good wife, and sharing her husband's bed is a price she is willing to pay.

Charlotte Lucas, who is 'about twenty-seven', is intelligent, matter-of-fact and Elizabeth's best friend. According to Mrs Bennet, Charlotte is 'very plain', and she has 'little fortune' with which to attract suitors. Her chances in the marriage market are slim, and the longer she stays single, the longer her sisters must wait to 'come out' and have their turn at finding husbands. And so, when an offer unexpectedly comes, Charlotte grabs her chance. In doing so, she gains the dignity of 'wife', the prospect of babies and a future home at Longbourn, and she benefits all her family: 'the boys were relieved from their apprehension of Charlotte's dying an old maid', an old maid they would have had to support financially. Charlotte makes a rational, practical decision. Some critics have wondered if she will grow like Mr Bennet, embittered by a stupid partner, but Charlotte is less self-centred, and far more aware of the idiocy of the partner she has chosen. As rational and controlled as Lydia Bennet is passionate and reckless, Charlotte marries with her eyes wide open.

Unfortunately for Charlotte, Mr Collins is a 24/7 commitment. As a parson, he works from home and is always there; she gets no breaks from his irksome society. How much better for her it would have been had Mr Collins been a naval captain, away at sea for months at a time, or a medical man out visiting his patients! However, Charlotte makes her arrangements, giving him the front room while she takes a dreary back room, encouraging his interest in gardening to get him out of doors, and inviting her own friends and relatives to stay so that her husband's company is 'diluted'. Sometimes she pretends not to hear his more moronic utterances. She manages him well, taking on herself the task of introductions and giving him few opportunities to expose his own absurdities. And her future prospects look brighter: when Mr Collins inherits Longbourn he will be busy about the farm and, away from Lady Catherine, might even grow very slightly more sensible.

But there's no doubt that Charlotte has a high price to pay for her rather mercenary attitude to life and matrimony. Her husband is a total embarrassment, a clumsy and pompous buffoon. Sequel writers have done their best for Charlotte by killing off Mr Collins and leaving her to enjoy her children and widowhood in peace, but Charlotte is an excellent household manager and Mr Collins is in rude health, so the melancholy truth is that she is far more likely to be burdened with him to a ripe old age.

At 'about twenty-seven' Jane Austen accepted a proposal of marriage from Harris Bigg-Wither. In 'a prudential light' it was a good match for her: he would inherit a fine property, she was fond of his sisters, and he could keep her in comfort. But he was 'very plain in person – awkward, & even uncouth in manner' (like Mr Collins), 'a big man' (like Mr Collins) and he had a speech defect and a rather ridiculous name. When Harris asked for her hand, Jane Austen said 'Yes'. The next morning she told him, with great embarrassment, that she had changed her mind. The Charlotte Lucas in her made her accept, but the Elizabeth Bennet in her prompted that 'No'. Charlotte's marriage to Mr Collins must have already been described in *First Impressions* by the time of that proposal, but probably as Jane Austen revised her manuscript, her own experience crept into that of Charlotte, giving her a new understanding of a woman who could agree to sleep with a man that no woman could possibly desire or love.

MERYTON INHABITANTS

'all the spiteful old ladies in Meryton'

Some of the good people of Meryton are clearly individualized by Jane Austen. There's Sir William Lucas, with his constant talk of the court of St James (a place he only visited once) who was one-time mayor of a nearby town. Civil and inoffensive, he is another of *Pride and Prejudice*'s delightful fools. His wife, Lady Lucas, is 'a very good kind of woman', and the couple have several children, including one son whose main ambition in life is to keep foxhounds and 'drink a bottle of wine every day', and silly young Maria Lucas.

Other Merytonians include poor freckled Miss King, who attracts no man until she comes into money and who has an uncle looking out for her interests; Mr Robinson, who attends the assembly ball; Mr Jones the apothecary, who prescribes for Jane when she is ill; Miss Watson, who keeps a shop; and Mr Morris the estate agent, who arranges the letting of Netherfield. Several servants are named: Mrs Hill and Sarah (also called Sally) at Longbourn, and Mrs Nicholls at Netherfield. The local butcher is mentioned, and there are Mrs Long and her nieces, the Goulding family of Haye-Park (one of whom is called William), and Harriet and Pen Harrington, who are friends of Mrs Forster's.

These are minor characters but they, and other unnamed residents of Meryton, all have a voice in *Pride and Prejudice*. They gossip, pass on news, exult in Lydia's disgrace, speculate about possible matches. En masse, they form 'the neighbour-hood' and Jane Austen is at her most ironic when dealing with what that neigh-bourhood has to say: 'To be sure it would have been more for the advantage of conversation, had Miss Lydia Bennet come upon the town; or, as the happiest al-ternative, been secluded from the world, in some distant farm house. But there was much to be talked of, in marrying her; and the good-natured wishes for her well-doing . . . lost but little of their spirit in this change of circumstances, because with such a husband, her misery was considered certain.'

MR WICKHAM

'He has been profligate in every sense of the word. That he has neither integrity nor honour. That he is as false and deceitful, as he is insinuating.'

In 1748 Jane Austen's favourite novelist, Samuel Richardson, published his episto-lary novel *Clarissa*. The book was hugely popular and set a new standard in novel-istic villains. Robert Lovelace is a glamorous satanic figure – he swashbuckles his way through the novel, abducts and rapes Clarissa in order to 'possess' her, fights duels, drinks heavily, deceives and manipulates. Lovelace (named for the Cavalier poet) is all a novel's villain ought to be.

Mr Wickham of *Pride and Prejudice* is a watered-down Lovelace, but is far more credible. He avoids a duel, fails in his first abduction, and is subdued into marriage at the end. Sponging, feckless, a spendthrift and a gambler, he wants (in the words of Sir Edward Denham of *Sanditon*) to be 'quite in the line of the Lovelaces', but he lacks the flair or abilities to make a success of the role.

George Wickham first appears in Chapter Fifteen, and his entrance is a dra-matic one. 'But the attention of every lady was soon caught by a young man, whom they had never seen before, of most gentleman-like appearance . . . His appearance was greatly in his favour; he had all the best part of beauty, a fine countenance, a good figure, and very pleasing address.' Added to that is an air of mystery about him – where has he come from, why does Mr Darcy snub him, what has taken place between these two men? Before many days have passed 'every girl in or near Meryton [is] out of her senses about him', including Elizabeth Bennet. Her 'first impressions' of Wickham are all good ones: 'when Mr Wickham walked into the room, Elizabeth felt that she had neither been seeing him before, nor thinking of him since, with the smallest degree of unreasonable admiration'. His physique, face and even his walk delight her, and when he sits down to talk to her, she is certain he could make the 'commonest, dullest, most threadbare topic' a scintillating one. But the red flag for danger ought to be going up in Elizabeth's mind, for with Wickham her first impressions are seriously wrong. Wickham's words about Darcy are insincere and indiscreet. He vows 'till I can forget his father, I can never defy or expose *him*', yet he proceeds to do just that. He manipulates the conversation and does his best to prejudice Elizabeth against Darcy (did he notice Darcy trying hard *not* to look at Elizabeth in the street?). But Elizabeth is blinded by physical attraction (just as her father once was) and is not on guard against him.

Son of Mr Darcy Senior's steward and also his godson (he has the distinction of being the only godson mentioned in any of Jane Austen's novels), Wickham grew up at Pemberley. His education at school and Cambridge University was generously paid for, something his own father (who has an extravagant wife) could never have afforded. He was then offered a church living. Claire Tomalin, in her biography of Jane Austen, speculates that Wickham resembles Henry Austen in his inability to fix on a career (Henry entered a militia unit and tried out two other careers as well). Certainly Wickham drifts, until he turns up like a bad penny at Meryton to enter the local militia there. He is popular, debonair and handsome and for some time all of Meryton is charmed.

But Wickham, like Lovelace, is a danger to women, especially those on their own. He has tried to run off with fifteen-year-old Georgiana Darcy,[2] but is stopped in time. He tries wooing Mary King when she suddenly inherits £10,000, but she is whisked away to Liverpool, beyond his reach. He ends up eloping with Lydia Bennet and marrying her only when bribed to do so. *Pride and Prejudice* is

2 Surely Mr Darcy Senior must have been named George, since his daughter is Georgiana (George for her father, Anne for her mother) and his godson s George.

a 'bright and sparkling' novel, but Wickham could so easily have brought misery and penury to all three women.

Wickham is civil to all the world, yet lacks courage, honesty and any true amiability. A 'gamester' in every sense, he is as irresponsible with female reputations as he is with money. His typical response to a problem is to run away from it. When last heard of in *Pride and Prejudice* he is off 'to enjoy himself in London or Bath' without his wife.

When Jane Austen was eighteen, a militia regiment was quartered in Basingstoke, the nearest big town to Steventon. Suddenly the streets were full of officers, and there were red-coated partners to dance with at Basingstoke assemblies. She drew on this experience when she wrote *Pride and Prejudice*,

Mr Wickham with Kitty and Lydia (illustration by Jane Odiwe).

depicting a militia quartered for a winter in Meryton and creating an excited feminine response to their presence. Her novel contains several officers: newly married Colonel Forster (another sensible man who has chosen a ditzy wife), Mr Denny, handsome Captain Carter, Pratt (how aptly named is this man who wants to dance with Lydia Bennet) and Chamberlayne (whom Lydia and Kitty encourage to indulge in a spot of cross-dressing). These, and other officers, attend the parties, fill the ballrooms and strut the streets of Meryton, making female hearts beat faster. They are generally a 'very creditable, gentlemanlike set' of men. In the end they are delighted to rid their ranks of Mr Wickham and send him off to 'an ensigncy' (a junior rank among infantry officers) in someone else's regiment in the north.

Wickham is an adventurer, out for what he can get. He's not a deep-dyed villain like Lovelace, but is more of a cad and a bounder. In being leg-shackled to Lydia Bennet, he gets exactly what he deserves.

MRS YOUNGE

'Mrs Younge, in whose character we were most unhappily deceived'

Mrs Younge is the only character in *Pride and Prejudice* linked with the Regency underworld. To begin with, she was governess to Georgiana Darcy. She failed in her duty of care, for when she escorted Miss Darcy to Ramsgate she connived with Wickham in his plan to elope with the heiress. Of course she was then summarily dismissed from her post.

Mrs Younge is next heard of as the keeper of a London lodging house, where she lets rooms to all and sundry. She must be prospering in this business venture, for it's a large establishment and when Wickham and Lydia go to her on arrival in London, she is 'not able to receive them into her house', so presumably it is full. Darcy's 'bribery and corruption' are effective and he eventually gets from her the information he needs.

Mrs Younge is in *Pride and Prejudice* as proof that Wickham can at least charm one female to the extent that she takes 'two or three days to betray him' for money. She is also there as evidence of Darcy's love for Elizabeth. How hard it must be for Darcy to beg from such a woman, 'a woman whom he must abominate and despise'! That he could visit her, and visit her again, and pay money for her information, shows how very deeply he loves Elizabeth and how much he wishes to rescue her family from disgrace.

Regency London must have been full of 'Mrs Younges'. Has she ever actually married, or is the 'Mrs' a courtesy title? There's certainly no mention of a 'Mr Younge'. Has she, in her past, been taken in by a plausible charmer such as Wickham? Is she a Lydia Bennet who had no family friend to make the man marry her? In her sinking from governess (a respectable, if impoverished, position) to keeper of a seedy boarding house, she provides additional commentary on the theme of 'unprotected women' in *Pride and Prejudice*.

THE LARGER WORLD

Jane Austen drops other names into her narrative to give a sense of a larger world. London is a place of business, so she mentions Mr Stone transacting business with

Mr Gardiner and Haggerston as the attorney Mr Gardiner consults. The Church was a major employer of the day, so Mr Collins' archbishop rates a mention, as do his parishioners. She adds to the sense that young ladies are all highly accomplished by a reference to Miss Bingley's acquaintance Miss Grantley, who designs tables. And Jane Austen adds to the picture of a large number of unmarried women in England – Lady Catherine recommends a governess called Miss Pope to her friend Lady Metcalfe, and there's a group of Miss Webbs known to Lady Catherine (more females hoping for single men with large fortunes). The gentry and aristocrats are waited on by plenty of servants: Dawson has the unenviable position of maid to Lady Catherine, John is man of all work to Mr and Mrs Collins, and another John is employed by the Gardiners. At Pemberley there is the loyal, sensible and so aptly named Mrs Reynolds to show off the picture gallery, while outdoors gardeners are ready to show the Gardiners around. Through such very minor characters, Jane Austen builds her pictures of Meryton, Hunsford, London and Lambton as real, populated places, wonderfully convincing settings for the characters she places in them.

- THE COMPANIONS -

Young well-bred single women needed chaperones once they were past the age of the schoolroom. Georgiana Darcy has first Mrs Younge (governess as well as chaperone), and then is under the charge of Mrs Annesley, 'a genteel, agreeable-looking woman', who is well bred enough to outclass Mrs Hurst and Miss Bingley when it comes to good manners at Pemberley. Georgiana lives with Mrs Annesley in London and is still learning the niceties of social etiquette from this sensible, polite woman.

Anne de Bourgh has Mrs Jenkinson as paid companion. She is described by Maria Lucas as an 'old lady' (though it should be borne in mind that to a teenager anyone over twenty-five looks old), she has 'nothing remarkable' in her appearance. Her job consists of escorting Miss de Bourgh on carriage rides, 'arranging her footstool', 'listening to what she said' and 'placing a screen in a proper direction before her eyes'. Mrs Jenkinson's life sounds the epitome of tedium. There's a pianoforte in her room, on which Lady

Mr and Mrs Collins talk to Miss de Bourgh and Mrs Jenkinson (illustration by C.E. Brock).

Catherine casually invites Elizabeth to practise, for she would 'be in nobody's way . . . in that part of the house'. That invitation reveals just how little Lady Catherine considers or respects her employee's privacy.

Impoverished gentlewomen often had to take work as companions to younger women. Charlotte Lucas probably avoids such a fate when she accepts Mr Collins. Such a position put a roof over a woman's head and food in her mouth, but it was a hard life – no sick leave or paid holidays, poor pay and no status. Mr Darcy is a 'good master', from which we understand that he would pay Mrs Annesley well and treat her with respect. His aunt, on the other hand, is rude and demanding with her daughter's companion. Georgiana Darcy has no mother and so really needs a chaperone, but Anne de Bourgh does have a mother. What Lady Catherine really requires is not a companion for her dull daughter but a slave, and poor Mrs Jenkinson fills that role. The economic insecurity and poor 'conditions of employment' of these three women add pertinent commentary to the 'position of women' theme in *Pride and Prejudice*.

The cover of a Hungarian edition of *Pride and Prejudice*.

Pride and Prejudice Goes Overseas

THE TRANSLATIONS

'no miraculous consequence of travelling'

Had Jane Austen by chance been visiting Switzerland six months after *Pride and Prejudice* was published in England, she would have been able while there to read her novel in a French translation. Or, to be more accurate, she would have been able to read something that was a seriously 'lop't and crop't' version of her book, a version adapted to suit the journal in which it was published and transformed to suit the Swiss reading market of the day.

The *Bibliothèque britannique* was a journal that popularized science, but included some good moral fiction as well. Maria Edgeworth was a favourite, in translation, within its pages. The publication was popular with French readers, both in Switzerland and in France. *Pride and Prejudice* appeared in England in January 1813. On 6 March the journal's editors received a copy from a London bookseller, and immediately arranged for translation to begin. The first instalment of *Orgueil et préjugé* came out in July 1813 (Part I took the reader up to Mr Collins' proposal) and the following instalments appeared in August, September and October of the same year. The translator was probably Charles Pictet, one of the editors, but his name was not added to the work.

The Swiss approved of heroines who were demure and obedient, rather than unconventional and witty. 'Elisabeth' (her name is given the European spelling) is therefore a sadly toned-down version of Elizabeth Bennet. She never jumps over stiles, or dreams of teasing Mr Darcy. Her speeches and her emotions are squashed or altered almost beyond recognition – her vivacity becomes decorum on every page. She blunders through the novel because there is no male mentor to tell her what to do; no sisterly relationship is depicted between her and Jane and she never contradicts her mother. In fact, the 'liveliness of [her] mind' disappears altogether.

'Monsieur Darcy' is also radically altered to appear as a proper Swiss gentleman. In *Orgueil et préjugé* he has nothing to learn because he is faultless from the
beginning, a magnanimous mentor whom 'Elisabeth' is lucky enough to gain for
life. Always cool, permanently in control, this is not a Darcy who could ever say,
'By you, I was properly humbled.' All blame is laid at the feet of the villainous
Wickham, who, it is clear from the beginning, is evil and debauched; all the problems of the novel result from his wicked ways, and not from any fault in the hero.

The Swiss, as a very democratic people, rather disapproved of those of high
rank. Almost the only irony retained from the original novel is that aimed at
'milady' Catherine in her 'château' of Rosings Park. With no other irony in its
pages, *Orgueil et préjugé* is sentimental and didactic. This bland, dull serialized
version must also have been confusing to those first French-language readers.
Forty out of the sixty-one chapters of the book are entirely left out, resulting in
the loss of two-thirds of the story. There is no Meryton assembly ball, the other
couples (Bingley and Jane, Charlotte and Mr Collins, Lydia and Wickham) gain
barely a mention, there is no social background of Meryton filled in with Mrs
Long, the Lucases and the Philipses, Miss Bingley is reduced to a mere caricature,
and the novel's three volumes are drastically chopped and re-moulded to fit a four-
instalment format. Sentences are flattened: the first sentence becomes '*C'est une
vérité reconnue, qu'un jeune homme qui a de la fortune doit chercher à se marier*', there
is no 'truth universally acknowledged' and no 'in want of a wife' – no tension and
no irony at all. Other sentences are completely rewritten, or moved elsewhere (the
novel ends with Mr Bennet's joke about being available to any young men wanting
to marry Mary or Kitty), summaries of missed action are inserted, emphases and
narratorial viewpoints are changed. All that could possibly be regarded as the
slightest bit subversive has been removed.

It is probably a good thing that Jane Austen never read this abomination of her
'darling child'. It is unlikely that she knew it even existed, and she certainly never
received any money for it. The word 'copyright' did exist (Jane Austen refers to
what she earned from the copyright of *Sense and Sensibility* in an 1813 letter), but
it was not the 'copyright' we know today, with laws and agreements protecting the

rights of the author. Certainly there was no international copyright, or any obligation for the *Bibliothèque britannique* to inform Jane Austen of their translation or send her any payment for it.

Although it was an abomination, the French did not lose all interest in Jane Austen's work as a result of this first abridged translation. Between 1815 and 1824 her six novels were all translated into French, and this included two translations of *Pride and Prejudice*. The first, which came out in 1822 (although dated 1822, it was actually issued late in 1821) as *Orgueil et prévention*, was translated by Mademoiselle Éloïse Perks (it cost 7.50 francs); and the second, *Orgueil et préjugé*, published in the same year in Geneva, was by an unknown translator. In 1815 *Raison et sensibilité* appeared in Switzerland and France, translated by Baronne Isabelle de Montolieu, who was a popular Swiss novelist and translator (she was the first to translate *The Swiss Family Robinson* into French). This was another very altered translation, turning *Sense and Sensibility* into a formulaic sentimental novel. Once again, Jane Austen was adapted to Swiss Protestant taste. Isabelle de Montolieu (who also went on to translate *Persuasion* as *La famille Elliot* in 1817) was well known, and Jane Austen suffered in comparison with the fame of her translator. Mademoiselle Perks, working on *Pride and Prejudice*, was heavily influenced by the Baronne's style and emendations, and publicly placed her own efforts under Isabelle de Montolieu's patronage. Right up until the mid-1990s, Montolieu's translations were being reissued by French publishers, without any explanations of the changes included or concerning the inaccuracy of the translation. Little wonder that Jane Austen's books remained almost invisible for French readers throughout the nineteenth century and most of the twentieth. The French clearly responded with 'pride' and with 'prejudice' to these feeble translations.

The next nation to translate *Pride and Prejudice* were the Germans, with *Stolz und Vorurteil*, translated by Louise Marezoll, appearing in 1830 (*Persuasion* had been translated as *Anna* 'by Johanna Austen' in 1822). The books were not popular with German readers and Jane Austen remained virtually unknown in Germany during the nineteenth century. In 1939 *Elisabeth und Darcy* was published, followed by several versions of *Stolz und Vorurteil* by various translators in 1948 (two that year), 1951, 1965 and 1977. The popular TV version of *Pride and Prejudice* in 1995 made Jane Austen much better known in Germany, and indeed throughout Europe, but it was only in the late 1990s that the first biography of Jane Austen written in German became available. Today all good German bookshops stock *Pride and Prejudice* in both German and English editions.

Jane Austen's writing was simply not recognized as important in the European novel tradition and there were no other translations of *Pride and Prejudice* in the nineteenth century. The early twentieth century saw a small spurt of activity by translators who made the novel available to those who spoke no English, and by the First World War, people could read it in about a dozen different languages. This minor flurry escalated dramatically in the 1940s, '50s and '60s, with Arabic, Bengali, Chinese, Czech, Danish, Dutch, Finnish, Greek, Gujarati, Hebrew, Hungarian, Icelandic, Italian, Japanese, Kannada, Korean, Marathi, Norwegian, Persian, Polish, Portuguese, Romanian, Russian, Serbo-Croat, Sinhalese, Slovene, Swedish, Tamil, Telugu, Thai and Turkish translations all being produced.

Pride and Prejudice has remained the most translated of all Jane Austen's novels (followed by *Persuasion*), but in Europe her books have never had the popularity gained by Sir Walter Scott, her contemporary, or by Dickens. Donizetti, having

LANGUAGES IN WHICH *PRIDE AND PREJUDICE* IS AVAILABLE

Albanian, Arabic, Bengali, Croat, Czech, Danish, Dutch, Finnish, French, German, Greek, Gujarati, Hebrew, Hindi, Hungarian, Icelandic, Iranian, Italian, Japanese, Kannada, Korean, Lithuanian, Marathi, Norwegian, Panjabi, Persian (Farsi), Polish, Portuguese, Romanian, Russian, Serbo-Croat, Sinhalese, Slovene, Spanish, Swedish, Telugu, Tagalog, Tamil, Thai, Tulu, Turkish, Urdu and Vietnamese.

made a successful opera, *Lucia di Lammermoor*, from Scott's *The Bride of Lammermoor*, was not then tempted to make Elizabeth and Darcy sing arias on stage to his music. Usually this lack of interest in Jane Austen's work arose from the poor translations; but sometimes it could also be put down to cultural differences. For many Europeans *Pride and Prejudice* was too unusual, too different. The French found the novel 'puritanical', but the Swiss thought it not puritanical enough. The Italians had little sympathy for 'Giovanna Austen' when she insisted that passion could be controlled (Italians adore Marianne Dashwood, who lets all that passion out): any good Romeo gave in to his emotions rather than struggled against them. The *Enciclopedia Italia* of the early 1930s condemned her books as 'all reason and no sentiment'. Interestingly, though, the Italians issued *Pride and Prejudice* in a cheap edition subtitled '*romanzo per ragazzi*' ('a novel for young boys'), so perhaps they felt that young Romeos could learn something from its pages. The Scandinavians were left cold by Elizabeth and Darcy. While the Spanish could relate to the challenges of marrying off five daughters with small dowries, they much preferred the writings of Maria Edgeworth. And in Russia (which first translated *Pride and Prejudice* only in 1967) the book remained the preserve of a few literary scholars and critics (though there is some evidence to suggest that Pushkin may have read it). Generally *Pride and Prejudice* generated little enthusiasm in Europe.

This lacklustre international reception was radically changed in the 1990s. Colin Firth can take much of the credit for this. When the 1995 BBC TV series was screened around the world, Darcy-mania went global, and a good translation became a commercially viable proposition. Today more than twenty different Italian translations of *Pride and Prejudice* exist, China currently has more than seventeen different translations available, and there are several Scandinavian ones, two in Serbo-Croat, several Turkish (a 2005 Turkish translation awoke huge interest in Jane Austen in that country), more than a dozen Spanish, numerous versions in Japanese, Portuguese and Arabic, as well as editions written in Hindi, Tagalog, Tulu and Croatian. *Pride and Prejudice* is today analysed and enthused over by members of Jane Austen societies in Argentina, Brazil, India, Japan, the Netherlands and Italy, while those societies in English-speaking countries (Australia, North America and the UK) have extremely international memberships. The movies and TV adaptations have been 'dubbed' and screened globally. The rest of the world has finally discovered the joy of *Pride and Prejudice* in a great variety of languages.

Once the novel was properly known, its universality began to be properly appreciated. Indians relate to the problem of marrying five daughters into the right families, the status of Mr Collins and the Church of England is still applicable in many African countries, while any nation which still contrives to find dowries for daughters, or which has a preoccupation with money, can sympathize with the problems of the Bennets. The gossip racing around Meryton is as true of any girls' school today as it was of Regency villages; and the struggles of Darcy and Elizabeth to find happiness and to improve as human beings are totally universal. A reader does not have to understand English to relate to all these and other aspects of the novel.

It must be acknowledged, in fairness to the many translators who have tackled the job, that translating *Pride and Prejudice* is a daunting task. The problem begins with the title. 'Pride' in English is both a good and bad quality: it is estimable to have pride in one's work or achievements, but not so worthy to be proud or arrogant with social inferiors. Darcy recognizes this when he says that pride, 'where there is real superiority of mind . . . will be always under good regulation' and Jane Austen examines both good and bad forms of 'pride' within her novel. The Dutch '*trots*' provides the positive meaning of the word, but leaves out its negative connotation. In French, should the translator use '*orgueil*' (pride/arrogance) or '*fierté*' (pride/dignity)? 'Prejudice' too brings challenges. It also can be favourable or detrimental (as in 'prejudiced for or against'). It implies pre-judgment as well. Does one choose '*préjugé*' (implying presumption) or '*prévention*' (implying suspicion)? The linguistic pitfalls are endless. Some translators have avoided them simply by choosing something else – *De Vier Dochters Bennet* (Dutch), *Les Cinq Filles de Mrs Bennet* (French), *Elizabeth og hennes søstre* (Norwegian) and *Love and Pride* (Hebrew) are some examples.

And then comes the challenge of the famous first sentence. For the Anishinaabe (Ojibwe), an American Indian people, the idea of 'possession' hardly exists linguistically, so in their language the opening of *Pride and Prejudice* becomes: 'It is true

living knowledge that when a man alone has something of value, women may want to walk with him.' While Elizabeth does come to 'walk with' Mr Darcy, this hardly captures Jane Austen's meaning at all. When 'must be in want of a wife' is transmuted into 'needs', when 'a truth universally acknowledged' is softened to 'everyone knows', so much of the irony and subtlety of those famous opening lines is lost.

Things don't get any easier in the rest of the novel. Should Mr and Mrs Bennet say '*vous*' or '*tu*' to each other in a French version? They might have shared a bed for twenty-three years, but they still formally address each other as 'Mr Bennet' and 'Mrs Bennet'. Would Lady Catherine patronize Elizabeth by using the German '*du*' instead of the more correct '*Sie*'? When would Jane Bennet begin to be on informal terms when she says 'you' to her friend Miss Bingley? These are all decisions that must be made, one way or the other. How does a translator convey the many connotations of such words as 'gentleman', 'character', 'extravagance', 'impropriety', 'nice' (a word which Henry Tilney of *Northanger Abbey* complains is grossly misused) and 'fortune'. Or accurately express all the associations of place names, when a 'park' can be a stretch of ground for the general public to walk in or a grand house in its own estate (such as Rosings Park)? If no such position as that of 'mayor' or 'attorney' exists in another country, how does one depict the profession of Sir William Lucas or Mr Philips? Should Jane Austen's long sentences be kept intact or broken up to make them easier for a modern reader? Should the translation sound nineteenth century, or should it be modernized to make it more appealing to this era's readers? Language is constantly changing and sometimes Jane Austen deliberately selects a 'trendy' word to say something about the person using it. Only Lydia Bennet ever speaks of having 'fun' – this was a newish word in English and disapproved of by that great arbiter of language Dr Johnson, who stigmatized it as 'low cant'. How does a translator show that Lydia is using slang? The social world of Regency England will be reasonably familiar to readers with an English-speaking background, but will a Polish reader know that 'gone to Gretna Green' means an elopement, will a Tamil pick up on how much money having 'a chaise and four' signifies, or a Thai understand that a 'morning visit' can take place at 2.00 p.m.? 'Red-coats', being 'out', an 'entail', 'dancing twice' with one man in the course of an evening, living in Gracechurch Street, being 'in trade' – these are just some of the many words in the novel that could well need explanations in a different culture. Explanatory notes can supply some of this knowledge, but inevitably verbal associations, deeper implications and linguistic subtleties will be lost.

When it comes to irony, that trademark of Jane Austen's style, the translator's task grows close to impossible. Irony involves the conveyance of meaning by words whose literal meaning is the opposite, or the giving of extra significance to words on the page, often a mocking one. When Mr Bennet tells his wife that he has 'a high respect' for her nerves, he is being ironic. *Pride and Prejudice* is rich in irony on almost every page, and pinning this down in another language is terribly hard. Another much-used aspect of Jane Austen's style, 'Free Indirect Discourse', is also a huge challenge in translation. It is no mean feat to replicate the subtle differentiation of the individual voices when the narrator moves almost imperceptibly from narrative voice to the voice of a character (usually Elizabeth's), while maintaining the sharpness of thought and style.

Translation is an art form in its own right. A true artist 'cannot do anything slovenly', Jane Austen once insisted. There have been slovenly translations of her novel, unfortunately, as there have also been fine ones. As Virginia Woolf said, Jane Austen is 'of all great writers, the most difficult to catch in the act of greatness'.

How much more difficult to 'catch' that genius in another language! Ultimately no translation will ever fully capture the wit, elegance, humour, exactitude and polish of Jane Austen's English in *Pride and Prejudice*.

THE OPENING SENTENCE IN OTHER LANGUAGES

'凡是有钱的单身汉，总想娶位太太，这已经成了一条举世公认的真理。'(Chinese)

'Het is een algemeen aanvaarde waarheid dat een alleenstaand man met een flink vermogen een vrouw nodig heft.' *Trots en Voorcordeel* (Dutch)

'C'est une vérité universellement reconnue qu'un célibataire pourvu d'une belle fortune doit avoir envie de se marier. *Orgueil et préjugés* (French)

'Es ist eine allgemein anerkannte Wahrheit, dass ein alleinstehender Mann, der ein beträchtliches Vermögen besitzt, einer Frau bedarf.'
Stolz und Vorurteil (German)

'Általánosan elismert igazság, hogy a legényembernek, ha vagyonos, okvetlenül kell feleség.' *Büszkeség és balítélet* (Hungarian)

'È verità universalmente ammessa che uno scapolo fornito di un buon patrimonio debba sentire il bisogno di ammogliarsi.'
Orgoglio e pregiudizio (Italian)

'Det synes å være en alminnelig og vedtatt oppfatning at en rik ungkar trenger en kone.' *Stolthet og fordom* (Norwegian)

'Es una verdad mundialmente reconocida que un hombre soltero, poseedor de una gran fortuna, necesita una esposa.' *Orgullo y prejuicio* (Spanish)

'Parası pulu olan her bekar erkeğin kendine bir yaşam arkadaşı seçmesinin kaçınılmaz olduğu, herkesçe benimsenmiş bir gerçektir.'
Aşk ve Gurur (Turkish)

PRIDE AND PREJUDICE.

She then told him what Mr Darcy
had voluntarily done for Lydia. He
heard her with astonishment

London Published by Richard Bentley, 1833.

Elizabeth and Mr Bennet in the first illustration of *Pride and Prejudice*
from 1833, with Elizabeth dressed in 1830s fashions.

'Pictures of Perfection'

ILLUSTRATING AND COVERING
PRIDE AND PREJUDICE

'As for your Elizabeth's picture, you must not attempt to have it taken, for what painter could do justice to those beautiful eyes?'

ILLUSTRATIONS FOR *PRIDE AND PREJUDICE*

Some novelists are intimately connected with an illustrator: think of Charles Dickens (Boz) and Hablot Knight Brown (Phiz) and their remarkable partnership with ten of Dickens's novels, or E.H. Shepard, who permanently formed readers' mental images of Winnie-the-Pooh and his friends when he illustrated A.A. Milne's books. Other writers have done the job themselves, like Thackeray with his *Vanity Fair*, and William Blake with his poems. But Jane Austen had no 'Phiz', and she lacked Blake's ability with a paintbrush. Cassandra kindly created some comically hideous kings and queens for Jane's juvenile work *A History of England*, but the early editions of *Pride and Prejudice* had no pictures.

Such things as illustrated books existed in Jane Austen's lifetime, and there was a big market for coloured prints (Mr Darcy is certain to have had some of Ackermann's volumes of hand-coloured aquatints in the Pemberley library), but these were expensive. It was only changes brought by the Industrial Revolution and an emerging prosperous middle class that resulted in illustrated novels becoming affordable. Alice in Wonderland might ask 'What is the use of a book without pictures', but not everyone liked the idea of an artist imposing his view on the reader. Jane Austen's contemporary Charles Lamb railed against the idea: 'To be tied down to an authentic face of Juliet! To have Imogen's portrait! To confine the illimitable!' So do we need to be 'shown' Mr Darcy, when the picture in our own minds is so vivid? Laurence Sterne famously inserted a blank page in his *The Life and Opinions of Tristram Shandy* so that readers could imprint there their own image of the most beautiful and desirable female imaginable. Should publishers do the same for Elizabeth Bennet?

The first illustrated *Pride and Prejudice* was published in 1833 after Richard Bentley purchased the copyright of Jane Austen's novels and produced them in a collected edition. There was only one picture, by William Greatbatch — a steel-engraved frontispiece depicting Lizzy and her father dressed in clothing of the 1830s, and a small engraved vignette on the title page. Then in 1849 *Pride and Prejudice* came out in Routledge's Railway Library series with a garish front woodcut picture on the cover, showing characters in Victorian dress.

The early 1890s saw an edition illustrated by William C. Cooke (who worked on drawings for all the novels for J.M. Dent & Sons), creating nine small collotype drawings for the book. He was the first to accurately portray the characters wearing Regency fashion. One very strange drawing depicts Darcy proposing to Elizabeth from a rather precarious perch. In 1892 American painter and bookplate maker Edmund H. Garrett illustrated all six Austen novels. His *Pride and Prejudice* pictures show a very cool and sophisticated Elizabeth and Darcy.

In 1893 the artist Hugh Thomson was commissioned by George Allen & Co. to illustrate *Pride and Prejudice* for the 'Peacock' series and the book was published the following year. Thomson (1860–1920) was a

Darcy proposes to Elizabeth and appears to be levitating off his footstool in an illustration by Rhys Williams from 1949.

pioneer of book illustration and his art had much to do with the future 'packaging' of Jane Austen. His drawings regularly appear in modern editions of the novel, and on tea towels, mugs, cards and other merchandise. His style verges on the 'chocolate-box', with added cherubs, idealized characters, ornamental initial letters at the beginning of chapters and pretty domestic details. He emphasized the rural and the quaint. E.M. Forster called him 'the lamentable Hugh Thomson' and others have complained that his work is kitsch. His drawings are certainly sentimental, but he did have artistic skill and can portray expressions and personality. His depiction of Mrs Bennet, 'unable to utter a syllable' upon hearing that Mr Darcy is to be her son-in-law, is excellent, and his Mr Collins has a wonderful mixture of pride and humility on his foolish face. Hugh Thomson did 160 line drawings (including illustrations within the text, head and tail pieces and ornamental letters) for *Pride and Prejudice*, making the 'Peacock' *Pride and Prejudice* the most lavishly illustrated edition ever published.

One year later *Pride and Prejudice* was illustrated by C.E. (Charles Edward) Brock. He and his brother Henry (H.M. Brock), who was also an artist, shared a Cambridge studio and a costume collection, and acted as models for each other when required. Brock worked initially in the style of Hugh Thomson, but developed his own drawings and became a talented colourist. One can see how much use was made of the costume collection – there is great detail of dress and furnishing – and sometimes the colour can be too much (his Elizabeth looks as if she's been at the rouge pot), but his illustrations have charm, and have been much reproduced over the years. His brother Henry created six coloured lithographs for *Pride and Prejudice* in 1898, for Dent & Sons. His efforts closely resemble his brother's, but are a little too busy and fussy.

Also in the 1890s was the edition illustrated by Chris (Christiana) Hammond, whose sepia-toned pen-and-ink drawings are both sensitive and confident, and reveal an accurate knowledge of the period.

The twentieth century has seen a great range of artists attempting to visually recreate scenes from *Pride and Prejudice*. Dent commissioned Blanche McManus in 1902 and in 1908 A. Wallis Mills (a *Punch* artist) did illustrations for a Chatto

& Windus edition. French art theorist and cartoonist Maximilien Vox (whose real name was Samuel Monod) made eight sepia drawings for Dent in 1933 after trying to 'attune [himself] to [Jane Austen's] art which never stresses, records only the essential, draws rather than paints'. Monsieur Vox was influenced by the then popular Art Deco style. In 1934 Lex de Renault produced pictures for a Collins' Clear-Type Press edition. His are rather melodramatic watercolours, featuring a Darcy who is awkward, middle-aged and extremely unattractive (he also looks very short). There is a Heritage Press edition (1940), illustrated with forty-two line drawings by children's illustrator Helen Sewell, depicting a very starchy Elizabeth, who is 'not handsome enough' to tempt any male reader. Artist Robert Ball illustrated the 1945 Doubleday edition with attractive colour pictures, including centrefold-style panorama scenes which give the feeling of having walked into Meryton. Edgard Cirlin did cartoon-like colour and black-and-white drawings for the World Publishing Company edition in 1946, and B. Gordon Smith did eight rather lifeless full-page sepia drawings and a collection of smaller illustrations for the 1949 Avalon Press edition. In the same year an American edition illustrated by D.W. Gorsline included full-colour illustrations as well as black-

LEFT TO RIGHT Elizabeth and Lady Catherine by Chris Hammond (1890s), Darcy and Elizabeth by Lex de Renault (1934), Elizabeth by Helen Sewell (1940).

and-white drawings. Gorsline's figures, while skil-
fully rendered, show little feeling or connection with
each other. He adds many pretty scenes, but conveys
no emotional impact at all. Indeed, in his illustrations
the reader often sees a character from the back, with
the face hidden. Rhys Williams did the pictures for the
1949 Kingston Classics edition (in one of them, Darcy
unfortunately appears to be levitating off a footstool),
and the artist Carabine created cartoon-like illustrations for a 1954 Nelson copy.

In 1957 wood engraver and typographer Joan
Hassall (the first female master member of the Art
Workers Guild) was asked to illustrate the six novels
for a Folio edition. *Pride and Prejudice* was the first
one she tackled. Her woodcuts have a good sense of
movement and energy, and she is very careful with

Illustration of Mrs
Bennet by Edgard Cirlin
(1946).

background detail, but her style is masculine and stark. The engravings are dark
and rather gloomy – fine for the Gothic-themed *Northanger Abbey* but perhaps not
so suited to the 'light and bright' *Pride and Prejudice*.

In 1951 Philip Gough did coloured pictures for a Macdonald & Co. edition,
with an interesting use of the colour pink in many of them. In 1962 Bernarda
Bryson produced stylized drawings for Macmillan, and the Heron Books edition
of 1968 included drawings by Sandra Archibald, with everyone dressed in flowing
'Gainsborough' style. Other artists who have tackled the task include Gertrude
Hermos (for Penguin), Helen Binyon (also for Penguin), Isabel Bishop (who
did rather gloomy sepia drawings for Dutton), and Barbara Brown, who drew
a commemorative card featuring a scene from *Pride and Prejudice* as well as the
1975 Mr Darcy British postage stamp. In 1980 Lynette Hemmant was allowed
double-page spreads for her pictures, thus giving a far wider vista for the outdoor
scenes and permitting much to be taking place in the background as well as the
foreground. As well as the colour spreads, Lynette Hemmant did black-and-white

pictures. One artist, Chris Duke (for the 1980 Oxford Library of World's Great Books), chose to do a gallery of individual character portraits, giving the reader a sense of being escorted through the Pemberley gallery by Mrs Reynolds. His is a rather attractive and pensive Elizabeth, but the unsmiling Jane Bennet is much more like haughty Miss Bingley, and Darcy is simply not handsome enough. Gene Sparkman created colour pictures for a 1984 Reader's Digest edition; and in 1985 Ian Beck tried a pointillist technique for the 'Century Jane Austen' edition, but the result is vague and overly sentimental, and could illustrate any romantic novel of the era. There have also been illustrations for children's editions of the novel – Joseph Miralles did very clear, almost comic-book like drawings for the 1997 Great Illustrated Classics for Children edition.

Most illustrations of *Pride and Prejudice* depict graceful females, all very busy with 'accomplishments' such as netting purses, covering screens, playing the piano, etc., who look at men admiringly and dance elegantly at balls. Usually the sharpness is lost – Elizabeth is not shown climbing over stiles. It must be admitted that Jane Austen never gave her illustrators much help. Her comments about a character's physical appearance are usually vague – a figure is 'correct' or 'pleasing', height is 'middling', and rarely is there is description of hair colour or skin tones. However, such a lack of physical detail can also give an artist free rein, resulting in both excellent and dreadful depictions. Mr Bennet read books in his library, not lying prone on the grass, as one illustrator has imagined him, and when a misspelled caption reads 'Elizabeth confronts D'Arcy' one has to wonder how well the artist knows the novel. Generally, however, artists try hard to be faithful to the text and produce a pleasing illustration. Probably it was for the sake of accuracy that the two most authoritative editions of Jane Austen's novels, R.W. Chapman's Oxford Illustrated edition and the recent Cambridge University Press edition, chose to illustrate the volumes not with imaginary portrayals of the characters but with contemporary prints of fashion, carriages and the Brighton military camp, etc. or with photographs of houses known to Jane Austen. Perhaps, in the end, readers are best left to their own imaginations: the Elizabeth and Darcy in our heads will always be better than any representation of them that even the most talented artist can create.

146

JANE AUSTEN SEEKS ILLUSTRATIONS
OF HER CHARACTERS

Mrs Quentin, engraved by W. Blake after François Huet Villiers, 1820.

Jane Austen had a strong mental image of her own characters, and when she visited a London gallery at Spring Gardens with her brother in 1813, she amused herself by trying to find portraits of women that resembled her heroines. She had some success and found one that resembled Mrs Bingley (the married Jane Bennet): 'Mrs Bingley's is exactly herself – size, shaped face, features and sweetness; there never was a greater likeness. She is dressed in a white gown with green ornaments, which convinces me of what I had always supposed, that green was a favourite colour with her.' The portrait she found of Jane Bingley is believed to be *Mrs Quentin* by François Huet Villiers (Mrs Quentin was wife of an army officer and rumoured to be mistress of the Prince Regent).

But she had no luck with Mrs Darcy ('but there was no Mrs Darcy'), whom she hoped to find dressed in yellow. Disappointed, she looked for her the next day at Somerset House and at a Sir Joshua Reynolds exhibition, but 'there was nothing like Mrs D. at either'. She wrote to her sister: 'I can only imagine that Mr D. prizes any Picture of her too much to like it should be exposed to the public eye. – I can imagine he wld have that sort of feeling – that mixture of Love, Pride & delicacy.' The idea of Jane Austen searching galleries for her own characters is an attractive one, showing how very real they were to her and how often they were in her thoughts.

If Mr Darcy did not like his wife's portrait being exposed to the public eye, what would he have thought of the representations of her, and of himself, which have appeared in illustrated editions over the years?

COVERS OF *PRIDE AND PREJUDICE*

According to the old adage, a book should never be judged by its cover. But publishers know better, so marketers and designers spend much time and thought on cover illustrations and colours, to create the most eye-catching book on the shelf – a cover that will appeal to the different prides and prejudices of potential buyers. A book's cover always has its own story to tell, about the target audience, the fashions of the day, publishing practice and the economic climate. A lot of thought goes into bindings, spines, typeface and jackets. The covers of *Pride and Prejudice* over 200 years have been no exception.

When Sir Walter Scott purchased his first edition of *Pride and Prejudice* (and began to wear it out with rereading), what he bought was visually a very dull book. Egerton, the publisher, had produced pages enclosed in a binding that consisted of 'boards' – plain, cardboard-like covers that protected the pages but were strictly utilitarian. As explained on pages 14–15, this meant that Sir Walter could then take the book to his local binder and choose a binding that matched the other novels in his library at Abbotsford. His books there, as was the case in other private libraries in stately homes of the era, look so harmonious with bindings and crests matching and complementing each other. On the spine of the novel Scott could read 'Pride and Prejudice' on a small label stuck on with glue. Today a first-edition *Pride and Prejudice* in its original boards and with label still attached is more valuable at auction than one that has been smartly bound in gilt and leather.

By the 1820s, when Bentley produced *Pride and Prejudice* as part of his 'Standard Novels' series, cloth was starting to replace boards. The 'feel' of a book became important (and in poorly lit bookshops touch was sometimes very important for a customer), so covers were often ornamented with patterns of bumps or indentations forming borders or decorating spines.

By the middle of the nineteenth century covers as we know them today were enclosing *Pride and Prejudice*. But nice leather covers were costly, and railway bookstalls meant that demand for cheap editions was increasing. Covers known as 'yellowbacks' appeared, with an illustration on the front cover and usually a small one on the spine as well. They were not always yellow, but they had to be bright and eye-catching to attract the train traveller in a hurry. Bound in straw boards covered with paper, they resembled the paperbacks of today. Routledge brought out *Pride and Prejudice* in 1849 in one of these editions, with advertisements on the back cover. Cover space was being seen as more and more important and the more melodramatic or sentimental the picture, the higher the chance the book would find a buyer; and the purchaser might also buy the Pears Soap or clothing advertised on the back. As Deirdre Gilbert explains in her article 'From Cover to Cover', an 1883 railway edition of *Pride and Prejudice* 'advertised patent medicines on its lower boards while its upper boards depicted the stomach-churning marriage proposal from Collins to Elizabeth – an unintended juxtaposition.'

Other publishers brought out *Pride and Prejudice* as part of a series – the 'Seaside Library' series, the 'Rainbow Library' series or 'Dick's English Library' series – so the covers of these editions had to conform to a pattern already established. This resulted in *Pride and Prejudice* appearing with the same cover as a popular thriller of the day. Through these series editions, *Pride and Prejudice* was read by greater numbers, but its cover didn't stand out from the rubbish often included alongside it. When Everyman began publishing its set of classics, Jane Austen was the first author to have all her novels published in the series and *Pride and Prejudice* was the first of the fifty books. It was sized for the pocket, with print that was easy to read, but the burgundy cover had no illustration and there was only a simple black label on the spine. Penguin soon followed with its classics in brightly coloured covers, but again no picture.

Those in the late nineteenth century or early twentieth century wanting a more durable and luxurious copy could purchase a Dent edition, bound in greenish-white cloth and gilt, with an Austen crest; or the George Allen 'Peacock' edition (its cover a riot of feathers and swirls); or the Chatto & Windus copy with its oval-coloured illustration by A. Wallis Mills. But the cheap editions continued, and it is on them that the greatest variety of cover pictures can be found. Penguin, in 1938, made *Pride and Prejudice* look different from its standard covers by placing a Helen Binyon drawing on the front, depicting Elizabeth waving goodbye to Jane as she rides off to Netherfield. Cover design was soon so important that by 1945

J.M. Dent and Co. edition, published in 1907.

the designer was being identified by name within the book. Much thought was being put into type styles, colour choice and spine decoration.

The Second World War, with its paper shortages and bombed book warehouses, produced 'austerity' covers. Soldiers were desperate for cheap and light copies (knowing they would be carried around and dirtied), and a similar demand for copies to soothe the minds of those in air-raid shelters resulted in unattractive buckram covers, or cheap and serviceable grey board covers. When there was money for a picture, the 1940 Greer Garson film was an influence or provided a cover photograph. Many 1940s and '50s *Pride and Prejudice* covers bore little relation to the text — sentimental heroines, anonymous men in uniform, or a stately home that could be Pemberley or Netherfield or Rosings might have attracted the eye, but did little to inform the reader of the contents of the book. This era saw little attempt at creating historically accurate cover designs.

In the 1960s the trend changed to 'historic' illustrations — landscape paintings, or portraits from the Regency. Usually of wealthy women, such portraits give a false impression of a novel which is about a far from wealthy heroine, but it was felt that such art would attract a buyer nostalgic for a pre-war world of good manners and elegance. The 1972 Penguin cover was decorated with Raeburn's portrait of Lady Colville, bedecked in pearls, while another Penguin edition displayed Sir Thomas Lawrence's painting of the Fullerton sisters (looking just as affectionate as Elizabeth and Jane Bennet); Dover Thrift had *Mrs Quentin* (the portrait that Jane Austen thought resembled Jane Bingley); and Oxford World Classics used the Sir Thomas Lawrence portrait of Mrs Edward John Littleton. Such 'art' covers are still popular today.

CLOCKWISE FROM TOP LEFT The George Allen & Co. 'Peacock' edition published in 1894; A Signet cover design from the 1960s; Historical-style cover by Penguin, featuring a portrait of Lady Colville, from 1972; A 2006 Headline edition with a chick lit-style cover, a popular choice in the last decade.

The last decades have seen publishers going for contemporary design fashion, choosing trendy colours (purple, pink and turquoise in the 1960s, for example), modern hairstyles (Lizzy with a fringe, Jane with her hair loose about her shoulders) and replacing period costume with stylized, less time-specific outfits. Many aim to give the impression that Jane Austen's classic is 'chick lit' or 'reading candy' for young women, packaging the novel in candy colours and pastels, and featuring romantic couples in the cover picture. Today the Pocket Penguin has a stylized dancing couple; Headline (in a cover designed by Ami Smithson) has a swallow flying past, a flower and a whip-wielding dandy, along with quotes from celebrities on the back and the promotion of Jane Austen as the 'grandmother of all romantic fiction'; the recent Vintage edition has two young ladies in pseudo-historic capes and gowns; while another displays silhouettes of two very trendy people about to kiss. Penguin Classics' design by Reuben Toledo uses a cartoon-like silhouette on the edition's cover to attract the younger reader. Other designers prefer to highlight texture, with cross-stitched covers, covers depicting gorgeous fabrics or soft rose-petals. Many publishers simply go for a safe option by adorning covers with such anonymous items as quill pens, rows of books, Regency rooms, parasols and bouquets. Publishers of scholarly editions play it even safer, either selecting a Regency print of a building or landscape (Norton Critical Edition has a print of a Regency cottage), or providing perfectly plain covers in green (Oxford Illustrated) or red (Cambridge University Press).

A *Twilight*-themed cover, published by Harper Teen.

An especially interesting recent example of *Pride and Prejudice* packaging is the edition produced by HarperTeen (an imprint of Harper-Collins), which links Jane Austen's classic with Stephanie Meyer's *Twilight* series, which has sold incredibly well around the world. The *Twilight* books all had covers with black backgrounds, featuring blood-red images (in keeping with the novels' vampire themes). The HarperTeen *Pride and Prejudice* uses very similar type and the same colours, features flowers, and in almost every way seeks to copy *Twilight* in the hopes of attracting the same teenage readership and riding on Stephanie Meyer's phenomenal success (Emily Brontë's *Wuthering Heights* has also been given a *Twilight*-style cover to attract teen readers). The back of the HarperTeen *Pride and Prejudice* offers readers a quiz: 'Which *Pride and Prejudice* Girl are You?' What would Jane Austen have made of a publisher who covered her novel with images redolent of vampires and blood-sucking heroes?

Films continue to influence design and Colin Firth and Jennifer Ehle, or Matthew Macfadyen and Keira Knightley, smile from present-day covers, just as Greer Garson and Laurence Oliver did from a 1940 edition (such covers are known as 'photoplays'). Here publishers are working from the premise that if you loved the film, you will be dying to read the book (and sales of *Pride and Prejudice* certainly sky-rocketed after the 1995 TV series was shown).

Some designers manage to get it seriously wrong – a Broadview Press edition anachronistically depicts Elizabeth in Victorian dress, while others opt for Edwardian bustles instead. Today there are hundreds of editions of *Pride and Prejudice* currently in print. Go into a bookshop and you can choose a copy bound with a trendy pastel cover, or adorned with an old-favourite Brock or Thomson illustration, or with a gracious artwork, or even with a plain binding. Or you can buy it as a 'Flipbook', where the cover has been turned round forty-five degrees, or a 'Spineless Classics' edition where the entire text of the novel is printed on just one page and a magnifying glass is needed to read it. Buyers are spoiled for choice.

But do *Pride and Prejudice* covers have a future? Today many readers download the novel on to a Kindle or e-book reader without any 'cover' at all. The book's 'binding' is the Kindle cover, which 'binds' not only *Pride and Prejudice* but every other book stored there as well. Audio versions in packaged boxes of CDs have covers, but when downloaded from the Internet again have no covers either. Perhaps the impersonal and dull 'boards' of Jane Austen's day have come full circle.

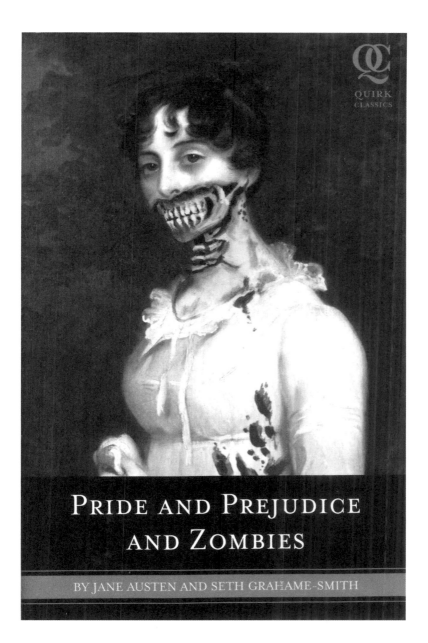

PRIDE AND PREJUDICE AND ZOMBIES

BY JANE AUSTEN AND SETH GRAHAME-SMITH

The best-selling zombie version of *Pride and Prejudice*.

Did They All Live Happily Ever After?

SEQUELS AND ADAPTATIONS

'it added to the hope of the future'

There is only one *Pride and Prejudice* and for many readers, that is simply not enough. They want more! And if Jane Austen could imagine lives for her characters after the ending of her novel – a clergyman husband for Kitty and one of Uncle Philips' clerks for Mary – why should not other authors do the same?

The Jane Austen sequels are a fascinating phenomenon. Dickens is a great and much-loved novelist, but no writer has written of the post-marital affairs of David and Agnes Copperfield, or told the tale of what sort of adult young Oliver Twist grew up to be. Emily Brontë's Heathcliff and Cathy are left safely dead and, while the occasional author has created afterlives for the citizens of Barsetshire, Trollope's characters have generally been left 'unpoached' by later novelists. Why does Jane Austen have such irresistible appeal to modern writers? Is it because, as William Deresiewicz speculates, 'she has an unsurpassed ability to make us feel as if we know her characters as well as we know the people in our own lives. They're friends of ours – no wonder we want to keep gossiping about them.' Is it for a more commercial reason: Jane Austen's name sells, so other writers jump on her bandwagon to sell their books. Or do we have a need to answer her story with more stories? After all, Jane Austen was inspired to write her juvenilia in response to the popular novels of the day; their stories provoked hers. Whatever the reason, literally hundreds of writers have felt the need to sequel, prequel, continue, adapt, re-tell and re-create with Jane Austen's characters. *Pride and Prejudice* has been subject to these uses and abuses far more often than the other five novels, and also more frequently than the unfinished novels (*The Watsons* and *Sanditon*), which it is understandable other writers might wish to complete.

MIXED SEQUELS

The first sequel to *Pride and Prejudice* was published in 1913. Sybil Brunton's *Old Friends and New Fancies*, set three and a half years after *Pride and Prejudice* ends, is a 'mixed sequel' in that it brings in characters from the other Austen novels, connecting them with the Darcy family. Actually, it brings in too many of them and is a seriously over-populated book, with characters rushing in and out from *Mansfield Park*, *Sense and Sensibility* and *Northanger Abbey*. There are many silly adventures and the novel ends with a dizzying number of probable and actual marriages: Colonel Fitzwilliam weds Mary Crawford, Isabella Thorpe catches Tom Bertram, Georgiana Darcy marries William Price, even though Kitty Bennet wants him (she has to find consolation with James Morland). Sybil Brunton did not provide an inspiring beginning to *Pride and Prejudice* sequels . . . but there was worse to come.

Mixed sequels have remained a popular sub-genre. *The Ladies: A Shining Constellation of Wit and Beauty* by E. Barrington, published in 1922, contains a novella, *The Darcys of Rosings*. In this melodramatic tale both Lady Catherine and Anne de Bourgh are killed off, and the Darcys spend much of the year at Rosings, where Willoughby's illegitimate son tries to elope with the Darcys' daughter, and the dastardly plot has to be foiled by Wickham. Colonel and Mrs Brandon also put in an appearance. While it is extremely hard to accept that the Darcys would ever have named their daughter after Caroline Bingley, to believe that Darcy could have an uncle named 'Lorenzo' is frankly impossible. Naomi Royde-Smith's *Jane Fairfax* is a prequel to *Emma*, which gives widowed Lydia Wickham the chance of a fling with gouty Admiral Crawford. Mr and Mrs Collins and Lady Catherine de Bourgh all wander into *Gambles and Gambols* written by 'Memoir', who was clearly too ashamed to connect her real name with this error-filled, Americanized 1983 abomination. *Consequences*, by Elizabeth Newark, has children from all six novels arriving at Pemberley for the birthday ball of Juliet Darcy, the Darcys' daughter. Among the party are Colonel Fitzwilliam's girls, Catriona and Torquil, who sound as if they have crept in from a Robert Louis Stevenson adventure by mistake. Ava Farmer's *Second Impressions* has Darcy leading Mr Knightley on a tour of the Pemberley collieries and confiding in Sidney Parker from *Sanditon*. One tale (*Old Friends* by Andrew Lang) even drags Mr Rochester in from *Jane Eyre*. Most of these mixed sequels are a muddle – characters are probably best left in their own novels.

CONTINUATIONS

By far the most popular style of sequel is the 'continuation', which either follows on directly where *Pride and Prejudice* leaves off, depicting the married bliss (or otherwise) of the newly wed Darcys and Bingleys, or moves into the next generation. The first of Jane Austen's novels to be so continued was *Sense and Sensibility* (in 1929 Jane Austen's great-great-niece wrote *Margaret Dashwood, or Interference*), but twenty years later it was *Pride and Prejudice*'s turn. *Pemberley Shades* by D.A. Bonavia Hunt was a creditable attempt, although Jane Austen is most unlikely to have ever named a character 'Horace Carlini'.

Most of these sequels marry off Kitty and Mary Bennet, Georgiana Darcy and even nasty Caroline Bingley and poor feeble Anne de Bourgh. In Jane Gillespie's *Deborah* Anne runs away and calls herself Deborah (de Bourgh) Smith. All her adventures come right in the end and she finds herself a husband. Julia Barrett's *Presumption* gives Georgiana her turn at romance, as does C. Allyn Pierson's *Mr Darcy's Little Sister*, while *Desire and Duty* finds husbands for Kitty and Mary Bennet. In *A Match for Mary Bennet* by Eucharista Ward, Mary does not want a husband and would prefer to follow 'God's path for her life', until she fortuitously discovers that 'the true union of a woman and a man is all part of God's plan' (Jane Austen would surely have been the first to scoff at such Evangelical claptrap). Even worse is Colleen McCullough's *The Independence of Miss Mary Bennet* which, after a series of extremely improbable adventures, ends with Mary giving birth to a son, Hamish Duncan Sinclair, and looking forward to the baby's circumcision.

Many continuations create problems in the Darcy marriage: the longed-for son and heir fails to arrive, Darcy is hopeless in bed, when she does give birth Elizabeth hasn't the milk supply to feed her baby. Burglars and impostors arrive at Pemberley and must be unmasked, the Collinses move too close for comfort, Mrs Bennet dies and Elizabeth must cope with the prospects of a new stepmother in Mrs Forster (widowed, of course), Aunt Philips is in prison for stealing lace and must be rescued: these are all scenarios from recent sequels. In others Mr Darcy has secrets (*Mr Darcy's Secret*, Jane Odiwe), a possible illegitimate child (*The Bar Sinister: Pride and Prejudice Continues*, Linda Berdoll), an obsession (*Mr Darcy's Obsession*, Abigail Reynolds), communication problems (*An Unequal Marriage*, Emma Tennant) – the list of afflictions heaped on Jane Austen's benighted hero is seemingly endless. His wife calls him 'Fitz' in some sequels, 'Fitzwilliam', 'Darcy dear' and 'Mr Darcy' in others, as hero and heroine are put through stilted dialogue, made-up dizzying adventures and unlikely scenarios before they can return to the happiness in which Jane Austen left them at the end of her novel. Some continuations simply provide mushy and sentimental portraits of a marriage that has no problems, as is the case with *My Dearest Mr Darcy: An Amazing Journey into Love Everlasting* by Sharon Lathan (Jane Austen would have been truly amazed by the title alone).

Other continuations take the Darcys and Bingleys through to the next generation. The Darcy children, variously named Richard, Julian, Juliet, Alethea, Letitia, Camilla, Cassandra, Edward, Miranda, Isabelle, Jane, Fitzwilliam, Henry, etc., meet their cousins Jonathan, Anne-Marie, Charles Junior and Beth Bingley, or Chloe and Bettina Wickham. Caroline and Darcy Gardiner, and Marcia and William Collins also wander in and out.

Many of these books try to imitate Jane Austen's title – *Honour and Humility*, *Affinity and Affection*, *Virtue and Vanity*, *Desire and Duty*, *Duty and Desire*, *Drive and Determination*, *Trust and Triumph* – but often that is where accurate imitation ends. Many are riddled with mistakes (seven people sitting down to play whist, a game for four; characters picking cranberries in nineteenth-century England; divorces obtained at the drop of a hat; women attending funerals), and a host of other inaccuracies occur. And as for some of the language! Jane Austen once had a character in a state of extreme emotional stress say 'Good God!', but 'Oh, shit', 'Hop to it', 'brat', 'put on the spot', 'contrary folks', 'stalking someone', 'looking sheepish' and 'bums up' were phrases unknown to her. One novel describes Elizabeth Bennet as 'elfin', which raises the suspicion that the author had possibly not actually read *Pride and Prejudice*. Such language fails dismally to ring true in a continuation novel.

RETELLINGS

Then there are all the retellings of Jane Austen's plot from a different angle, such as *Lydia Bennet's Story: A Sequel to Pride and Prejudice* by Jane Odiwe, which gives Lydia a chance to have her say. *Darcy's Story* by Janet Aylmer is a popular example of this sub-genre. The novel reveals more of Darcy's relationships with his aunt, sister and friend, and the reader sees Elizabeth and her relations through Darcy's eyes. Much of Jane Austen's text is used or paraphrased, but all with a different slant. It is hard to imagine Mr Darcy keeping a diary from the age of ten, but he does in Marjorie Fasman's *The Diary of Henry Fitzwilliam Darcy*. One third of the way through he meets Elizabeth, and then the diary continues on after the point where Jane Austen ends her novel, to record his wedded bliss, often quite explicitly. *The Private Diary of Mr Darcy: A Novel* by Maya Slater, *Darcy's Passions: Pride and Prejudice Retold Through His Eyes* by Regina Jeffers and *An Assembly Such as This* by Pamela Aidan are other examples. P.O. Dixon has penned *To Have His Cake (& Eat it Too): Mr Darcy's Tale*, which is followed up by *What He Would Not Do: Mr Darcy's Tale Continues*.

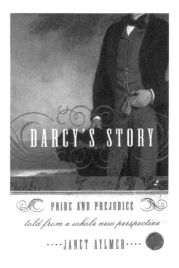

Darcy's Story, a retelling of *Pride and Prejudice* from Darcy's point of view.

Providing only Mr Darcy's point of view is far too tame for some writers: they need to give him further adventures as well. A large number of authors have created 'what-if' continuations, pausing *Pride and Prejudice* at a certain point and sending it flying in some other direction, before eventually

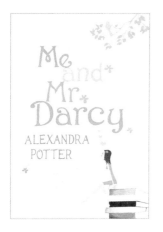

A modern adaptation by Alexandra Potter.

returning it to its original conclusion. In *Mr Darcy's Undoing* Elizabeth accepts another man's proposal; in *Beloved* she is adopted out; in *Darcy and the Duchess* she is married when Darcy first meets her; and in *Fitzwilliam Darcy: An Honourable Man* he flees to Scotland when Elizabeth turns him down. The past decade has seen a flood of such novels. *Mr Darcy's Proposal* speculates on what might have happened if Darcy hadn't proposed when he did; in *The Perfect Bride for Mr Darcy* it is his cousin Anne de Bourgh who helps bring about his marriage with Elizabeth; in *Only Mr Darcy Will Do* he finds Elizabeth working as a governess in London; *Pride and Prejudice: The Jewess and the Gentile* asks how the story might have gone had Elizabeth Bennet been Jewish and the victim of anti-Semitism; and in *An Arranged Marriage* the Bennets all leave Longbourn when Mr Bennet dies, so Darcy misses his chance to propose. *Darcy and Fitzwilliam: A Tale of a Gentleman and an Officer* examines his relationship with Colonel Fitzwilliam, *The Mistress's Black Veil: A Pride and Prejudice Vagary* rewrites *à la Northanger Abbey* the fate Jane Austen gave her hero, while *Mr Darcy's Angel of Mercy* drops him into the American Civil War. Abigail Reynolds has written *A Pemberley Medley* of five variations of Darcy's story, and Mary Lydon Simonsen has had at least three goes at making Darcy do what she wants him to do. Perhaps readers should pause over *Mr Darcy Takes the Plunge* to ask what depths this hero must be further expected to plumb?

MODERN RETELLINGS AND ADAPTATIONS

Generally the modern retellings of *Pride and Prejudice* are better than the historical ones. *Pride, Prejudice and Jasmin Field* by Melissa Nathan is an entertaining recasting of Jane Austen's characters into twentieth-century London, in which Jasmin, a young journalist, is acting the part of Elizabeth Bennet in a play, and the man directing it turns out to resemble Darcy off-stage as well as on. *Jane Austen in Boca* by Paula Marantz-Cohen is also enjoyable. It transports *Pride and Prejudice*'s characters to a Jewish retirement village in Florida very credibly. Then there is *Perfect Fit: A Modern Tale of Pride and Prejudice* by Linda Wells, in which Elizabeth Bennet is a twenty-first-century writer of mystery novels, and Sara Angelini's *The Trials of the Honourable F. Darcy* in which the modern Darcy is a judge. In *Lions and Liquorice* Kate Fenton retells the *Pride and Prejudice* plot in a Yorkshire setting, where a production company is making a film of a Jane Austen novel. *First Impressions* by Debra White Smith has a modern Darcy who is a handsome young rancher who must protect his heroine, 'Eddi', from tornadoes; *Prawn and Prejudice* by Belinda Roberts moves the story to a seaside setting in Devonshire; *A Little Bit Psychic: Pride and Prejudice with a Modern Twist* depicts Elizabeth doing her Ph.D. in London – and there are many other examples. Some modern versions are in short-story form. Chawton House, now a centre for the study of early woman writers, has held two short-story competitions and the result has been *Dancing with Mr Darcy*, an anthology of tales inspired by Jane Austen and her works, and *Wooing Mr Wickham*, which has short fiction inspired by her villains and heroes.

Retellings move into a variety of epochs as well. *1932* by Karen M. Cox has an Art Deco American setting. *Pemberley Ranch* places Beth Bennet at the end of the American Civil War in a *Pride and Prejudice*-meets-*Gone with the Wind* scenario, while *Pride and Prescience* depicts a Lizzy-like heroine saving Regency England from an alien invasion in a sort of historical/futuristic mix. American Bennets meet up with English Bennets, or the story becomes entirely American, as in *A Single Man, Good Fortune (Must Want Wife): American Pride and Prejudice: Book I*, which is followed by *Book II* and *Book III* for those desperate to learn what happens.

In yet other versions young women visit England on *Pride and Prejudice*-themed tours, and encounter Mr Darcy on their travels. Sometimes he's a ghost, as in Alexandra Potter's popular *Me and Mr Darcy*, in which the heroine meets a modern-day corporeal Darcy as well as the phantom one. *Austenland* by Shannon Hale runs along similar lines. And in Victoria Connelly's *A Weekend with Mr Darcy* a university lecturer ('the only thing keeping professor Katherine Roberts sane is Jane Austen') goes off on a Jane Austen-themed weekend in Hampshire and meets a surprise Mr Darcy there.

Time-travel sequels resembling the film *Lost in Austen* have also sold well. In *Confessions of a Jane Austen Addict*, by Laurie Viera Rigler, Los Angeles girl Courtney Stone wakes up one morning in Regency England and finds that not even her love of the Jane Austen world has prepared her to cope with chamber pots and nineteenth-century standards of hygiene.

MURDER MYSTERIES

According to P.D. James, doyenne of detective fiction, if Jane Austen were alive today she would be writing murder mysteries, and doing it brilliantly. In 2011 P.D. James combined her two enthusiasms – for murder and for the novels of Jane Austen – by writing *Death Comes to Pemberley*. Her story is set in 1803, when Elizabeth and Mr Darcy have been six years married and have two children. The murder victim is Captain Denny and Mr Wickham is found in the woods of Pemberley bending over his friend's blood-soaked body. Darcy and Elizabeth do not become detectives themselves, but are involved and deeply interested observers of the outcome of Wickham's trial. P.D. James's novel is well crafted, but her Elizabeth and Darcy are rather dull characters and there are some historical errors – it's nowhere near as good as one of her Dalgleish detective novels. Some enjoyable references to characters from *Emma* and *Persuasion* are brought in at the end. This is a murder mystery that is a murder mystery in its own right, but it is also a pleasing homage to *Pride and Prejudice*. However, the reader misses a sparkling Elizabeth, Mrs Bennet rarely appears, Mr Collins is missing, and Lady Catherine has been killed off at the very beginning. Without those brilliant comic creations, *Death Comes to Pemberley* is left curiously flat.

P.D. James is not alone in introducing murder and other crimes into a *Pride and Prejudice* sequel. A survey of female readers in Britain, carried out in 2011, identified Mr Darcy as the literary character most women wanted to meet (preferably romantically), but out of the next six heroes chosen, five were detectives or solvers of crime (this included Inspector Morse, Sherlock Holmes and James Bond). This means that those sequel writers who combine Darcy and crime are working with an appealing mix. Combining crime and *Pride and Prejudice* is also appropriate given Jane Austen's own interest in criminal activities. She even visited a prison once, which was an unusual thing for a Regency lady to do. Her juvenilia is packed with crimes of various degrees of iniquity and *Jane Austen and Crime* reveals how the crimes of duelling, poaching, theft, gambling and elopement are all to be found in her mature novels as well.

American novelist Stephanie Barron has picked up on this interest and made Jane Austen the solver of crimes in her series of mystery novels, starting with *Jane and the Unpleasantness at Scargrave Manor*. But Carrie Bebris feels that it is not Jane Austen but her Mr and Mrs Darcy who make more likely detectives. Her popular series of six novels takes the couple on a perilous journey through all of the Austen novels, finding 'who-dunnit' at Mansfield, Northanger, Highbury and at Lyme. *Pride and Prescience* is the *Pride and Prejudice* book of her series and in it the Darcys have not even had time to enjoy a honeymoon before crime, the supernatural, Miss Bingley's American fiancé and the threat of madness almost overwhelm them. They must search out the truth, universally acknowledged or otherwise. Of course, prescience wins the day and all comes right in the end. *The Phantom of Pemberley: A Pride and Prejudice Murder Mystery* by Regina Jeffers also features the husband and wife team and uses the classic murder device of a snowstorm trapping a party of assorted guests at Pemberley.

Other mystery novels inspired by *Pride and Prejudice* move forward in time so that it is Elizabeth and Darcy's descendants who must solve the crime. *Darkness at Pemberley* by T.H. White was published in 1932 and has a classic 1930s English setting (the 1930s were the Golden Age of the English detective novel). It involves Sir Charles Darcy and his sister Elizabeth but, while Pemberley is a location and bits of Darcy family history are inserted, there is not a great deal of connection with Jane Austen's novel. Tracy Kiely's *Murder at Longbourn: A Mystery* (which has been described as being in the genre of 'rom-com-crime') has a modern-day setting with aspects of *Pride and Prejudice* in the plot and characters. Elizabeth Parker attends a 'How to Host a Murder' party and must shelve her hopes of finding her own Mr Darcy while she solves the mystery. The same is the case with its follow-up, *Murder on the Bride's Side*, in which Elizabeth Parker reads *Pride and Prejudice* for comfort and encounters a cat named 'Lady Catherine,' and which contains more re-imagined themes and characters from Jane Austen's novel. Both these books are set in the US, and author Tracy Kiely has satisfied her desire to mix and match her two favourite English writers, Jane Austen and Agatha Christie.

Surprisingly no crime novelist inspired by *Pride and Prejudice* has ever murdered Lady Catherine de Bourgh, who is surely the character in the book most deserving of some particularly gruesome end.

PORNOGRAPHIC VERSIONS

It is a truth universally acknowledged – universal, that is, among a sub-group of sequel writers – that a single man in possession of a large fortune must be in want of a good bonk! There are writers who have been unable to resist the temptation of describing Darcy's sex life, and even that of Mr Collins. Every reader knows that Charlotte's wedding night must have been grim indeed, but do we really want to know the gruesome details?

The craze for 'sexing-up' Jane Austen began with *Pride and Promiscuity: The Lost Sex Scenes of Jane Austen* by Arielle Eckstut and Dennis Ashton. Purporting to be a missing manuscript that was miraculously found, this book contains 'missing' chapters from the various Austen novels. Three of these are devoted to *Pride and Prejudice*. They describe Jane Bennet, ill at Netherfield, enjoying lesbian sex with Caroline Bingley and her sister Louisa Hurst; Elizabeth and Darcy getting passionate against a tree in the grounds of Pemberley before 'she arrange[s] him on the grass' and straddles him; and finally Charlotte Collins enlivening her sex life with her husband by dressing in one of Lady Catherine's old gowns to excite him, and then using a whip on him. The book was more of a send-up than a serious attempt at pornography – the authors were catering to readers' expectations of passion, rather than describing love-making in full detail. However, it demonstrated that sex and *Pride and Prejudice* could be a profitable combination.

After this book, it appeared to be open season for porn writers. *Fire and Cross: Pride and Prejudice with a Mysterious Twist* by Enid Wilson brings in whips, spies and even murder, as well as steamy sex. *Mr Darcy Vibrates*, by the same author, is a collection of stories inspired by *Pride and* Prejudice which is not for the faint-heart-

Illustration from *Pride and Promiscuity* by Arielle Eckstut and Dennis Ashton.

ed, while her *Really Angelic: Pride and Prejudice with a Paranormal Twist* promises more steamy sessions, along with angels, in a book that 'transcends dimensions'. Barbara Tiller Cole's *White Lies and Other Half Truths* claims to be the Regency sex manual Jane Austen would have written, if only she'd thought of it.

Other writers have agreed that Mr Darcy's sex life is in want of a boost, whether he appears in historical or modern sequels. *Fitzwilliam Darcy, Rock Star* by Heather Lynn Rigaud is a 'sexy romance', and when Elizabeth arrives on this musician's scene, she 'rocks his world' in more ways than one. She is a member of a female band, 'Long Bourne Suffering', and the novel is the tale of her sweaty, raunchy relationship with long-haired and tattooed Fitzwilliam Darcy. In *My BFF: A Friendly Romance* by Ruth Phillips Oakland Darcy is a billionaire, weary of the sex he has with models, which satisfies his baser needs, but which is pretty meaningless emotionally. He then meets Professor Elizabeth Bennet. His trousers tighten uncomfortably every time he looks at her and soon they indulge in 'erotic interludes'. Lucy Steele gets a brief mention as a porn star, which is a nice touch, but it is totally unconvincing that Mrs Bennet would happily offer one of her daughters up to be raped. In Linda Wells's *Chance Encounters* the well-stocked library at Pemberley is so well stocked that it contains the *Kama Sutra* (first printed in English only in 1883, but perhaps Darcy read Sanskrit) and Darcy and Elizabeth put its teachings into practice in the woods, in their carriage, in their bedroom, in front of an audience and in plenty of other places, during more than 400 pages. *Chance Encounters*'s sequel, *Fate and Consequences*, has more bodice ripping along similar lines.

Other novels change the gender preferences of the main characters. *Pride/Prejudice: A Novel of Mr Darcy, Elizabeth Bennet, and Their Forbidden Lovers* by Ann Herendeen imagines Darcy, Bingley, Elizabeth and Charlotte as bisexuals, all enjoying same-sex affairs as well as more conventional ones. The author states that she has 'queered Jane Austen's novel'. Her book might have won a minor literary award in a 'bisexual fiction' category, but most readers of *Pride and Prejudice* will shudder at the mere thought of Darcy nightly assaulting his dear friend Bingley, with the two men glued together 'in a sticky love-scented mess', and at the idea of Charlotte finding consolation in the embraces of Anne de Bourgh when she loses Elizabeth as her lover.

Pride and Prejudice: The Wild and Wanton Edition by Jane Austen and Miranda Pillow removes some original scenes from the novel to make room for the erotica. Lydia is a total slut, Darcy masturbates, and almost every character loses no opportunity to get hot and sweaty with someone else, but the result is a desecration, fit only for the garbage bin. And the latest in this line of sleaze fiction is *Pride and Prejudice: Hidden Lusts* in which the lusts are anything but hidden. Mitzi Szereto depicts Mr Collins indulging in oral sex with a groom, and the housekeeper Mrs Hill committing indecencies with Mr Bennet under the library table, while Caroline Bingley (who has mysteriously become 'Lady Caroline' in this version) is 'pleased to discover the flap of [Darcy's] breeches in a state of disturbance' when he looks at her. Sexy gypsies wander into the fields of Longbourn, Wickham runs a bawdy house and the phrase 'behaved in a more gentleman-like manner' takes on a whole new meaning! The result is a complete muddle that is successful neither as an adaptation of *Pride and Prejudice* nor as an erotic novel.

Jane Austen was almost certainly a virgin, but that does not mean she was entirely ignorant of sexual behaviour. In her fiction and letters she comments on adultery and prostitution, she made naughty jokes and she was all too aware of the prevalence of incest, rape and sex for sale within Regency society. But she respected the privacy of the lovers she created, leaving them in peace even at the moment of successful proposals. She respected those emotions that are intimate. Never would she have followed her characters into the bedroom. For Jane Austen love was about something far deeper than two bodies joining physically; it was about the meeting of minds as well. A hand almost kissed, the meeting of eyes across a ballroom, deep blushes and breath caught short from emotion – Jane Austen knew that these can be far more erotic and moving than anything described in pornography. Readers who have met Captain Harville and Captain Benwick in the pages of *Persuasion* do not want to be informed that they are actually pimps, as in Grania Beckford's novel *Virtues and Vices*. It is all so tasteless and so unnecessary. Every reader knows at the end of *Pride and Prejudice* that Elizabeth and Darcy will have fun in bed; we do not need to be told the details. However, clearly there are some readers who do have such a need, for pornographic sequels to *Pride and Prejudice* do get published (many are self-published) in large numbers, and they do sell. The www.steamydarcy.com website gets thousands of visitors each month, and that is not the only website specializing in Austen erotica. There are even porn movies such as *Porn and Penetration* for sale. But surely it's the missing bits that fascinate us about Jane Austen, the places where we are forced to use our imaginations. Those readers who follow her characters into the bedroom to watch what another writer thinks they do between the sheets are perilously close to resembling Nancy Steele of *Sense and Sensibility*, who eavesdrops on her sister with her lover, or other characters who peep through keyholes. Do we really want or need to be the Peeping Toms of Jane Austen's world? 'Seldom, very seldom does complete truth belong to any human disclosure,' Jane Austen wrote in *Emma*. It is a great pity that sequel writers have not followed this advice and left us to the wonderful personal imaginings created by *Pride and Prejudice*.

PRIDE AND PREJUDICE MEETS ZOMBIES AND ALIENS

In 2009 zombies and aliens invaded *Pride and Prejudice*. Publisher Quirk Books came up with the idea of mixing a well-known classic novel with popular zombie fiction, and the result was what is now known as a 'mashup'. *Pride and Prejudice and Zombies* by Jane Austen and Seth Grahame-Smith was the first of this genre, and by far the most popular. Its lurid cover, depicting a ghoulish Jane Austen in a blood-spattered muslin gown, immediately attracted attention, as did its unusual mix of genres, and the book shot to No. 3 on *The New York Times* bestseller list.

Most of the novel is in Jane Austen's words (about 80 per cent), but the remainder introduces some extraordinary changes. Seth Grahame-Smith felt that *Pride and*

Prejudice 'was just ripe for gore and senseless violence' and that is certainly what he introduces into the story. The Bennet girls have been well instructed by their father in martial arts and Elizabeth in particular is a deadly slayer of the 'undead'. Darcy too is a monster-hunter, while the militia are there to deal with all the dead bodies with which the English countryside is soon littered, and Lady Catherine never travels without her escort of ninjas. Elizabeth and Darcy take an instant dislike to each other and such is her hatred of him that she is actually about to behead him when he deflects her attention by proposing marriage. When she goes travelling with the Gardiners, it is for the purpose of hunting down and exterminating zombies, but she is unable to save Wickham, who is turned into an incontinent quadriplegic. All ends with 'the sisters Bennet . . . brides of man, their swords quieted by that only force more powerful than any warrior', but with the dead still continuing 'to claw their way through crypt and coffin alike, feasting on British brains'.

Such was the success of the novel that it spawned a host of imitations. Some were of Jane Austen's novels – *Sense and Sensibility and Sea Monsters* by Jane Austen and Ben H. Winters, and *Mansfield Park and Mummies: Monster Mayhem, Matrimony, Ancient Curses, True Love, and Other Dire Delights* by Jane Austen and Vera Nazarian – but it soon appeared that no classic novel was safe from zombie infiltration. *Android Karenina, Little Women and Werewolves, The Adventures of Huckleberry Finn and Zombie Jim* and *Jane Slayre* soon followed. Quirk Books, delighted by the commercial success of their idea, then published a prequel, *Pride and Prejudice and Zombies: Dawn of the Dreadfuls* by Steve Hockensmith, which describes how Elizabeth Bennet trained to be such a successful zombie-hunter. That was then followed by another continuation by the same author, *Pride and Prejudice and Zombies: Dreadfully Ever After*, in which Darcy is nipped by a 'rampaging dreadful' while on honeymoon. Elizabeth knows that the only option is to behead him, and then burn his corpse, but luckily there is a miracle antidote which saves Darcy, so the honeymoon can happily continue. The original book was then turned into a graphic novel and a video game, and in 2011 an interactive e-book version was announced, giving readers the chance to slay zombies for themselves.

Other writers have seized their own opportunities to create Jane Austen mashups or zombie-filled sequels and make money from them. *Mr Darcy, Vampyre* by Amanda Grange was published in 2009, as was *Vampire Darcy's Desire* by Regina Jeffers (also issued under the title of *Darcy's Hunger: A Vampire Re-telling of Jane Austen's Pride and Prejudice*), in which Darcy's vampirism is a hereditary curse which has made him long for Elizabeth's blood. *Mrs Darcy Versus the Aliens* ('The truth is out there, though it is not yet universally acknowledged') by Jonathan Pinnock mixes Regency bonnets with ghouls, ghosts and a lunatic named Mr Firth, and was published in 2011.

For author Michael Thomas Ford it has all gone too far. He responded first with *Jane Bites Back*, a 'fang-tastic satire' in which an 'undead' Jane Austen is disgusted by this latest craze for adapting her books, and then with *Jane Goes Batty: A Novel* in which she is taking 'How to be a vampire' lessons because a blood-sucking Brontë sister is rumoured to be coming to finish her off. His most recent effort is *Jane Vows Vengeance*.

This extraordinary craze was all started by *Pride and Prejudice* being mixed up with zombies. It is surely a craze that is bizarre enough to almost make Jane Austen 'undead' through all the turning she must be doing in her grave.

OTHER ADAPTATIONS AND CONTINUATIONS

Jane Austen enjoyed poetry, but was no great poet herself. This has not stopped admirers from turning her *Pride and Prejudice* into poetic form. *Roses and Thorns* by Selene Goodman tries to capture the thoughts of various characters from the novel in verse form, but the elegance of Jane Austen's prose is lost in such lines as:

> Mistress Mary, quite contrary,
> Her nose within a book.
> Come between her and the page,
> You'll surely get a look.

Goodman's sequence of verses seems trite and pointless. The Internet displays various poems inspired by Jane Austen and her writings, but it is easy to see why these works are self-published on the web, rather than produced commercially in book form. They are saccharine rather than witty, trite rather than insightful, and they bear no resemblance to Jane Austen's famously concise and brilliant style. Cedric Wallis (who wrote a film script and a play of *Pride and Prejudice*) also turned his hand to a theatrical sequel in *The Heiress of Rosings* in which Anne de Bourgh gets married and Mr Collins has a fling with a chambermaid.

There are abridged versions of the novel for younger readers such as the *Pride and Prejudice* adapted for children by Gill Tavner, with illustrations by Ann Kronheimer. The volume provides a list of characters at the beginning to help readers of the eight-to-ten age group sort out who is who, and ends with some useful historical notes and the excellent suggestion of reading the full novel very soon. Of course, much has been deleted, but the volume is an attractive introduction to Jane Austen for those too young to read a nineteenth-century novel by themselves. For those even younger, there is a 'learn-to-count' unchewable board book based on *Pride and Prejudice, Little Miss Austen: Pride & Prejudice* by Jennifer Adams, which integrates elements from the novel while counting from one to ten, with two being the '2 rich gentlemen' who arrive at the start of the novel and ten for 'ten thousand a year'. Also for toddlers is *Mr Darcy*, the story of a very proud duck who is invited to have tea with female ducks, Lizzy and her sisters. His pride results in an embarrassing fall 'in an enormous puddle' where he sinks into 'thick, brown, squelchy mud' and needs rescuing by Lizzy. It is charmingly illustrated and ends happily with Mr Darcy feeling 'quite loved and not alone at all'.

When Marvel Comics decided to turn a Jane Austen novel into a graphic novel, they chose to begin with her *Pride and Prejudice*. Serious abridging must occur for the story to fit into a comic-book format, but the word bubbles contain mostly Jane Austen's own dialogue and the illustrations, while somewhat modernized, are vibrant and detailed. The whole is likely to appeal to younger readers and could make a good introduction for any who go on to read the real thing. There is also a Japanese comic version (*Hana Yori Dengo*) which is loosely based on *Pride and Prejudice;* and there is the graphic novel *Mary King* by Sophie St Clair, which tells the story of the freckled girl Wickham flirts with when she inherits money.

Pride and Prejudice now seems to have become a sort of Bible for modern life and advice culled from its pages has been used for dating guides. Lauren Henderson's *Jane Austen's Guide to Dating* offers quizzes so that you can find out if you are most suited to marriage with a Mr Bingley or a fling with a Mr Wickham. It also provides rules for finding your very own Mr Darcy. There is more of the same in Sarah Arthur's *Dating Mr Darcy: The Smart Girl's Guide to Sensible Romance* and Patrice Hannon's *Dear Jane Austen: A Heroine's Guide to Life and Love*, while the web offers 'The Jane Austen Dating School'. An American episode of *Who Wants to Marry a Millionaire?* was inspired by *Pride and Prejudice*, with fifty women competing for the attentions of a Mr Darcy-style bachelor. If you really want to be Elizabeth Bennet, you can create your own Jane Austen adventure, accept Darcy's proposal, or even rewrite *Pride and Prejudice* just the way you want it, by reading *Being Elizabeth Bennet* by Emma Campbell Webster. Need some financial wisdom? Don't despair – all the economic advice you need is in Jennifer's Forest's *Mr Darcy's Guide to Money: How to Marry Well, Never Work Again and Live at Pemberley*. If your relationship with God needs sorting out, then *Pride and Prejudice* can help you: *A Walk with Jane Austen: A Journey into Adventure, Love and Faith* by Lori Smith, and *Conviction: A sequel to Jane Austen's Pride and Prejudice* by Skylar Hamilton Burris, can guide you on to the path to true faith. But if it's bad manners that are your problem, then *Jane Austen's Guide to Good Manners* by Josephine Ross teaches you correct etiquette, and *A Year in High Heels: The Girl's Guide To Everything from Jane Austen to the A List* by Camilla Morton can assist with fashion and socialite ambitions. While such guides take their advice from all six Austen novels, most of the pearls of wisdom come from *Pride and Prejudice*.

Illustration by Ann Kronheimer from the Real Reads abridged version of *Pride and Prejudice* by Gill Tavner for younger readers.

Mrs Bennet would be delighted to know that she has inspired a song, but as it is a rock song perhaps the noise may be too much for her poor nerves. The American band Glass Wave uses famous literature as inspiration for their lyrics and their 'Mrs Bennet' gives her a chance to boast of her success in marrying off so many daughters.

CHICK LIT AND REGENCY ROMANCES

Pride and Prejudice is the 'mother' of chick lit. Jane Austen's classic novel pioneered the genre of plucky modern heroine searching for Mr Right (chick lit is defined as light, often funny fiction which deals with issues of romance for modern women). For her *Bridget Jones's Diary*, which made her a millionaire, Helen Fielding admitted in an interview to 'stealing' Jane Austen's plot, and made the link between her novel and *Pride and Prejudice* even clearer by naming her hero Mark Darcy. Hundreds of other chick lit novelists have followed in those footsteps. Publishers such as Headline showed how strongly they credited Jane Austen as the progenitor of chick lit when they gave *Pride and Prejudice* chick lit style covers (see pages 151–2). Jane Austen might have started the chick lit genre, but in comparison with her books these modern novels seem unsubtle, unironic and rather clunky. It's very much a case of 'first was best'.

Pride and Prejudice also inspired the Regency romance. The plots and stylistic conventions of this sub-genre of historical fiction all derive from Jane Austen. They are expected to contain intelligent, likeable heroines and handsome, inscrutable heroes, along with elopements to Gretna Green, the chance of a duel, rascals who steal a young lady's virtue, fortune-hunters, etc. – all the elements of *Pride and Prejudice*. Georgette Heyer is by far the best writer of the Regency romance, and she is sometimes called 'the twentieth-century Jane Austen'. But she knew that witty and accurate as her own novels were, she was not in the same class at all. When a fan once wrote to say she had been 'wading through *Pride and Prejudice*' and that it was like a Georgette Heyer book but 'with too much padding', Heyer tore the letter up in disgust. There have been many other writers of romances with a Regency setting, and some romance publishers have their own 'Regency lines', but all are feeble imitations of the real thing to be found in *Pride and Prejudice*.

No other nineteenth-century novel has inspired anything like the huge number of sequels, prequels, adaptations, songs, poems, crime novels, pornographic novels and other genres of fiction as has Jane Austen's *Pride and Prejudice*. Devoted admirers simply cannot get enough of it, and keep luring the Bennets, Darcy, Bingley et al. into their own books. The books mentioned above are far from being a comprehensive list, and it's a safe guess that between the writing of this book and its publication, at least a dozen more will have appeared. Today the web has a group called 'Austen Authors' who discuss their next planned sequels and comment on each other's work. The various continuations are also discussed on other websites, such as 'The Republic of Pemberley' and 'Austenprose – the Jane Austen Blog'. 'Pride and Prejudice' put into Google brings up 14 million websites. The Internet has made mass and group intimacy with *Pride and Prejudice* possible for readers from all over the world. The possibilities for more adaptations are global and seemingly endless.

But are these other books vital, enhancing our enjoyment of a masterpiece, or simply derivative rubbish we can live without? Of course much depends on the talent of the writer. Some authors display accurate knowledge of the era and a true appreciation of the characters, and create new books in genuine tribute to Jane Austen. P.D. James and Georgette Heyer write as an act of homage to a writer they recognize as infinitely greater than themselves. Well-written sequels can be fun to read and make the reader think sensibly about the eventual fates of the characters. Others merely jump on the bandwagon, using Jane Austen's name to make sales of their own, dashing off silly books filled with sex or crimes that might add to mass-market appeal. When an early Jane Austen sequel was published in 1929, a reviewer remarked: 'we hope that a fashion in unauthorizable addenda will not be set'. How astonished that reviewer would have been if he could see, going on for a century later, how many unauthorized novels there now are! For with *Pride and Prejudice* it has turned out that 'The End' was really just the beginning.

A poster for the 1940 MGM film starring Laurence Olivier
and Greer Garson.

Bonnets and Bosoms

FILM AND THEATRICAL VERSIONS

'Give a loose to your fancy . . .'

As mentioned on page 147, Jane Austen, after writing *Pride and Prejudice*, attended an art exhibition in London to see if any other artist might have created their version of her fictional creations; she could imagine a painter depicting, by chance, her Elizabeth Darcy or Jane Bingley. Possibly she could have also imagined her characters on a stage, although turning novels into plays was not yet customary. But never, in her wildest imaginings, could she ever have dreamed that millions of people (in fact, more millions than existed in all Great Britain when she wrote *Pride and Prejudice*) would sit in the comfort of their own homes, push a button and watch on a strange metallic and glass box portrayals of her very own Elizabeth and her very own Mr Darcy getting married. Nor could she have even started to imagine that more millions would go and sit in darkened public places and again, on a screen, see her characters 'come alive', speaking the words she had written for them. Yet over 100 years after her death, BBC and Hollywood began to 'repackage' *Pride and Prejudice*, taking Jane Austen's novel to a whole new audience and giving her book extraordinary on-screen lives.

Films have diminished vital aspects of *Pride and Prejudice* and enhanced others; they have eroticized the novel, cheapened it and reinvented it. Without any doubt, they have hugely popularized it. It has become a truth most truly acknowledged universally that *Pride and Prejudice* is a joy to movie-makers. As the heroine of *Confessions of a Jane Austen Addict* confesses, 'If there were fifty adaptations of *Pride and Prejudice*, I'd see them all.'

FIRST IMPRESSIONS ON TV: THE 1938 VERSION

BBC TV, 60 mins, black and white

Screenplay: Michael Barry

Starring: Curigwen Lewis as Elizabeth, Andrew Osborn as Darcy

The BBC only began to produce its own television programmes in 1932, but very early on it recognized the appeal of a good costume drama and turned to *Pride and Prejudice*. Welsh actress Curigwen Lewis played Elizabeth. She was in her early thirties and too old for the part. As this is such an old television version, there is virtually no information available about it, but wouldn't it be fascinating to watch this very first screen adaptation of the novel?

FIRST IMPRESSIONS ON FILM: THE 1940 VERSION

MGM Feature Film, 114 mins, black and white

Director: Robert Z. Leonard

Screenplay: Aldous Huxley and Jane Murfin

Producer: Hunt Stromberg

Starring: Greer Garson as Elizabeth, Laurence Olivier as Darcy, Edna Mae Oliver as Lady Catherine

It has the wrong period costumes, it turns Lady Catherine de Bourgh into Cupid and it contains some memorable historical clangers, yet the 1940 movie of *Pride and Prejudice* starring Greer Garson and Laurence Olivier still holds an affectionate place in the memories of many older men and women. It was their first *Pride and Prejudice* and 'first impressions' can be very lasting.

The original idea for the film is supposed to have started with Harpo Marx. In 1935 he went to see a theatrical version of *Pride and Prejudice* written by Helen Jerome (her play *Pride and Prejudice: A Sentimental Comedy in Three Acts* is listed in the film's credits) and he suggested that MGM should try turning it into a movie. Plans were made to star Norma Shearer (wife of MGM producer Irving Thalberg) as Elizabeth and Clark Gable as Mr Darcy, but Thalberg died only weeks before production was due to start, and the project fizzled out.

However, in 1939 the idea was revived, with director Robert Z. Leonard in charge. Englishman Aldous Huxley and American Jane Murfin were commissioned to write a script. MGM should have noted the advice of Mary Crawford in *Mansfield Park*: 'such half and half doings never prosper'. Jane Murfin had made her name writing screwball American comedies, while Huxley was a serious literary novelist with *Brave New World* and *Eyeless in Gaza* behind him. The resulting script is an odd mix of broad humour and lack of credibility in many places, and it keeps none of the intricacies of Jane Austen's *Pride and Prejudice*. The studio wanted wholesome family entertainment. There is a kiss between Elizabeth and Darcy at the end, but it's an extremely chaste one, and while Greer Garson appears in her underwear, there's little flesh on display. Indeed, the film is so 'proper' that Mr Collins has a change of profession and becomes Lady Catherine's librarian, just in case anyone might object to a clergyman being made a figure of fun.

What is especially interesting about this version of *Pride and Prejudice* is its propaganda message. Huxley signed his contract days before the Second World War broke out and while filming took place there were air raids and wartime shortages to cope with. The British wished Americans to enter the war and did not miss this opportunity to remind them of all that was at stake if they refused. So the film hints that the world of 'ye merrie olde England' could disappear for ever. An archery contest (with all its connotations of Agincourt and Robin Hood) is staged during the film and there are references to war in the script (including a hilarious line given to Mrs Bennet about the Battle of Waterloo, which had not yet taken place). Family harmony is stressed: the Bennets seem to move about en masse and even Mr and Mrs Bennet live without marital tension. The film creates an unreal world, stuffed with flowers and finery, where it is always spring, and the British aristocracy (in the form of Lady Catherine and her nephew Mr Darcy) capitulates to the middle classes (represented by the Bennets) in an effort to cater to more democratic American tastes.

The film constantly stresses and even broadens the comedy of *Pride and Prejudice*. Farce is introduced – Lady Catherine sits on Kitty's music box, Mr Collins chases Elizabeth round the garden and she plays hide-and-seek with him. Aldous Huxley managed to persuade the director not to add a duel to the script, but there is a wild carriage ride, Kitty Bennet gets tipsy, and Lady Catherine (played by Edna Mae Oliver, who wanted her character to turn out 'nice') pushes Elizabeth and Darcy together at the end. 'What you need', she tells him, 'is a woman who will stand up to you. I think you've found her.' The film begins with an advertisement – 'Bachelors Beware! Five Gorgeous Beauties are on a Madcap Manhunt'. It nears its ending with Mr Bennet saying to his wife of their daughters: 'Perhaps it's lucky we *didn't* drown any of them at birth, my dear.' What comes in between is really just more of the same. The Bennets are played only for comedy and even Jane lacks decorum and bats her eyelashes just as much as her sisters. Plain Mary looks like getting her man by the end, and there's a great deal of gushing and frolicking among them all.

Regency costumes were deemed not decorative or flattering enough, so pelisses and empire gowns went out, and crinolines and vampish black dresses came in. The costumes give a first impression of coming straight from *Gone with the Wind* (which had premiered the previous year), but they are a peculiar mixture, from no actual historical era. Elizabeth wears ties, Miss Bingley comes to the ball in black, and huge picture hats have replaced bonnets and caps.

The film was shot against stage sets; nothing was filmed in the real outdoors. Its 'decorators' Cedric Gibbons and Paul Groesse won an Academy Award for their efforts. The makers of the truckloads of paper flowers used to create Longbourn and Netherfield gardens should probably have won one too – for sheer hard work.

In spite of all the inaccuracies and changes from the original novel, the film does have its charms, and it was both a popular and critical success. Greer Garson was too old to play Elizabeth Bennet (she was in her mid-thirties), but she is beautiful and she brought to the role a certain éclat. The script often forces her to speak very rudely, and she is often overly bold, but she remains a likeable Elizabeth in spite of it all.

Laurence Olivier had played Heathcliff in the 1939 film of *Wuthering Heights*. Most readers would question why being a good Heathcliff should qualify him to be a good Darcy, but MGM needed no convincing. Olivier had many script challenges to contend with in *Pride and Prejudice* – his interest in Elizabeth is too sudden, he is never seen at Pemberley, and he is forced to do lots of standing about looking haughty. Being Olivier, he carried it off. His is one of the better performances in the film.

The movie is still for sale on DVD and today is fascinating as a period piece. But it made a strong impression on many viewers and it would be sixty-five years before any movie director was brave enough to tackle *Pride and Prejudice* as a movie again.

ABBREVIATED: THE 1949 VERSION

NBC Philco Television Playhouse, 60 mins, black and white
Director: Fred Coe
Screenplay: Samuel Taylor
Starring: Madge Evans as Elizabeth, John Baragrey as Darcy

In 1949 NBC (American National Broadcasting Company) produced a one-hour, black-and-white Philco TV Playhouse adaptation of *Pride and Prejudice*. Along with the 1938 version, this is the shortest film ever made of the novel. Evidently it entirely leaves out the visit to Hunsford, but as it is no longer available, it is impossible to see what else was omitted. It included an actor playing Jane Austen, who provides an ironic voiceover, explains the characters and gives transitional information when the plot takes huge leaps. She appears at the beginning saying 'It is a truth universally acknowledged . . .', before the screen 'dissolves' into the first act.

Elizabeth was acted by Madge Evans (who turned forty that year) and Darcy was acted by John Baragrey. Both were Americans. Evidently the film concludes with 'Elizabeth' asking 'Darcy' his Christian name. 'Fitzwilliam,' he replies, at which she sighs happily and responds, 'Ah, how nice.' While it would be interesting to see this TV version, it doesn't sound as if viewers are missing much through its unavailability.

Madge Evans and John Baragrey in the 1949 NBC production of *Pride and Prejudice*.

ENTER 'SHERLOCK HOLMES': THE 1952 VERSION
BBC mini-series in six parts, 180 mins, black and white
Director/producer: Campbell Logan
Screenplay: Cedric Wallis
Starring: Daphne Slater as Elizabeth, Peter Cushing as Darcy, Prunella Scales as
Lydia Bennet

Peter Cushing is today associated in the public mind with the famous sleuth
Sherlock Holmes; he acted in *The Hound of the Baskervilles* and sixteen episodes
of Holmes's stories. He was also well known in horror films such as *The Curse of
Frankenstein* and *Dracula*. He once remarked that if he played Hamlet, 'they'd call
it a horror film'. He took on the role of Mr Darcy before acting these other parts,
but he still seems an odd choice. Once again the six-part TV series is no longer
available, so it is impossible for us to judge. At nearly forty, Cushing was too old
for the part, and his beaky nose and receding hairline do not qualify him to look
the part of a 'tall, dark and handsome' hero.

Daphne Slater played Elizabeth in this BBC mini-series. Eight years later she
was given the part of Anne Elliot in a BBC *Persuasion*, so clearly she impressed. As
a teenager she had acted Viola in *Twelfth Night* at Stratford and her performance
there was reviewed as 'impulsive and warm-hearted', which does make her sound
suitable as Elizabeth.

What must surely have been memorable in this adaptation is the performance
of Prunella Scales as Lydia Bennet. She was a twenty-year-old actress, at the start
of her illustrious career. Playing opposite her as Mr Collins was Lockwood West
(father of Timothy West, Prunella Scales's future husband). She would go on to
play other Jane Austen roles, such as Miss Bates in the 1996 ITV production of
Emma, as well as making memorable audio readings of Jane Austen's novels.

The screenplay by Cedric Wallis was good enough to impress Colonel Austen
B. Knight, who wrote to congratulate the BBC: 'I have never had so much pleasure
from one of my great-great-Aunt Jane's romances before,' he enthused. Once
again, Jane Austen is a 'character' in the series, providing commentary as needed.

THE 'SCREENPLAY REPEAT': THE 1958 VERSION

BBC mini-series in six parts, 180 mins, black and white

Director/producer: Barbara Burnham

Screenplay: Cedric Wallis (same as 1952)

Starring: Jane Downs as Elizabeth, Alan Badel as Darcy

Cedric Wallis's screenplay was recycled for this BBC version, made only six years after the last. The previous version must have been popular, or a second version within the decade would not have been risked, but the BBC obviously decided to economize on scripting costs. This time the role of Darcy went to Alan Badel, whose voice was so rich it was once described as 'the sound of tears'. He was at the start of what would be a distinguished stage and television career and his Darcy is remembered by those who saw it as an excellent portrayal.

Jane Downs took the part of Elizabeth. In her early twenties, she was the right age and had striking and attractive eyes.

Once again, this version is disappointingly unavailable.

OUTDOORS AND INTO COLOUR: THE 1967 VERSION

BBC1 mini-series in six parts, 180 mins, colour

Director: Joan Craft

Screenplay: Nemone Lethbridge

Producer: Campbell Logan

Starring: Celia Bannerman as Elizabeth, Lewis Fiander as Darcy

Today we take it for granted that a film of *Pride and Prejudice* will include gorgeous shots of stately homes and depict actors striding through Derbyshire, windswept or rained on, with landscape scenery enriching almost every shot. But it was only in this 1967 version that such things began to happen (the BBC had brand-new equipment that allowed this) and the National Trust village of Lacock (later used in the 1995 *Pride and Prejudice* and the 1996 *Emma*) and the National Trust's Dyrham Park in Gloucestershire were used as locations. There is a rather odd contrast, however, between the naturalistic exterior shots and the less realistic indoor scenes, which were created in the studio rather than shot in the rooms of Dyrham Park. This was also the first colour *Pride and Prejudice* film. It was directed by Joan Craft, one of the few female TV directors in that era, who was well used to period drama (she had recently completed *David Copperfield*).

Celia Bannerman played Elizabeth, while Australian actor Lewis Fiander was Darcy – his first major role. Their love affair is completely lacking in sexual tension; all is very proper and correct. They were dressed rather too much in the style of the 1960s, with bouffant hairdos, too much eyeliner and fussy gowns. Mrs Bennet, played by Vivian Pickles, seems to have crept in from *David Copperfield* and her histrionics are seriously overdone. Mary Bennet is eliminated from this version.

This was a version of *Pride and Prejudice* aimed at an audience who had never read the book. It is frothy and amusing, but is generally agreed by those who saw it to have been pretty forgettable.

GETTING IT RIGHT AT LAST: THE 1980 VERSION

BBC2 mini-series in five parts, 226 mins

Director: Cyril Coke

Screenplay: Fay Weldon

Producer: Jonathon Powell

Starring: Elizabeth Garvie as Elizabeth, David Rintoul as Darcy

Conveying the charm of Elizabeth Bennet on screen is not an easy task. Elizabeth Garvie achieved this and her performance as Lizzy is the real highlight of this five-part TV adaptation. Elizabeth Garvie was in her early twenties, fresh out of drama school, and the role of Elizabeth was her big break. She captures the 'sweetness and archness' of the heroine, and conveys her intelligence and playfulness, along with a hint of vulnerability as well. For almost every viewer with a good knowledge of the novel, Elizabeth Garvie remains the definitive Elizabeth Bennet.

David Rintoul, playing Darcy, is more controversial. Physically he is right for the part – tall, handsome and distinguished. He plays the part very closely to the Darcy of the novel – proud, aloof and inscrutable. Right up until he proposes at the end of the novel, Elizabeth is troublingly uncertain of his true feelings for her, and his first proposal comes as a total shock to her. David Rintoul conveys this inscrutability (whereas any woman would have to be blind to be on the receiving end of one of Colin Firth's smouldering looks and not know just what he felt for her.) Certainly, in comparison with Colin Firth's Darcy, Rintoul's is stiff, awkward and formal, but as the series progresses he does smile more and the viewer does see him change as he learns the lessons Elizabeth has to teach him. He just doesn't give away his feelings with every look and so has been deemed 'wooden' by many critics. Nor is there between this Darcy and Elizabeth the obvious sexual attraction that sizzles from Colin Firth and Jennifer Ehle.

This series has some other excellent actors. Priscilla Morgan's Mrs Bennet is wonderful. She does not make a shrill caricature of the part as Alison Steadman does in the 1995 adaptation. She portrays a Mrs Bennet who could believably have attracted Mr Bennet twenty-five years earlier, but without losing the silliness and vulgarity that are so essential an aspect of Mrs Bennet. Moray Watson acts a stern Mr Bennet, speaking more maliciously to his foolish wife and daughters and clearly unhappy with his chosen lot in life. The deeply flawed Mr Bennet of the novel is perhaps emphasized at the expense of the comedy also associated with his character, but it is a thought-provoking rendition. Judy Parfitt is rare in being Lady Catherine de Bourgh's age (most casting directors choose an elderly actor for the role), and Mr Collins, in being less slimy than David Bamber (who plays Mr Collins in the 1995 version), is closer to the 'tall and heavy looking' young man of the original novel.

Fay Weldon, a highly esteemed novelist herself, wrote the screenplay. A few years later she wrote *Letters to Alice: On First Reading Jane Austen*, which is a delightful tribute to Jane Austen and an interesting exploration of the craft of writing fiction. Jane Austen purists generally agree that this is the version that sticks most faithfully to the original book. Most of the dialogue is lifted from the novel (although it is sometimes given to another character to say) and, apart from a strange and totally unfunny scene of Mr Collins wading into a pond wearing an aqua-hat, the scenes are believable and ring true.

However, the series was made on a low budget, and shot on video rather than film, and economy dictated that most of the scenes were shot indoors (which is where most of the action of the novel takes place). Charlotte Brontë famously criticized Jane Austen's novels for lacking 'fresh air' and 'open country', and her charge could justly be applied to this TV version. It has a studio-bound feel. Beautiful Renishaw Hall in Derbyshire (home to the intriguing Sitwell family) is used as Pemberley, and characters travel in carriages and on horseback through pretty countryside, but nevertheless the viewer is left longing for a good gust of wind to blow away the sense of sometimes being trapped in a televised stage play. Production values and advances in fifteen years would make a huge difference to this aspect of the 1995 BBC *Pride and Prejudice*.

Costumes too were badly affected by the lack of lavish financing. They are unexciting and overly modest (too much lace in most of the bodices) and they look like 'costumes' rather than clothes their wearers are comfortable in. A few truly dreadful 1980s perms make the actors look slightly ridiculous and dated. Again, this mini-series suffers when its costumes are compared with the beautiful and well-planned outfits of the 1995 production and with the 'arty' and very modern-looking styles chosen for the 2005 movie.

This *Pride and Prejudice* was screened on TV in Britain, America, Australia, New Zealand and many other countries, and then was released on video. It is now available on DVD. Aspects of it seem 'fuddy-duddy' to a modern young viewer, but it remains an admirable adaptation, extremely true to Jane Austen's novel, and made memorable and enchanting by Elizabeth Garvie's absolutely wonderful Elizabeth Bennet.

SEXY: THE 1995 VERSION

BBC/A & E mini-series in six parts, 300 mins

Director: Simon Langton

Screenplay: Andrew Davies

Producer: Sue Birtwistle

Starring: Jennifer Ehle as Elizabeth , Colin Firth as Darcy

'Settle Down for an Orgy of Austen!', 'Prepare to be Shocked', 'Sexed-up *Pride and Prejudice*', 'Sex Romp Jane Austen', 'Mr Darcy Strips' – these were some of the headlines warning viewers what to expect of the BBC *Pride and Prejudice* that screened in

1995. Scriptwriter Andrew Davies (veteran of many excellent period dramas adapted from the classics) said that Jane Austen's novel was 'packed with a lot of young people dying to get at each other', and that all he had to do was to let all this rampant sexuality out. He did so with a vengeance, and the world was enthralled.

This is the 'sexy' adaptation of *Pride and Prejudice*. Generous cleavages and heaving bosoms, gorgeous men with steaming horses between their powerful thighs, hair let down in candle-lit bedrooms, glances so smouldering they could set the screen on fire and, most famously, a Darcy so 'hot' he is forced to cool his fiery passion with a plunge in a lake – there is sexual energy everywhere. It's no surprise that it ignited not only Jane Austen's fictional creations, but the actors playing them as well. Jennifer Ehle and Colin Firth had an off-screen affair during filming. Viewers see Wickham cuddling a half-naked girl, Lydia frolics in her underwear, plenty of unbuttoning takes place and there is an abundant use of the Wonderbra. We see gorgeously physical males who fence, ride, stride and ogle. Female viewers universally ogled in response.

This is the version of *Pride and Prejudice* that created 'Darcymania' and the phenomenon of 'Darcy parties'. Actor Colin Firth had never read Jane Austen's novel before taking the part (he thought it was just 'girlie stuff') but once he started to read, he was hooked. His role does not require him to say a huge amount; so much of his Darcy is conveyed by looks, rather than through dialogue. His intense physicality is intended to inform Elizabeth, and the female audience, that just as he excels at physical sports such as riding, fencing, swimming and dancing, so he will be magnificently physical in the bedroom. Even when he is absent from the novel, he is still kept in the film viewer's eye – attending Lydia's wedding, seeking out Wickham, etc. No one is allowed to forget this Mr Darcy for an instant. He leans against mantelpieces, he paces the festering streets of Georgian London and he mutters forcefully, 'I will conquer this! I will conquer this.' He saves his young sister from a fate worse than death, runs a great estate efficiently, writes good letters, and in every scene he looks sexy, handsome and memorably brooding. He often stands near mirrors, so viewers get not one image of him, but two. The role made Colin Firth a universal heart-throb. He was so inundated by fans that he fled to Tunisia to escape them. Websites sprang up whose sole purpose was to adore Colin Firth (including gay ones), fans rushed to any place in Britain where they had a hope of spotting him, and his film career took off from that moment.

He is not an aloof Darcy, whose emotions are hard to fathom. It is clear from the beginning that this Darcy is smitten by Elizabeth and can make little effort to resist her attraction. With added scenes that are not in the book (Darcy fencing, Darcy in Cambridge, Darcy diving into cold water) this Darcy is made more accessible. Watching women felt they could not get enough of him and were ecstatic to have Colin Firth as accessible as possible. There are female viewers today who sit and watch the DVD by fast-forwarding to all the scenes in which Colin Firth appears, getting a 'Darcy fix' as efficiently as possible.

Another huge 'plus' of this BBC adaptation was the gorgeousness of locations, costumes and film techniques. With a $13 million budget, there were funds to allow shooting at stunning stately homes (Belton House, Sudbury Hall, Lyme Park, Luckington Court), and the entire village of Lacock could be taken over and turned into Meryton. Everything was filmed on location, with more scenes taking place out of doors than is the case in the novel. There are lavish ball scenes, stylish props, rich fabrics and elaborate food on dinner tables. It is an opulent series, rich in detail, with natural yet interesting film techniques. There is no 'studio feel' about it at all. This is a film, not photography of a book.

No BBC period drama has ever been so popular. When the last episode was screened in Britain, motorways were jammed with people desperate to get home in time to watch Elizabeth marry Mr Darcy. Thousands of viewers who had never read the novel (poor things) phoned the BBC asking for assurance that there would be a happy ending for hero and heroine. The video, released midway through screening, sold out in the first two hours, and the novel started selling 20,000 copies per week in Britain (how Jane Austen would have loved receiving royalties from those sales!). The series won awards (Jennifer Ehle gratefully thanked her wig in her BAFTA Award speech), it garnered favourable reviews, it created 'Austenmania'.

Yet, like any film of *Pride and Prejudice*, it failed to satisfy every viewer and it does have its faults. Jennifer Ehle's Elizabeth is an Elizabeth Bennet for the late

CLOCKWISE FROM RIGHT
Elizabeth and Darcy:
Kiera Knightley and
Matthew MacFadyen (2005);
Jennifer Ehle and Colin
Firth (1995); Aishwaria Rai
(Lalita) and Martin Henderson
(2004); Greer Garson and
Laurence Olivier (1940);
Elizabeth Garvie and David
Rintoul (1980).

twentieth century – she tramps across fields like a woman more used to wearing jeans than a Regency gown, she has an overly sweet smile, is just too voluptuous, and lacks the charm of Elizabeth Garvie's portrayal, although she exudes more sexual energy. Alison Steadman's Mrs Bennet is abrasive and 'Dickensian' rather than 'Austenian'; for some viewers (including this one) she ruined every scene in which she appears. She resembles more a pantomime dame than Jane Austen's marvellous mixture of nerves and inanity. Perhaps too (inevitably, probably, in a script written by a man) the male perspective dominates at the expense of the female one (and the novel is written from the female point of view and famously includes no scene where there is no woman present). The sexuality of the film is far more explicit than that of the novel – Jane Austen is brought perilously close to Jackie Collins or Jilly Cooper. Jane Austen's characters actually thrive on inhibition, but there is no inhibition in this version.

This is the adaptation that introduced *Pride and Prejudice* to the masses. It started the 'reign of Jane' among film-makers, turning Jane Austen's novels into a multi-million-dollar industry. Jane had 'arrived' as far as film directors were concerned (although some of them were disappointed to find that she had died and would not be available for film-tie-in book signings). The series' 'wet-shirt' scene became an iconic moment in film history (so memorable that Andrew Davies later felt obliged to insert another 'wet-shirt' scene into his adaptation of *Sense and Sensibility*) and it made Colin Firth the preferred eye-candy and the definitive Mr Darcy of an entire generation of women. When the series ended, people felt bereft. This weekly fix of *Pride and Prejudice* had been something very special indeed.

'MUDDY HEM': THE 2005 MOVIE VERSION

Working Title Films, 128 mins, movie version

Director: Joe Wright

Screenplay: Deborah Moggach

Producers: Liza Chasin, Debra Hayward

Starring: Keira Knightley as Elizabeth, Matthew Macfadyen as Darcy, Brenda Blethyn as Mrs Bennet, Donald Sutherland as Mr Bennet, Judi Dench as Lady Catherine

After Colin Firth had made his Mr Darcy internationally famous, it took a brave actor to tackle the role. All that Matthew Macfadyen could do was to make his Darcy very different. He plays Darcy as shy rather than haughty, awkward rather than arrogant. There's lots of inner conflict going on – he is a troubled Darcy, instead of a proud one. Macfadyen's is a sensitive Darcy, in considerable emotional pain. However, viewers do not see him change; he remains the same troubled and sensitive Darcy throughout.

Keira Knightley was exactly the right age to play Elizabeth Bennet, but she is perpetually Keira Knightley and never Jane Austen's witty and sparkling heroine of the novel. The camera worships Keira in every scene, rarely leaving her alone, focusing obsessively on her lips (she is often open-mouthed), her hands, her thin body as she moves. She is certainly highly photogenic, but the focus is on her body, not on her mind, and the absence of an intelligent, thoughtful Elizabeth is a serious problem in this movie. Jane Austen's Elizabeth would never smirk, giggle too much, pout, eavesdrop at doors, seductively lick her fingers and roam outdoors in a nightie, but Keira Knightley's Elizabeth does. She is unable to keep still, she is too vapid, and she dispenses too violently with decorum and manners.

The 1995 TV series was very much an 'outdoors' *Pride and Prejudice*, but this 2005 version is even more so. Characters battle with rain and wind, farm animals and rock-climbing. Darcy's first proposal takes place in a rain-soaked temple, his second at dawn on misty moors. The Bennets' home is a warren of pigs, geese, hay and dirt, all of which need to be scattered or dealt with as the Bennets walk in and out. Seven different historic houses were used as locations, and the socio-economic divide between Darcy's Pemberley and the Bennets' Longbourn is strongly stressed through location choice and visuals. Everyone in this film is less formal – hair is greasy or falling down, men have designer stubble not only at 5.00 p.m. but all day, hems are often very muddy, and rooms are untidy and cluttered. At times the scenes are visually very beautiful, but they are never truly convincing as Georgian England.

Director Joe Wright and scriptwriter Deborah Moggach (who is a novelist) should have taken Georgian etiquette lessons. Single men did not enter the bedrooms

Mrs Bennet and her daughters: Brenda Blethyn, Rosamund Pike, Carey Mulligan, Talulah Riley, Keira Knightley and Jena Malone in the 2005 film adaptation.

of unmarried women as Bingley does when Jane is ill in this film, Lady Catherine would never have paid a call when the Bennets were all in their nightgowns, and Elizabeth would not have wandered unescorted through Pemberley This is a *Pride and Prejudice* film for those who have not read the novel and who know little of the era.

The film, however, does have its merits. There is very interesting camera work, with the camera acting like a bystander. At the Meryton assembly ball, the viewer feels like one of the dancers taking part. The 'sculpture gallery' scene at Pemberley (where Elizabeth gazes lingeringly at a statue of Darcy, rather than at his portrait) is very beautiful (but unfortunately all wrong as well, because the Darcy portrait in the novel 'smiles' at Elizabeth, whereas a statue is cold marble and can show no warmth of smile or look). There are lovely landscapes, sumptuous houses, decorative costumes (in the style of the late eighteenth-century *First Impressions* rather than the early nineteenth-century *Pride and Prejudice*) and gorgeous horses.

There are also lovely faces. This is the first filmed *Pride and Prejudice* to have a stunning Jane – Rosamund Pike is even more beautiful than Keira Knightley. There is interesting casting of Mr Collins, providing a reason for his bumptiousness in 'small-man syndrome', as Tom Hollander is very short. Dame Judi Dench makes an icy and formidable Lady Catherine (but is too old for the part), and Brenda Blethyn is an excellent Mrs Bennet – foolish and nervous, but recognizably a human being at the same time.

The film received four Academy Awards, won one BAFTA, and did well at the box office. The daughters of the women who had seen Colin Firth as their ultimate Darcy, and the granddaughters of those for whom Laurence Olivier had filled that role, found their Mr Darcy in Matthew Macfadyen. The movie charmed a new generation of viewers and, fortunately, persuaded many of them to read the novel.

ITALIAN

In 1957 Italian TV audiences were introduced to *Pride and Prejudice*, or rather to *Orgoglio e pregiudizio*. The black-and-white version was screened in five episodes produced by RAI, with a screenplay by Eduardo Anton. The series is not available commercially, but several episodes from it can be watched on YouTube.

Even the credits of this version are amusing – Jane becomes Jenny Bennett [*sic*], Lady Catherine becomes Lady Katherine, Miss Bingley is Carol instead of Caroline, and Sir William Lucas is abbreviated to Sir Lucas. 'Colonello Forster' has a lovely ring to it! The theme music played at the opening and as the background to several scenes is 'I'll Take You Home Again, Kathleen'. A sentimental Irish ballad from the wrong era (it was written in 1875), it creates a sense of dislocation for the viewer from the beginning.

Franco Volpi plays Mr Darcy. One would have thought the Italians would have had no trouble finding a 'tall, dark and handsome' actor for the part. Volpi was in his mid-thirties and looked even older, and he makes a stodgy and very unromantic Mr Darcy. Virna Lisi as Elizabeth is pretty, with very attractive eyes. There is an intriguing 'Signora Bennett', played by Elsa Merlini, who is more like a Borgia than a Bennet – she looks as though she could happily poison her husband, Mr Darcy and possibly some of her four daughters (there is no Kitty in this version) into the bargain. This Mrs Bennett, in true Italian style, makes full use of gesticulation, dramatics and hysterics.

This version makes some radical changes to Jane Austen's novel – for example, Mr Wickham is turned into Darcy's illegitimate half-brother.

DUTCH

A few years later, in 1961, it was the turn of the Dutch to have a go at *Pride and Prejudice*. The five episode TV series, *De Vier Dochters Bennet* (The Four Bennet

Daughters), used the script written by Cedric Wallis (used twice by the BBC in the 1950s), and this was translated into Dutch and somewhat altered by Lo van Hensbergen. The series was directed by Peter Holland and was shown over five months. With such big gaps between episodes, the Dutch audience needed a monthly reminder of what had already taken place, so each episode begins with the diary entry from one of the four Bennet sisters (poor Kitty has again been deemed surplus to requirements). While this version is, once again, not for sale, one scene (Darcy's proposal to Elizabeth – or 'Elisabeth', as she becomes in the credits) can be viewed on YouTube and it has been watched and very much enjoyed by members of the Jane Austen Society in the Netherlands. It was entirely shot in studios, and extremely fake trees can be seen blossoming in the background of the YouTube scene.

Ramses Shaffy (a popular singer as well as actor) makes a creditable and rather vulnerable Darcy. In the proposal scene he informs Elizabeth that his decision to propose is 'the final result of weeks of nagging doubt' which sounds far from Austenian. His 'Elisabeth' looks suitably unimpressed, as he does so. Lies Franken (playing Elisabeth) looks too old – she was thirty-one – and seems sarcastic rather than angry. According to one reviewer (who managed to view the film in the Dutch archives), the Mr Bingley of this version is wonderful. It feels rather odd to hear Jane Austen's elegant prose expressed in Dutch, and a Dutch pancake

On the set of the *De Vier Dochters Bennet*, the Dutch TV series.

pan (*poffertjespan*) on the table does not help convince the viewer of a Regency England setting. The costumes are a very strange mixture, with waists too low for the Regency period and huge lapels on the men's coats reminiscent of the enormous collars of the 1970s. This adaptation gives a sense of having seriously lost its way in history.

SPANISH

The Spanish had watched the 1940 movie of *Pride and Prejudice* as *Más fuerte que el orgullo* (Stronger than Pride) and Jane Austen's novels were quite popular in radio versions in Spain in the late 1950s. In 1966 a ten-episode television version of *Pride and Prejudice* (*Orgullo y prejuicio*) was screened, as it was felt the story fitted nicely into current strict Spanish codes of morality – after all, the book encouraged matrimony and correct feminine behaviour. The script was subject to Franco's censorship, which would remove anything politically or morally incorrect. The director was Alberto González Vergel, the script by José Méndez Herrera (who had won an award for his translations of Shakespeare), and the main roles were played by Pedro Pecci (Darcy) and Elena María Tejeiro (Elizabeth, but renamed 'Isabel' in the film). No effort was made to create an English setting – the houses are clearly Spanish, and the girls appear to be wearing mantilla-like headdresses. The costumes date from the Victorian era rather than the Regency. This version is not commercially available and may well have been destroyed.

MORMON

The Mormons are not into kissing in their movies, so there is no kiss in this version. A kiss might have improved it! *Pride and Prejudice: A Latter Day Comedy* was made in 2003 by Bestboy Pictures and was directed by Andrew Black.

The movie is set in modern Utah, where Elizabeth Bennet (played by Kam Heskin) is a student at Brigham Young University and an aspiring novelist. In town on a visit is Will Darcy (Orlando Seale), a British businessman who treats her with condescension. Parents have disappeared from this version and Elizabeth has housemates instead of sisters. The film follows the rough outlines of Jane

Austen's novel, and there are some cute Austen references, such as Lydia owning a pug named 'Austen' and Elizabeth's flat being on Longbourn Street.

The Mormon references are not overpowering, but the lack of physical contact between twenty-first-century lovers creates an odd note. These days, in a modern movie, we expect to see some physical contact between lovers. However, the Mormon expectation of women marrying so that little Mormons can be created (one suitor suggests to Elizabeth that they should go forth to 'multiply and replenish the earth') does tie in quite nicely with the financial and social imperatives faced by Mrs Bennet and her daughters. There are only light hints of the religious convictions of the characters and the occasional reference to Bible study; there's no alcohol, Wickham is criticized because he has stopped attending church, and Mr Collins is a returned missionary who is told by an angel in a vision that he should marry Elizabeth (or at least, that's what he tells her). It's odd that in such a strict religious culture, Elizabeth doesn't seem to mind about the religious faith of any of her suitors.

This is a frothy, extremely forgettable film. There are some good-looking actors, but it got poor reviews when it came out and is a superficial rendition of a deep and complex novel.

INDIAN

This is an infinitely more satisfying and clever version of *Pride and Prejudice*, although it doesn't have a kiss either. Bollywood is a term that usually means Hindi-language films, and this film is in English (although with some Hindi and Punjabi dialogue), but it has all the extravagance, music and colour of a typical Bollywood production. *Bride and Prejudice* was screened in 2004. Directed by Gurinder Chadha (of *Bend It Like Beckham* fame), it is only loosely based on Jane Austen's novel. However, swapping Regency bodices for Indian saris works surprisingly well, and the scenario of an Indian Mrs Bakshi who is desperate to marry off her four daughters is most convincing.

Will Darcy is a Beverly Hills hotel owner who comes to Amritsar with his friend Balraj and there meets, and argues with, Lalita Bakshi, the Elizabeth Bennet figure of the movie. Eventually, of course, they fall in love. Johnny Wickham, Mr Kohli (Mr Collins), Lakhi (Lydia), Will's snooty mother Catherine (Lady Catherine), are all faithful in essence to Jane Austen's characters and the plot even includes an elopement and the rescue by Darcy of the Bakshi family reputation when he saves Lakhi, just in time, from the clutches of Wickham.

Being a Bollywood film, this includes music. The sisters singing and dancing, Mr Kohli singing about his bathrooms, and a grand finale of a double wedding with elephants, sequins galore and vibrant colour everywhere – all make this a visually sumptuous adaptation. It helps also that

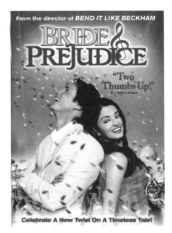

The film poster for *Bride and Prejudice*, directed by Gurinder Chadha.

the four main actors are almost breathtakingly gorgeous. Aishwaria Rai, who plays the heroine, was Miss World of 1994, while Namrata Shirodkar (who plays Jaya Bakshi, the Jane Bennet figure) was Miss India the year before. Martin Henderson as Darcy and Daniel Gillies as Wickham are real eye-candy too. According to Bollywood rules, there can be no kiss, but this production supplies much else, including a clever script. This Indian *Pride and Prejudice* is fun and memorable.

ISRAELI

In 2008 Israeli Television produced a six-part mini-series adaptation of *Pride and Prejudice* set in Galilee in the twenty-first century. Irit Linor had completed a Hebrew translation of the novel before she wrote the screenplay.

Its modernized Mr Darcy (played by Nimrod Artzi) is a worker in the high-tech industry, on a very large salary. He travels to northern Israel with his friend Ben Gal and their sisters, and there meets Anat and Alona, two divorcees in their thirties. Alona (Elizabeth) even has a teenage child. She can look Darcy up on his web page to check him out. Country houses become bed-and-breakfasts.

The series is not commercially available, but once again there is a clip on You-Tube to watch. Judging solely from that, there appears to be a wonderful Mrs Bennet – a large Jewish mama, who looks as though she could feed the world on chicken soup.

SCI-FI, ALIENS, SINGLETONS AND TIME-TRAVELLERS: OTHER VERSIONS
In 1995 the PBS American children's show *Wishbone* based one episode on *Pride and Prejudice*. Wishbone is a dog (a Jack Russell terrier) with an extremely active imagination – he played Mr Darcy. The episode was titled *Furst Impressions* (*sic*).

The science fiction sitcom *Red Dwarf* created a 1997 episode from *Pride and Prejudice*. In 'Beyond a Joke' the crew of a spaceship are introduced to a virtual reality rendition of 'Pride and Prejudice Land', where Elizabeth Bennet is played by Julia Lloyd.

Helen Fielding's bestselling book *Bridget Jones's Diary* was turned into a movie in 2001. The novel and film have fun playing with Jane Austen's *Pride and Prejudice*: Bridget is addicted to watching the 1995 Colin Firth mini-series of the novel, she has an obsessive mother desperate to marry her off, she meets a proud man called Mark Darcy, and there is a cheating womanizer to contend with. Colin Firth was given the part of Mark Darcy, an intended irony which doubled the Darcy appeal for viewers. Another connection with the 1995 *Pride and Prejudice* is that Andrew Davies wrote the *Bridget Jones's Diary* screenplay. The film was followed up by *Bridget Jones: The Edge of Reason*, loosely based on Jane Austen's *Persuasion*.

The 2008 four-part TV mini-series *Lost in Austen* is a time-travel *Pride and Prejudice*. Amanda Price, from Hammersmith, who loves reading the novels of Jane Austen, finds herself transported through a bathroom portal into the plot of *Pride and Prejudice*. The story keeps threatening to go off track (Bingley gets keen on her instead of Jane) and Amanda (played by Jemima Rooper) must steer it back on the right path. Meanwhile, Elizabeth Bennet has moved forward in time into twenty-first century London and there totally embraces modern life. She chats on her mobile, finds herself a job and takes public transport to work. In the end each woman elects to stay where she is – Amanda in the past, where she gets Mr Darcy

(Elliot Cowan) and Pemberley, Elizabeth in the future. The clever script won critical praise, and the series inspired several blogs. There are currently plans to turn it into a movie.

Other films that pay tribute to *Pride and Prejudice*, or borrow from it in some way, include *Becoming Jane*, a film about Jane Austen's romance with Tom Lefroy, where an invented character named Lady Gresham is clearly based on Lady Catherine de Bourgh; and *You've Got Mail* (1998), in which the heroine reads the novel and enters an Elizabeth/Darcy-like conflict with the rich and powerful hero. Stephanie Meyer acknowledges that she based her hugely successful *Twilight* series of novels on characters and events from *Pride and Prejudice* and her novels have been turned into movies. An episode of *Footballers' Wives* has a lavish *Pride and Prejudice*-themed wedding in which the groom (who turns out to be a bigamist) gets stuck in his Mr Darcy costume. Elton John's film company, Rocket Pictures, is currently working on *Pride and Predator* (inspired by a comic of the same name), a film about an alien landing at Longbourn with the aim of attacking the residents and leaving them without either sense or sensibility. This creature *must* be defeated. However, as the film was supposed to be ready for release in 2010 and nothing has recently been heard of it, perhaps gremlins got into the production company and caused havoc there too. In 2008 Stephen Fry planned to create a modern version of *Pride and Prejudice*. *Jane Austen Handheld* was to be a modern retelling of the story through the lens of a fly-on-the-wall documentary crew. Stephen Fry intended to play Mr Bennet, which sounds like fun, but nothing has been heard of this production for some time; it too seems to have been held up indefinitely.

MUSICAL VERSIONS

Jane Austen played the pianoforte every morning before breakfast and bestowed musical accomplishment on several of her characters. But she was not so fond of public performances, and sometimes she even tried to escape from the sound of the music. What would she have made of musical adaptations of her novel?

Turning *Pride and Prejudice* into a stage musical has been a fairly recent trend, especially among Americans. The first published version dates from 1962, when Abe Burrows adapted his *First Impressions: A Musical Comedy* from Helen Jerome's stage play. This two-act musical was first performed in the US in 1959, with Hermione Gingold as Mrs Bennet. In 1964 *Pride and Prejudice: A Musical Comedy* with music and lyrics by Nico Carstens and Mark Eldon was performed. It included seventeen songs, with much dancing by villagers and local labourers. In 1993 Bernard Taylor wrote his version, *Pride and Prejudice*, which premiered in Illinois and went on tour to Britain, New Zealand, Australia and Germany. It recounts Jane Austen's plot through twenty-one songs, including 'An Offer I Must Refuse', 'Have I Been Wrong?' and 'Thank God They're Married'. Lawrence Rush, in 2008, wrote lyrics and music for *Pride and Prejudice: The Musical*. He was a veteran of such adaptations, with musical versions of *Jane Eyre* and *Les Misérables* to his credit. In the same year there was *Jane Austen's Pride and Prejudice: The New Musical*. American Rita Abrams created her musical *Pride and Prejudice*, which includes nineteen songs (Lydia sings 'I Like a Man in Uniform'), and in 2011 Americans Lindsay Warren Baker and Amanda Jacobs co-wrote *Jane Austen's Pride and Prejudice: A Story of First Impressions and Second Chances*, including songs entitled 'I Can't Resist a Redcoat' and 'Fine Eyes'. In 2011 this musical was a sell-out in New York, but the songs were sung in an odd mix of British and American accents. There has even been a modern adaptation musical, with the Off-Broadway production *I Love You Because* (lyrics by Ryan Cunningham, music by Joshua Salzman), set in New York City, with a reversal of genders in the main roles. The hero and heroine are Austin Bennett and Marcy Fitzwilliams.

While some of these versions have been moderately popular, musical versions have failed to grab public attention and none appear to have been particularly memorable.

THEATRICAL VERSIONS

Martin Amis has likened writing a film script of a Jane Austen novel to 'artistic midwifery', by which he means that one must get the thing off the page and on to the screen in as undamaged a state as possible. But film directors at least have the opportunity to move their characters around easily – Derbyshire one minute,

Hertfordshire the next. Playwrights are more limited, as Pamela Whalan, who has adapted most of the Austen novels, explains:

> There are two major problems that must be considered when adapting this novel for the stage. The first is dealing with the number of characters that are brought to life in the novel. Any stage adaptation must limit the number of actors who appear on stage for practical reasons and it is impossible to establish and develop too many characters in a presentation that cannot greatly exceed two hours. The second problem is in creating appropriate settings for the action to take place. The story involves Elizabeth's growth of understanding of herself and others. It is not until Elizabeth physically journeys outside her familiar environment that she begins to question her judgment and this removal from her comfort zone needs to be portrayed with minimum disruptive set adjustment. Of course, the greatest challenge for anyone who attempts this task is to retain Miss Austen's wit and the charm of her leading character.

However, many have risen to these challenges of getting Jane Austen's words on to the stage and, thanks to its dramatic dialogue and witty comedy, *Pride and Prejudice* has been chosen for adaptation more than any other of her novels.

The very early theatrical versions were mostly scenes from the novel, prettily adapted for drawing-room readings or elocution exercises. In 1895 *Duologues and Scenes from the Novels of Jane Austen, Arranged and Adapted for Drawing-room Performance* by Rosanne Filippi included two scenes from *Pride and Prejudice* among its total of seven scenes. *Mr Collins Proposes* and *Lady Catherine is Annoyed with Elizabeth Bennet*, both by Phosphor Mallam, are examples from 1912. The first full play of the book came in 1902 with *Pride and Prejudice: A Play Founded on Jane Austen's Novel* by Mrs Steele MacKaye. The first foreign language play was an Indian one, written in Marathi, in 1912.

The 1920s saw more 'dramatic scene' scripts. *Scenes for Acting from Great Novelists* by Guy Pertwee included Lady Catherine's visit; *A Dramatic Reader* had Mr

Collins's proposal, as did *Elizabeth Refuses* by Joseph Williams. Ivor Novello took the part of Mr Bingley in a 1929 full-stage version of the book (*Pride and Prejudice: A Play in Four Acts* by Eileen H.A.Squire and J.C. Squire), and another version written by Anne Johnson-Jones came out the following year.

As with musical adaptations, the majority of stage versions have been written by Americans (the power of Broadway?). Helen Jerome brought out hers, *Pride and Prejudice: A Sentimental Comedy* in 1935, getting in just ahead of Englishman A.A. Milne, who didn't have much luck with the timing of his *Miss Elizabeth Bennet*. Milne wrote:

> On the day upon which it was finished I read that a dramatized version of *Pride and Prejudice* was about to be produced on the New York stage . . . There was still England. Should one hurry to get the play on with any cast that was available, or should one wait for the ideal Elizabeth, now unavailable? In the end the risk was taken; arrangements were made for the early autumn; the Elizabeth I had always wanted began to let her hair grow; the management, the theatre, the producer, all were there . . . and at that moment the American version arrived in London.

His play premiered in Liverpool in 1936 and 'in the absence of Miss Austen', Milne made a brief and modest speech, but it was Helen Jerome's inferior play, which completely ignores Jane Austen's scorn of the sentimental and which has the heroine saying 'I am abased' and uttering platitudes, that was chosen as the basis for the 1940 movie script. In the same year there was *I Have Five Daughters*, a three-act play by Margaret Macnamara, and in 1937 more dramatic readings, 'arranged by Doris Baxter'. The 1940s saw *Pride and Prejudice* by Jane Kendall and the one-act *The Wedding at Pemberley* by Anne and Arthur Russell.

Over the next decades theatrical versions appeared on a regular basis. There was a play by John Kennett in 1955, *The Heiress of Rosings* by Cedric Wallis (whose script had been used for two of the film versions) in 1956 (all the action takes place in Lady Catherine's drawing-room), *Pride and Prejudice: A Play* by Constance

Cox, and *Jane Austen's Pride and Prejudice* by Brainerd Duffield, both in 1972. There was even a one-act adaptation especially for performance by young people, published in a 1951 magazine and written by Deborah Newman.

Recent decades have produced more staged *Pride and Prejudices*, with versions by Brian J. Burton, Joseph Hanreddy and J.R. Sullivan, James Maxwell, Jon Jory, Gerald P. Murphy, Christina Calvit, Catherine Sheehy, Paula K. Parker, Lissa Creola and Tom Woods. Australian Pamela Whalan has adapted all of Jane Austen's novels except *Northanger Abbey*; her *Pride and Prejudice* premiered in Australia in 2010 and has been successful in several countries.

— —

'In any picture or play', Aldous Huxley commented in 1940, 'the story is essential and primary. In Jane Austen's books, it is a matter of secondary importance (every dramatic event in *Pride and Prejudice* is recorded in a couple of lines, generally in a letter) . . . the insistence upon the story as opposed to the diffuse irony which the story is designed to contain is a major falsification of Miss Austen.' And films, musicals and plays have 'falsified' *Pride and Prejudice*, making houses and dresses, horses and romances more important than ironic subtlety or depth of character. Serious themes are usually lost, while the love story, landscapes and beautiful clothes take centre stage.

The films succeed mainly because they put into full technicolour glory the erotic potential of the novel. They glamorize the men, and many create extra scenes to add to the sexiness of these males. Yet in *Pride and Prejudice* it is emotional self-restraint that reveals the true worth of the hero. Wickham (the villain) elopes with an under-age girl because he wants her in his bed, but Darcy (the hero) never even gets to give his Elizabeth a kiss.

We lose much and we gain much when we watch a film or a play of *Pride and Prejudice*. We get thoroughly enjoyable entertainment, but we do not truly get Jane Austen's classic. The films will come and the films will go, but the novel has lasted 200 years and has not yet delighted us for long enough.

Jane Austen 1775-1817 Mr Darcy

11^p

1975 British postage stamp featuring Mr Darcy.

Mugs and Skateboards

SELLING *PRIDE AND PREJUDICE*

'something in the opposite shop'

In 1799 Jane Austen went shopping in Bath. She wished to purchase something to decorate Cassandra's hat. 'Though you have given me unlimited powers concerning Your Sprig', she wrote to her sister, 'I cannot determine what to do about it . . . We have been to the cheap Shop, & very cheap we found it, but there are only flowers made there, no fruit – & as I could get 4 or 5 very pretty sprigs of the former for the same money which would procure only one Orleans plumb, in short could get more for three or four Shillings than I could have means of bringing home . . . Besides, I cannot help thinking that it is more natural to have flowers grow out of the head than fruit. – What do you think on that subject?' As Jane Austen searched the Bath shops soon after finishing *First Impressions* (there is no record of whether Cassandra preferred fruit or flowers 'sprouting' from her bonnet), she could never have imagined that 200 years later tourists would also suffer shopping dilemmas, as a result of her novel. Decisions must be made as to whether that *Pride and Prejudice* quote is shown to best advantage on a T-shirt or on a bumper sticker. Is a photo of Colin Firth as Darcy most enjoyed on a coffee mug or on a key ring? Would Mum prefer to have a *Pride and Prejudice* jigsaw puzzle or a *Pride and Prejudice* board game for her birthday?

Literary merchandise was not unheard of in Jane Austen's day. When Samuel Richardson's *Pamela* came out in 1740, *Pamela*-things were suddenly all the rage. Had Jane Austen's grandparents been so minded (or had more spare cash than they did), they could have purchased *Pamela* prints for the walls, *Pamela*-style gowns, fans, waxworks or a set of *Pamela*-decorated playing cards, all of which were easy to find in the shops of London or Bath. When Lord Byron awoke and found himself famous in 1812, he soon saw his own handsome face replicated and for sale on countless prints, while illustrations to his poems rolled off the presses and his clothes and hairstyle were imitated and marketed. However, it was not until after Jane Austen's death, when literary memorabilia became cheaper and easier to produce, that spin-off merchandising really took off. Dickens's *The Pickwick Papers* led to Pickwick cigar boxes, canes, Toby jugs, etc., while Beatrix Potter's animal tales and the rights to her illustrations have kept her publisher in business ever since, as manufacturers pay to put Peter Rabbit and his friends on bedspreads, china, gardening implements and toys. Today the merchandise connected with *Harry Potter*, or with the *Twilight* novels (novels that owe a considerable debt to *Pride and Prejudice*), is quite extraordinary, and a multi-million-dollar industry.

Jane Austen was fond of shopping. Her letters list many purchases – stockings, gauzes, sponge cakes and books – but she'd have enjoyed it more had her purse been better filled. However, she rarely gives shopping as an occupation for her characters, Mrs Allen in *Northanger Abbey* is her only true shopaholic, and that lady's obsession with muslins and fitting herself out in the latest fashion is made a subject of ridicule within the novel. *Pride and Prejudice* has few shoppers – the Misses Bingley have a 'habit of spending more than they ought', and the Bennet girls go to Meryton 'to pay their duty to their aunt and to a milliner's shop just over the way', but soon officers become more interesting than headgear. There is only one mention of a purchase there, when Lydia blows all her allowance: 'Look here, I have bought this bonnet,' she tells Jane and Elizabeth. 'I do not think it is very pretty, but I thought I might as well buy it as not. I shall pull it to pieces as soon as I get home, and see if I can make it up any better.' And when her sisters abused it as ugly, she added, with perfect unconcern, 'Oh! but there were two or three much uglier in the shop.' One suspects that many current manufacturers of *Pride and Prejudice* merchandise are aiming for the tastes and pockets of the Lydia Bennets of this world. There are some lovely things to buy that can increase the joy of *Pride and Prejudice* or act as delightful reminders of it, but there is also a great deal of kitsch and other objects of about as much use as Lydia's deconstructed bonnet.

Before Colin Firth linked his handsome face with *Pride and Prejudice* merchandising was generally tasteful and reasonable. 'It is a truth universally acknowledged . . .' and 'You must allow me to tell you how ardently I admire and love you' were printed on mugs and notepaper, and Hugh Thomson's illustrations of Mrs Bennet, or Jane and Mr Bingley, adorned tote bags and postcards. The Jane Austen House Museum gave over part of the entrance room of the house to shopping space and after a visit there a customer could write a note on *Pride and Prejudice*-themed notepaper, place it in a matching envelope, and then post it off with Mr Darcy on the stamp. A set of four Jane Austen postage stamps was issued in 1975 to mark the bicentenary of her birth (it remains a mystery why the Royal Mail did not commission a set of six – one for each novel). The 11 pence stamp featured a haughty Mr Darcy, in a blue caped greatcoat, leaning against a pillar. Cupid, ready to shoot his arrows, hovers in the background.

However, when the BBC *Pride and Prejudice* screened in 1995, the novel, the TV series, and especially Mr Darcy became a marketing phenomenon. Colin Firth's photo adorned key rings and tote bags, mugs and badges, note cards and fridge magnets, posters, bookmarks and calendars. Even without Colin Firth's image (or Matthew Macfadyen's after the movie was shown in cinemas), Mr Darcy with his £10,000 per year is worth far more than that sum in shops around the world. Women can stretch Darcy slogans on T-shirts across their chests – 'Mr Darcy is mine!' announces one such garment; but if that's not the message you want to convey, you can choose from many others: 'Looking for Mr Darcy', 'Pemberley Coat of Arms' or simply 'I love Mr Darcy' (T-shirts with this slogan come in women's styles and sizes, but also men's, for Darcy's gay fans). Your tote bag can tell the world that 'In vain have I struggled'), or boast 'Dibs on Darcy – you can have Wickham'; your mug can read 'Searching for Mr Darcy', 'I married my Mr Darcy', 'Call me Mrs Darcy' or just plain 'Mrs Darcy' (so that every women who sees you will envy you?). The Elizabeth Bennet who so proudly claims that she is Darcy's equal would not have been impressed by a T-shirt reading 'Property of Mr Darcy'; while Jane Austen would surely have smiled over one that asks 'What do you mean Mr Darcy isn't real?'. Then there is the fridge magnet with 'I

Want Darcy for Christmas', a mobile phone case with 'From Darcy' on its cover, thong underwear that proclaims the wearer's intimate connection with Darcy, 'I Love Darcy' lip balm (in four flavours, including spearmint and avocado – both of which would have been unknown to Darcy in the Pemberley dining room) – and even 'Mr Darcy' earrings to dangle from your earlobes. Very brave men can order for themselves a T-shirt that states emphatically, 'I am Mr Darcy!'

Elizabeth Bennet cannot compete with her admirer financially either within the novel or in today's marketplace. There are Royal Doulton and Franklin Mint figurines and metal statuettes of Elizabeth to place on the mantelpiece, needle-work samplers (though Jane Austen tells us that Elizabeth was not fond of sewing) on which one stitches the words 'Mrs Darcy of Derbyshire', jars of 'Lizzie [*sic*] Bennet hand cream' (scented with rose oil) and Elizabeth (together with Darcy) hanging on a pendant; there are even Elizabeth's words replicated on a beer stein. But generally marketers assume customers are females wanting to buy a bit of sex appeal rather than something connected with another woman (and the woman who gets Mr Darcy at that).

Other characters from *Pride and Prejudice* have not been totally neglected in the flood of memorabilia. There are little statuettes of Mr and Mrs Bennet, Kitty, Lydia, Bingley and Wickham; there is a 'Longbourn perfume set', an 'I love Mr Bingley' tote bag and a tank top stating its wearer is 'Mrs Bingley'. Other merchandise simply uses quotes from the book – the famous opening sentence appears on the usual range of mugs, beach towels, shopping pads, drawer liners, key rings, stationery, badges, a silver charm in the shape of a book and bookmarks – or uses illustrations of the

characters. It's possible to buy pictures of Elizabeth and Darcy on top of an expensive Limoges box, on mouse pads, tea towels, postcards, carrier bags, crockery and clothing. Today you can find your favourite *Pride and Prejudice* words and people on pet bowls, diaries and journals, tiles, calendars, coasters, linen, Christmas tree decorations, a wall clock, jewellery, toys, cosmetics, chocolate

ABOVE Elizabeth and Mr Darcy paper dolls; OPPOSITE *Pride and Prejudice* Trivia Game.

wrappers, embroidery samplers, magnets and china. There are other things that are more generally Jane Austen than specifically *Pride and Prejudice*, such as a Jane Austen action figure, or a quill pen with which one can write a Mr Collins letter. Such items can be purchased at the well-stocked shop in the Jane Austen Centre in Bath, or at the lovely gift shop in Chawton cottage, or at Chawton House, or at stalls set up by Jane Austen societies around the world, such as the Jane Austen Society of Australia's Regency Fair or the New York group's 'Pug's Parlour', or at hundreds of sites on the web. It's even possible to design your own *Pride and Prejudice* merchandise these days: online shops offer the chance to select your own quote from the novel and match that up to a garment, piece of china, toy or stationery.

Some merchandise shows that the manufacturer has not read *Pride and Prejudice* without picking up at least some of its humour. The apron that announces 'Let's BBQ Wickham' deserves to sell well, as does the T-shirt that asks 'Who invited Mr Collins?' Many a woman has bought 'Mr Darcy Soap' so that she can rub herself all over with Mr Darcy when she takes a shower, and it is to be hoped that a runner whose shoes proclaim 'Team Darcy' on their sides will out-run all the Wickhams in the race to win a Lizzy Bennet. Other unusual *Pride and Prejudice* objects currently for sale include glass votive candles made from recycled pages of a copy of the novel, hair clips or a corsage made from the same source, bunting also made from pages of the novel with which to decorate a room for your next party, clothes pegs (in a set of six) with tiny snippets of the novel's sentences on both sides (useful for hanging out on the line all those clean Darcy T-shirts), and thimbles, cravats and nighties – all 'advertising' the novel in some way.

No one, it seems, is too young to be a *Pride and Prejudice* customer. An expectant mother can wear *Pride and Prejudice*-themed maternity wear (taken from a drawer scented with Pemberley rose sachets) and then dress her baby (which will, of course, be named either Elizabeth or Darcy) in rompers that announce 'In vain have I struggled' (which rather dubiously suggests that the poor baby has constipation) or state that the infant will grow up to become Mr Darcy or Elizabeth Bennet. Little girls can cut out Elizabeth, Darcy, Jane, Bingley, Wickham and Lady Catherine paper dolls (how tempting to remove Lady Catherine's elegant gown and replace it with one of Lydia's low-cut slutty dresses instead!), or play with a *Pride and Prejudice* teddy bear (whose stomach is adorned with a picture of Jane Austen writing the novel), while boys and girls can zoom down a ramp on a skateboard covered in *Pride and Prejudice* quotes.

Anyone can have fun playing the *Pride and Prejudice* Trivia Game (a version of Trivial Pursuit) or the *Pride and Prejudice* Board Game (the aim being to win your way to the parish church where you will be married, hopefully to Darcy, Elizabeth, Jane or Bingley, and not to Mr Wickham, Mr Collins or Lydia), or do online quizzes about the novel, play Jane Austen charades online, or submit a photo of your cat named Mr Darcy to the online 'Mr Darcy Cat Contest'.

Henry Austen wrote of his sister after her death: 'No accumulation of fame would have induced her, had she lived, to affix her name to any productions of her pen . . . In public she turned away from any allusion to the character of an authoress.' This is not strictly true. While Jane Austen did not wish to be lionized, she did 'write only for Fame', and she certainly wanted any money that her 'character of an authoress' generated. The merchandise created in the name of *Pride and Prejudice* would have astonished, amused and possibly also appalled her, but she'd have been the first to appreciate any revenue it brought her way. 'Though I like praise as well as anybody, I like what Edward [her brother] calls Pewter too,' she wrote in a letter to a niece. What a shame that money from the weird and wonderful merchandise which *Pride and Prejudice* has inspired never benefited her financially, or enabled her to head off on a reckless shopping spree in Bath!

Jane Austen jigsaw puzzle.

PRIDE AND PREJUDICE TOURISM

'What delight! What felicity!' Elizabeth exclaims when her Aunt and Uncle Gardiner invite her to go travelling with them. 'Adieu to disappointment and spleen. What are men to rocks and mountains? Oh! what hours of transport we shall spend.' By going to the Lakes and the rocky and mountainous north of England, Elizabeth is proposing to be a literary traveller. Wordsworth's *Guide to the Lakes* had been published a few years before, the new idea of a 'tour of pleasure' had been promoted by William Gilpin in his *Tours*, and poets such as Wordsworth, Coleridge and Southey had made the north fashionable. Elizabeth's language ('Adieu to disappointment and spleen') is deliberately affected in imitation of travellers of 'sensibility'. But unlike those modish travellers, Elizabeth plans to notice properly and remember this part of England, which is new to her: 'And when we *do* return, it shall not be like other travellers, without being able to give one accurate idea of anything. We *will* know where we have gone – we *will* recollect what we have seen. Lakes, mountains, and rivers, shall not be jumbled together in our imaginations . . . Let *our* first effusions be less insupportable than those of the generality of travellers.' Of course, in the end Elizabeth never gets to the Lakes; her travels are confined to Derbyshire and 'all the celebrated beauties of Matlock, Chatsworth, Dovedale, or the Peak'. These were also places enthused over by Gilpin, in *Observations* (1786), by Thomas Whateley in his *Observations on Modern Gardening, Illustrated by Descriptions*, and also by seventeenth-century writers Thomas Hobbes, Charles

Cotton and Daniel Defoe (and Matlock was painted by Turner), so Elizabeth's 'tour of pleasure', although curtailed, still has literary associations.

Millions of tourists have followed Elizabeth Bennet's excellent example as a traveller, and today *Pride and Prejudice* tourism is big business. The first 'pilgrims' of the book were those in the 1860s who went to find Jane Austen's grave in Winchester Cathedral, so that they could pay their respects and think gratefully of all the reading pleasure she had bequeathed them. The cathedral's verger had no idea why so many were seeking that particular grave: 'Can you tell me was there anything particular about that lady?' he asked. Her home in Steventon was no longer standing (current excavations on the site are uncovering its exact position and dimensions), but Chawton cottage was. Run-down and shabby, it was inhabited by workers on the Chawton estate and was much changed since Jane Austen's day, so it wasn't much of a 'shrine'. The grave in the cathedral had to do. As the grave's inscription fails to mention *Pride and Prejudice* (or any of her novels), it wasn't terribly satisfactory either. In 1900 a memorial window of stained glass was installed near by. It too fails to credit *Pride and Prejudice* to Jane Austen, but still it was enough for Kipling, an ardent Janeite, to go out of his way to visit whenever he was in the area, and to call it 'the holiest place in England'.

The next 'shrine' was the cottage at Chawton, which was rescued for the nation by Thomas Carpenter in 1947, in memory of his 'Janeite' son who'd been killed in the war, and turned into a museum. 'Relics' (Austen furniture, Jane Austen's jewellery, a lock of her hair) were collected, donated, bought back and then displayed, and the literary tourists paid to see them. They arrived in steady numbers, happily bought their *Pride and Prejudice* postcards and mugs adorned with *Pride and Prejudice* quotes, and went away.

The popular films of the novel changed the constant trickle of visitors into a flood. In the year that the Firth/Ehle television series was screened in Britain, such hordes trooped through Chawton cottage that the museum had to extend its opening hours and hire more staff. The tourists' money financed essential roof repairs, but the wear and tear on the small house created other problems. A major rethink by the Jane Austen Memorial Trust resulted in the redesigning of rooms and display cases, a new bookshop built out the back and the opening up of the old kitchen as part of the museum (this work was all done by 2009, the 200th anniversary year of Jane Austen's arrival at the cottage). Today's visitor can gaze rapturously at the tiny table on which *Pride and Prejudice* was revised and polished (just to see this table moves many a visitor to tears), and can purchase from a far greater selection of Lizzy/Darcy/Pemberley merchandise in the enlarged gift shop.

Colin Firth's parents lived in Winchester and busloads of adoring women roamed the district hoping for a glimpse of him being a dutiful son. But if Colin was busy elsewhere, *Pride and Prejudice* tourists could still seek places he had been to, and imagine him there. Lyme Park in Cheshire was a quiet place for decades – the odd visitor strolled or picnicked in its park and admired the pond and extensive grounds – but after Colin Firth dived into that particular pond (or rather, a stunt man impersonating him did), the pond was like a magnet. In their thousands the tourists arrived. They sighed over the famous wet-shirt scene, and left feeling they had experienced some genuine *Pride and Prejudice* magic. Lyme Park's fame as Pemberley has taken on a life all of its own.

Houses used for interior scenes in the films also benefited from 'the Pemberley effect' and drew the crowds. Luckington Court in Wiltshire is in private hands and its owner, Angela Horn, had a great deal of fun admitting producers and camera crew and sharing her home with the Bennets, Bingleys and co. for some months. She occasionally opens her house for special tour groups. Belton House in Lincolnshire (which was Rosings), Sudbury Hall in Derbyshire (used for Pemberley's interior scenes) and the Old Rectory at Tegn in Leicestershire (Mr Collins' 'humble abode') all found, after filming was over, that visitor numbers escalated, or that far more cars were being driven very slowly past the gates. In 1996 the Historic Houses Association recommended fees of £2,000 per day for filming interior scenes and £1,600–£1,700 for exterior scenes. It was lucrative business to connect your home with a home from *Pride and Prejudice*.

The same thing occurred after the Macfadyen/Knightley movie was screened in 2005. Chatsworth (Pemberley) found its visitor numbers doubled, Basildon Park (Netherfield) had a 76 per cent increase in its number of coach visitors, and Burghley

Chatsworth Estate in Derbyshire (illustration by Alexander Francis Lydon) where scenes for the 2005 movie were filmed.

House (Rosings) also received fabulous advertising from its *Pride and Prejudice* connection. All who came spent money on tickets, but also spent big in the cafés and gift shops of these properties. The National Trust closed Basildon Park during filming, in recognition of the fact that revenue from connecting the property with *Pride and Prejudice* would be far greater than any income made from the usual trickle of National Trust members. Today the place hosts 'Jane Austen Weekends' in the summer ('It's easier to follow in the footsteps of Lizzy and Darcy than you might think . . .', they promise visitors), offers a 'Jane Austen Children's Trail', and puts on Regency talks and 'Living History' displays – evidence of the power of the *Pride and Prejudice* brand of tourism. Those who resemble Lizzy in being good walkers have set off across the Derbyshire Peak District National Park to find the exact rock upon which Keira Knightley stood in the movie (it's at Stanage Edge), coat swirling behind her in the wind as she gazed wistfully towards Pemberley.

There are even entire villages and towns to satisfy *Pride and Prejudice* fans who travel. The historic village of Lacock in Wiltshire, totally owned by the National Trust, is unspoiled and beautifully preserved, so its rows of cottages needed little changing when the place became the 1995 'Meryton'. The parking lot just outside the village is now always full of coaches, spilling out people anxious to lunch at the Red Lion Inn, where the Meryton assembly ball was filmed, to take a photo in the street where Darcy snubbed Wickham and rode angrily off, or to purchase something from the shop where the Bennet girls bought their bonnets. The market town of Stanford in Lincolnshire is also stuffed with historic buildings (and had been effectively used in a movie of *Emma*), so was an obvious choice for Joe Wright's 'Meryton' when he made the 2005 movie. Today the town sells postcards of the filming, so one can stand in the same spot as the cameraman to see what changes were made to turn Stanford into the headquarters of a regiment and the place the Miss Bennets visit 'three or four times a week'.

Many tourists don't wish to seek these places out on their own, or prefer to share their *Pride and Prejudice* passion with like-minded companions. The web lists a great number of different organized excursions – *Pride and Prejudice* weekends, *Pride and Prejudice* day outings, three-week Jane Austen tours including every place connected with her life and novels, 'film location' tours, *Pride and Prejudice* study tours – while members of Jane Austen societies frequently arrange visits to *Pride and* Prejudice-related spots. One can even board a Jane Austen cruise, and discuss *Pride and Prejudice* on a ship sailing from England to Holland, Guernsey, Spain and France (countries never visited by Jane Austen). There are also more general literary tours, such as 'Exploring the Literary Landscapes of England', which include Jane Austen properties and sites, offer specialist guides and arrange for visits into properties not generally open to the public. Devotees are spoiled for choice.

Pemberley, Netherfield Park and Rosings are all fictional, but Jane Austen might have based aspects of them on actual places she saw, and it is fun to travel around England seeking out landscapes and buildings that might have played a part in the creation of this beloved novel, and speculate. The Rutland Arms Hotel, a beautiful Georgian inn in Derbyshire, advertises itself as 'the place where Jane Austen wrote *Pride and Prejudice*'. There is no accuracy whatsoever in this claim, but that doesn't stop tourists from visiting, and feeling a special thrill at the connection, no matter how spurious it is. Those entering Derbyshire are not confronted with a sign announcing 'Mr Darcy's County' (in the way that Hampshire advertises 'Jane Austen's County' on its welcoming signs), but any true pilgrim will not fail to think of Mr Darcy when entering Derbyshire ('With the mention of Derbyshire, there were many ideas connected. It was impossible for her to see the word without thinking of Pemberley and its owner'), and Hertfordshire must inevitably conjure up thoughts of the Bennets. Tourists from around the world pay happily for such privileges; the Jane Austen travel industry is delighted to take their money and is flourishing as never before.

'Behold Me Immortal'

PRIDE AND PREJUDICE
NOW AND IN THE FUTURE

But tell Jane Austen, that is, if you dare,
How much her novels are beloved down here.
She wrote them for posterity, she said;
'Twas rash, but by posterity she's read.
'A Letter to Lord Byron' W.H. Auden

In Karen Joy Fowler's novel *The Jane Austen Book Club*, five women and one man join together to form the 'Central Valley/River City all-Jane-Austen-all-the-time book club' so that they can talk about *Pride and Prejudice* and Jane Austen's five other novels. As they read and discuss these books, they learn about themselves, each other, about love and their world. Each member recognizes that it is 'essential to reintroduce Jane Austen into your life regularly'.

We live in an age when so many forms of entertainment compete for our time. So why, some readers ask, should time be spent *rereading Pride and Prejudice* when there are so many other good books waiting to be read? But do those same readers listen only once to a Beethoven symphony and then tick it off as something done, never to be done again? Do they never return to the art

The cast of *Pride and Prejudice* (illustration by Liz Monahan).

gallery to study that Vermeer, believing that once they have viewed it, there's no need to look at it a second time? Rereading *Pride and Prejudice* is as necessary as listening again to favourite music or looking once more at a much-loved painting. For really no one ever reads the same *Pride and Prejudice* twice. A first reading alters you; by a second reading you are a slightly different person. Every subsequent reading reveals different things about you and your world. A starry-eyed teenager will find a romantic *Pride and Prejudice* on first perusal, but thirty years later that same reader, now a parent to five daughters, will discover a very different *Pride and Prejudice* on re-opening its pages. Every reading of *Pride and Prejudice* is a new one.

But how is *Pride and Prejudice* being read and reread today? It's no longer essential to get a *Pride and Prejudice*-fix from paper and ink. Recent reading changes have been quite incredible.

In 1932 the 'Talking Book Machine' was invented and within a short time *Pride and Prejudice* was recorded so that the blind could listen to it. Soon others were enjoying the first audio versions too. Today the ribboned cassettes of such machines seem decidedly old-fashioned and the technology for playing cassettes of Irene Sutcliffe reading *Pride and Prejudice* has almost disappeared. CDs came next and the story of Elizabeth and Darcy was put on shiny metal discs. These were soon readily available through bookshops and libraries, and indeed still are. Now it's downloads as mp3s – an audio version can go from the computer to an iPod, an iPad or even a mobile phone. A person can 'read' *Pride and Prejudice* while running in the park, driving a car or doing the housework. Audible.com (the audio book branch of Amazon) currently offers over twenty different audio versions. However, half of those are abridged and NO ONE should listen to a shortened *Pride and Prejudice*! (The full version should last about eleven to twelve hours, but Audible has for sale one audio version that lasts fifty-four minutes. Imagine a *Pride and Prejudice* with 92 per cent of the story chopped out – what on earth is left?) Also available on audio are several dramatized versions, a children's version, Spanish and Italian translations, various vampire, pornographic and sequel offerings, and even a Cliff Notes to *Pride and Prejudice* recorded on CD. Readers have such choice: a customer can select whether to have the novel read by a woman (Emilia Fox, who played Georgiana Darcy in the 1995 BBC series, is one reader; Joanna David, who played Aunt Gardiner in the same adaptation, is another; others include Joanna Lumley, Juliet Stevenson, Jenny Agutter, Lindsay Duncan, Angela Lansbury and Jane Lapotaire) or by a man (Neil Conrich is one male reader), by someone with an English accent or an American one.

Digital technology is changing the book format too. Now the novel can be downloaded on to a Kindle, an iPad, a Kobo or some other electronic reading device. More and more readers are growing comfortable with these new technologies, and the technologies are changing and developing at an incredible speed. Austen's novels are especially popular on such devices because they can be downloaded for free, as their copyright has expired. Project Gutenberg, the world's oldest digital library, offers *Pride and Prejudice* at no charge; so do Google, Facebook and Twitter.

Reading *Pride and Prejudice* on a Kindle has pluses and minuses. It is cheap (or free) once the Kindle has been purchased, has less environmental impact, and is amazing for travel (no more heavy suitcases, when thousands of books can be loaded on to one Kindle). However, an electronic version lacks the memories associated with a printed book, in which that coffee ring near Darcy's proposal reminds you of reading the scene in a Paris café or the curled pages bring recollections of laughing over Mr Collins while reading on the beach. No one can furnish a room with Kindle books, whereas a precious Jane Austen collection brings wonderful memories to its proud owner. Myriad ideas associated with a physical book are absent from a Kindle. And a Kindle homogenizes books – a reader has no sense of differing weights, different degrees of quality when *Pride and Prejudice* and *Fies and Prejudice* pop up in identical formats on the same screen. On a Kindle *Pride and Prejudice* weighs as much in an abridged edition as in the uncut one. Should one read a book in the way its author visualized it going out into the world, or do we all opt for convenience, cheapness and change? Or is what really matters the connection between the mind of the author and that of the reader, which is still there in an electronic version? Reading technologies have altered rapidly in the last twenty years and another 200 years could bring almost anything. If, as Elizabeth Bennet advises, you 'indulge your imagination in every possible flight which the subject will afford', you will still never be able to gain an accurate idea of how books will be read in 2213.

Preacher Charles Spurgeon once advised, 'Master those books you have. Read them thoroughly. Bathe in them until they saturate you. Read and reread them . . . digest them.' When you have read, reread and digested *Pride and Prejudice*, the next impulse is likely to be to want to talk about it. Jane Austen's earliest fans wrote of it excitedly in correspondence, and discussed it in their circulating libraries. In the twentieth century Jane Austen societies were formed for the purpose of providing forums for just such talk. Today, lectures, workshops, conferences, dinners, quizzes, journals and newsletters all provide opportunities for discussion, argument and debate. Il Club Sofa and Carpet di Jane Austen (the Italian society) hosts a Regency ball, offering prizes for those who can out-dance Darcy and Elizabeth; the Jane Austen Society of Australia holds regular study days on *Pride and Prejudice*; the Jane Austen Society of North America gives a scholarship for writers to research *Pride and Prejudice* (or another Austen novel) at Chawton House; and the Jane Austen Society of the Netherlands offers monthly balls in Dutch stately homes. Jane Austen societies provide opportunities to discuss themes, characters, setting, irony, comedy, films, sequels, romance, structure, marriages, food, travel, historical background, hero, heroine, style, time frame, continuing relevance, morality, feminism, Marxism, influence, criticism and many other aspects of *Pride and Prejudice*.

The novel is being talked about in the academic world too. Universities publish scholarly articles on a vast range of Austenian topics. Professor Douglas Bush ponders the phallic significance of Mr Gardiner's fishing tackle in an article entitled 'Mrs Bennet and the Dark Gods'; in another Eve Kosofsky Sedgwick writes an essay to establish which of Jane Austen's characters are into regular masturbation. Articles examine the ways in which Gaskell's *North and South* is inspired by *Pride and Prejudice*, or how the novel was inspired by Samuel Richardson's works. D.W. Harding famously examined the 'regulated hatred' to be found in the novel, while Margaret Kirkham sought out its feminism. Today's academics are still finding plenty to write about *Pride and Prejudice*. Austen classes at universities currently attract far higher numbers than classes on any other nineteenth-century novelist; university extension courses and summer school programmes for adults keen to learn more about *Pride and Prejudice* are immensely popular. From China to New

Zealand, Sri Lanka to Japan, students are kept busy writing essays about *Pride and Prejudice*; and lectures and seminars devoted to in-depth analysis of the novel are currently taking place all over the world.

Today, discussion is also taking place on the worldwide web. In 1943 Sheila Kaye-Smith and G.B. Stern (both novelists) sat down to write up their discussions about Jane Austen's novels. The result was *Talking of Jane Austen*. Reading their book is like eavesdropping on two friends chatting over a cup of tea about their favourite novels. In 2008 Steve Chandler and Terence N. Hill wrote *Two Guys Read Jane Austen*, a book that consists of chat conducted by email, as they ponder the importance of Jane Austen in their lives. Although they lived in different parts of the US, distance was no barrier to their holding a literary conversation. Now conversation about Jane Austen is global. There are hundreds of chat rooms, blogs, archives, discussion sites and Internet forums dedicated to her works. One of the best known, 'The Republic of Pemberley', was formed 'for people addicted to *Pride and Prejudice*', so that they could 'feel free to gush , and today 'Pemberleans' from around the world enthuse, argue, inform and gush to their heart's content. 'Austenprose – the Jane Austen Blog' daily celebrates the brilliance of *Pride and Prejudice*. There are online polls, web quizzes, chat rooms devoted to the films and scholarly sites. Those wanting to talk about *Pride and Prejudice* or hear what others have to say can visit an 'I Love *Pride and Prejudice* Group', austenacious.com, austenonly.com, 'All Things Austen', the 'Mr Darcy Fan Club' (or the Internet fan clubs specializing in Elizabeth Bennet, or Jane and Bingley), 'November is *Pride and Prejudice* Month', firth.com, 'Firthness' (offering 'All Darcy, all the time') or 'The *Pride and Prejudice* Paradise'. The BBC is bringing the world of Jane Austen to Facebook in 2012, with 'Jane Austen's Rogues and Romance', the first online social game dedicated to Wickham, Darcy and co. There's an awful lot of happy cyberspace taken up by people talking about *Pride and Prejudice*.

Pride and Prejudice is rare as a novel in making the highbrow and the lowbrow want to discuss it. It has mass appeal. Today many of those talking about it are female, although 100 years ago the book was read more by men than by women; films have made the book mistakenly appear to be more a female experience than a male

one. But there are male enthusiasts too and many fine modern critics have been, and are, men. Gender, geography, age, nationality
and religion are all unimportant – around the world this novel is
forcing a universal response.

Pride and Prejudice is an invitation: it demands to be talked
about. It asks readers today, and readers to come, to enter its
world, engage with its characters and issues, find answers for
the questions it poses. It makes us think about friendships, about
relationships with parents and siblings, about finding happiness
in marriage, about demanding employers, about chance and
the role it plays in human affairs (for example, Darcy walking
across his lawn at Pemberley just as Elizabeth is doing the
same), about clergymen and military men and their role in
society, about social rankings, about self-knowledge, about
. . . The list goes on and on. It encourages us to find role
models in its finer characters, to strive for self-awareness, to
learn how to cope with aggressive bosses or false friends.
Human nature has not changed in 200 years and so *Pride
and Prejudice* can still tell us what makes people tick. And
of course it forces every reader to consider the many forms
of 'pride' and 'prejudice' encountered by everyone every
day in this world in which we live. Professor Amanda
Vickery, who recently presented a documentary on *The
Many Lovers of Miss Jane Austen* (screened in Britain on the BBC in late 2011),
summed it up very well: 'I think the key to her adaptability is her restraint. Austen
leaves room for the reader's intelligence and fantasies, which has the uncanny effect
of allowing each new generation to see themselves reflected back from her pages.'
Surely in 200 years new readers will still be seeking themselves in the pages of
Pride and Prejudice. As Anthony Trollope remarked, this is a novel 'full of excellent
teaching'. There is every hope that *Pride and Prejudice* will continue to teach its
invaluable lessons to many generations to come.

PRIDE AND PREJUDICE AS BIBLIOTHERAPY

The ancient Greeks put up signs in their libraries announcing them to be 'healing places for the soul'. Any reader knows that books make you feel better, but today there's a word for it: bibliotherapy. It's an expressive therapy which uses novels, poems and the written word to fight depression and psychological problems. Bibliotherapy gives confidence to children, facilitates dialogue in troubled relationships, occupies a patient in a healthy and productive way, and brings catharsis and resolution to trauma. Bibliotherapy can take place in a professional environment, with trained therapists, in the classroom or at home. *Pride and Prejudice* is high on the list of books recommended by professional bibliotherapists.

Bibliotherapy is not a new concept, even if its name is a new one. Many a reader over the last two centuries has turned to *Pride and Prejudice* as a pick-me-up. As we have seen, in the trenches of First World War the Bennets and Bingleys brought comfort to men desperately in need of something to smile about ('Jane Austen has taken her fragrant way into a surprising number of dugouts', one contemporary commentator remarked) and Kipling wrote in 'The Janeites' of the group therapy the novel provided for weary men and the sense of companionship that *Pride and Prejudice* gave. He found solace in its pages when his only son was killed in France. A.A. Milne read it as he recuperated in a war hospital and in its pages forgot the horrors of the Front. Thousands took copies of *Pride and Prejudice* into bomb shelters in the Second World War. Anxieties over whether Darcy and Elizabeth would finally unite drove away greater anxieties about the exploding world outside. For two centuries *Pride and Prejudice* has soothed, cheered, calmed, inspired confidence, overcome emotional problems and lessened the hurts of life. Reading it makes you feel good. Who needs Mogadon when there is a copy of *Pride and Prejudice* on the bookshelf?

EXAMPLES OF *PRIDE AND PREJUDICE* AS BIBLIOTHERAPY

'Let me have only the company of the people I love . . .'

A friend I love has been precious to me for sixty years. A giving friend who is never demanding and expects nothing in return, a friend who provides delight and humour when I seek escape, solace in times of worry or grief, a friend who willingly shares acquaintances who are guaranteed to reveal the unexpected at each encounter. My treasured friend? *Pride and Prejudice*!

Marlene Arditto, Vice President, Jane Austen Society of Australia

'How can you be so silly,' cried her mother, 'as to think of such a thing, in all this dirt! You will not be fit to be seen when you get there.'

'I shall be very fit to see Jane – which is all I want.'

What better escape from the disruptive impact of an earthquake could there be than to dip into *Pride and Prejudice*? Against a background of ongoing quakes with associated damage, traffic delays and recurrent liquefaction, how could I not identify with Elizabeth Bennet when she arrives at Netherfield, her petticoats six inches deep in mud? Her example cannot fail to inspire. She thinks not of presenting a pristine appearance but of the need to support her sister. What a heroine! In a similar way, Christchurch may be damaged, but remains unbowed. Lizzy's imperfect appearance actually meets the approval of those who matter in the novel. Hard hats and high visibility vests are modish in my home town! In the midst of abnormal conditions, *Pride and Prejudice* is a never-failing source of inspiration, entertainment and a welcome distraction from life in quake-affected Christchurch.

Ruth Williamson, JASA member in Christchurch, New Zealand

What books are best when I am feeling low? It's not always escapist fantasy that fills the bill. Sometimes what is most comforting is to be reminded of an ordered world in which integrity wins the day, good manners are a reflection of a good heart, and love is generous not self-serving. For that, *Pride and Prejudice* is the perfect therapy: a timeless story which is at one and the same time both profound and vastly entertaining. How many books are there where, even though you have known the ending since you were 12, you still can't wait to find out what happens? The seriousness, the sanity, the exquisite sense of fun of Jane Austen's world in this novel combine to put everything back into perspective – and life begins to look up again.

Dr Joanna Penglase, editor of JASA journal *Sensibilities*

Even when I think I know the book so well, every re-reading turns up new delights of wit and humour and always makes me feel better. Jane Austen's portraiture in words is wonderful. Her succinct, clever, insightful and elegant language is a joy. I always laugh at Elizabeth's verbal fencing matches with Darcy, the Bingleys and Lady Catherine, at Mr Bennet's dry comments, at Mrs Bennet's twittering and at the never to be forgotten verbosity and pomposity of Mr Collins! Who can beat her?

Maureen Kelly, chairman of the Scottish branch of the Jane Austen Society

Since 2012 is a presidential election year in the USA, it is a *Pride and Prejudice* year for me. Although sorely tempted, I try to refrain from demonizing adherents of either political party. I do, however (as a Janeite) depend upon being entertained – virtually daily – by ridiculous, ludicrous, hyperbolic statements, accusations and charges made by candidates and the media types who report on their antics. Given the emptiness of political discourse in these polarized times – most people strive only to reinforce their own preferences and prejudices – I have been known to interrupt a political exchange, online or in-the-flesh, with this personal maxim: 'Forget politics. Read Jane Austen.' This year, of all years, my novel of choice for sense, sanity, stability and civility must certainly be *Pride and Prejudice*.

Elsa Solender, past president of JASNA, author of *Jane Austen in Love: An Entertainment*

PRIDE AND PREJUDICE,

A NOVEL.

BY

JANE AUSTEN.

*This is not to be borne. Miss Bennet.
I insist on being satisfied. Has he, has
my nephew made you an offer of marriage?*

ABOVE The first illustrated edition of *Pride and Prejudice* published in 1833; OPPOSITE 'Three daughters married! . . . I shall go distracted.' An illustration by Ann Kronheimer from the Real Reads abridged edition of *Pride and Prejudice* retold by Gill Tavner.

Pride and Prejudice is a diamond of a novel. The marvellous dialogue, beautifully constructed plot, wit and superb characters all sparkle from the page. It radiates light and energy, throwing off many shades and reflections from its facets. Like a diamond, it refuses to crack under pressure: it survives the onslaughts of filmmakers, sequel writers, critics and fans. Like a diamond, it's the universal symbol of Love. Critic Tony Tanner once remarked that *Pride and Prejudice* is the story of a man who changes his manners and a lady who changes her mind, but it's also the world's greatest love story. Like a professionally cut stone, *Pride and Prejudice* has exquisite symmetry. Those looking into its glittering depths find beauty, order and balance, but they also discover there what they want or need to see. There's nothing fake about this gem of a novel – it took great effort to forge its sparkle – and its glittering perfections have not worn away after two centuries of hard wear. Like a diamond, it is timeless and universal. Just as man has always lusted after jewels, *Pride and Prejudice* too evokes a powerful response.

It is not surprising, then, that readers' polls regularly place *Pride and Prejudice* in No. 1 position. It has been voted the 'Most Romantic Novel of all Time' and it was 'No. 1 Most-Loved Book' in a World Book Day poll. *Pride and Prejudice* is the book that people do not want to be without. In lists of '100 Books You Should Read Before You Die', *Pride and Prejudice* is there again. In so many ways, the world has acknowledged its uniqueness and its immense popularity.

It has been said that a classic is a book that has never finished saying what it has to say. *Pride and Prejudice* has now been 'speaking' for 200 years, and there is every reason to believe that it will go on speaking to readers for ever.

Bibliography

Auerbach, Emily, *Searching for Jane Austen*, University of Wisconsin Press, Wisconsin, 2004

Austen, Jane, *Jane Austen's Letters* (ed. Deirdre Le Faye), Oxford University Press, Oxford, 1997

—, *The Annotated Pride and Prejudice* (ed. David M. Shapard), Pheasant Books, New York, 2004

—, *Pride and Prejudice*, Cambridge University Press, Cambridge, 2006

Austen-Leigh, James Edward, *A Memoir of Jane Austen*, Folio Society, London, 1871

Austen-Leigh, W.A., Austen-Leigh, R.A., and Le Faye, Deirdre, *Jane Austen: A Family Record*, The British Library, London, 1989

Birtwistle, Sue, and Conklin, Susie, *The Making of Pride and Prejudice*, Penguin, London, 1996

Bottomer, Phyllis Ferguson, *So Odd a Mixture: Along the Autistic Spectrum in 'Pride and Prejudice'*, Jessica Kingsley Publishers, London, 2007

Boyle, Laura, *Pictures at an Exhibition*, The Jane Austen Centre, www.janeausten.co.uk

Cecil, David, *A Portrait of Jane Austen*, Constable, London, 1978

Chandler, Steve, and Terrence N. Hill, *Two Guys Read Jane Austen*, Robert D. Reed Publishers, Bandon, 2008

Cossy, Valérie, *Jane Austen in Switzerland: A Study of the Early French Translations*, Editions Slatkine, Geneva, 2006

Deresiewicz, William, 'Guest Essay', *Jane Austen's Regency World* magazine, September/October 2011

Donini, Dr Filippo, 'Jane Austen in Italy', *Collected Reports of the Jane Austen Society, 1966–1975*, Wm Dawson & Sons, Folkestone, 1977

Fullerton, Susannah, and Harbers, Anne (eds), *Jane Austen: Antipodean Views*, Wellington Lane Press, Sydney, 2001

Fullerton, Susannah, *Jane Austen and Crime*, Jane Austen Society of Australia, Sydney, 2005

Gay, Penny, *As She Likes It: Shakespeare's Unruly Women*, Routledge, London, 1994

Gilbert, Deirdre, 'From Cover to Cover: Packaging Jane Austen from Egerton to Kindle', *Persuasions On-Line, Vol. 29, No. 1*, Jane Austen Society of North America, 2008

Gilson, David, *A Bibliography of Jane Austen*, Oak Knoll Press, Delaware, 1997

Glancy, Kathleen, 'What Happened Next? Or The Many Husbands of Georgiana Darcy', *Persuasions No. 11*, Jane Austen Society of North America, December 1989

Grey, J. David (ed.), *The Jane Austen Handbook*, Athlone Press, London, 1986

Halperin, John, 'Inside *Pride and Prejudice*', *Persuasions No. 11*, Jane Austen Society of North America, 1989

Hardy, John, *Jane Austen's Heroines*, Routledge & Kegan Paul, London, 1984

Harman, Claire, *Jane's Fame: How Jane Austen Conquered the World*, Text Publishing, Melbourne, 2009

Hassall, Joan, 'On Illustrating Jane Austen's Works', *Collected Reports of the Jane Austen Society 1966–1975*, Wm. Dawson & Sons, Folkestone, 1977

Jenkyns, Richard, *A Fine Brush on Ivory: An Appreciation of Jane Austen*, Oxford University Press, Oxford, 2004

Jones, Hazel, *Jane Austen and Marriage*, Continuum, London, 2009

Kaye-Smith, Sheila, and Stern, G.B., *Talking of Jane Austen*, Wyman & Sons Ltd., London, 1943

—, *More About Jane Austen*, Harper & Brothers, New York, 1949

Kloester, Jennifer, *Georgette Heyer: The Biography of a Bestseller*, William Heinemann, London, 2011

Lane, Maggie, and Selwyn, David (eds), *Jane Austen: A Celebration*, Fyfield Books, Manchester, 2000

Le Faye, Deirdre, *Jane Austen: The World of her Novels*, Frances Lincoln, London, 2002

Macdonald, Gina and Macdonald, Andrew F., *Jane Austen on Screen*, Cambridge University Press, Cambridge, 2003

Mandal, Anthony, and Southam, Brian (eds), *The Reception of Jane Austen in Europe*, Continuum, London, 2007

Martin, Angus, 'Jane and Isabelle: The First French Translation of *Sense and Sensibility*', *Sensibilities No. 22*, Jane Austen Society of Australia, Sydney, 2001

Mazzeno, Lawrence W., *Jane Austen: Two Centuries of Criticism*, Camden House, New York, 2011

Moler, Kenneth, 'Group Voices in Jane Austen's Narration', *Persuasions No. 13*, Jane Austen Society of North America, 1991

Monaghan, David, Hudelet, Ariane, and Wiltshire, John, *The Cinematic Jane Austen: Essays on the Filmic Sensibility of the Novels*, McFarland & Co., Jefferson, North Carolina, 2009

Morris, Ivor, *Mr Collins Considered: Approaches to Jane Austen*, Routledge & Kegan Paul, London, 1987

Nicolson, Nigel, *The World of Jane Austen*, Weidenfeld and Nicolson, London, 1991

Parker, Keiko, 'Illustrating Jane Austen', *Persuasions No. 11*, Jane Austen Society of North America, 1989

Parrill, Sue, *Jane Austen on Film and Television: A Critical Study of the Adaptations*, McFarland & Co., Jefferson, North Carolina, 2002

Parry, Sarah, 'The Pemberley Effect: Austen's Legacy to the Historic House Industry', *Persuasions No. 30*, Jane Austen Society of North America, 2008

Perry, Ruth, 'Sleeping with Mr Collins', *Persuasions No. 22*, Jane Austen Society of North America, 2000

Ram, Atma, 'Jane Austen in India', *Collected Reports of the Jane Austen Society, 1976–1985*, Anthony Rowe Ltd., Chippenham, 1986

Robbins, Ruth M., 'Without the Gift of Tongues', *Collected Reports of the Jane Austen Society, 1966–1975*, Wm. Dawson & Sons, Folkestone, 1977

Sánchez, Mari Carmen Romero, 'A la Señorita Austen: An Overview of Spanish Adaptations', *Persuasions On-Line, Vol. 28, No. 2*, Jane Austen Society of North America, 2008

Smith, Ellen, 'Spanish Translations of *Northanger Abbey*', *Persuasions No. 7*, Jane Austen Society of North America, 1985

Spence, Jon, *Becoming Jane Austen*, Hambledon, London, 2003

Teachman, Debra, *Understanding Pride and Prejudice: A Student Casebook to Issues, Sources, and Historical Documents*, Greenwood Press, Westport, 1997

Tekcan, Rana, 'Jane Austen in Turkey', *Persuasions On-Line, Vol. 28, No. 2*, Jane Austen Society of North America, 2008

Thwaite, Ann, *A.A. Milne: His Life*, Faber & Faber, London, 1990

Tomalin, Claire, *Jane Austen: A Life*, Viking, London, 1997

Troost, Linda, and Greenfield, Sayre (eds), *Jane Austen in Hollywood*, University Press of Kentucky, Lexington, Kentucky, 2001

Tucker, George Holbert, *Jane Austen The Woman*, Robert Hale, London, 1994

Tyler, Natalie, *The Friendly Jane Austen: A Well-Mannered Introduction to a Lady of Sense and Sensibility*, Viking, New York, 1999

Vaughan, Margaret, *Tea with the Bennets of Jane Austen's 'Pride and Prejudice'*, Allison and Alderson Associates, Leyburn, 1996

Vickery, Amanda, '200 Years On: Why Jane Austen Lovers Find New Reasons for their Passion', *The Observer*, 18 December 2011

Whalan, Pamela, 'In Defence of Mrs Bennet', *Sensibilities No. 16*, Jane Austen Society of Australia, June 1998

Williams, Deb, 'Austen Illustrated or Jane Austen had no Phiz', Jane Austen Society of Australia, www.jasa.net.au

TRANSLATIONS OF *PRIDE AND PREJUDICE*

Büszkeség és balítílet, transl. Szenczi Miklós, Könyvmolyképzö Kiadó, Szeged, 2010

Orgoglio e Pregiudizio, transl. Maria Luisa Agosti Castellani, Rizzoli, Milan, 1997

Orgueil et préjugés, transl. V. Leconte and Ch. Pressoir, Librarie Plon, Paris, 1932

Orgullo y prejuicio, www.webitera.com

Stolthet og fordom, transl. Eivind and Elisabeth Hauge, Messel, Oslo, 1997

Stolz und Vorurteil, transl. Helga Schultz, Artemis & Winkler, Munich, 1997

Trots en Vooroordeel, transl. Elke Meiborg, BoekWerk, Groningen, 1996

SEQUELS/CONTINUATIONS/ADAPTATIONS

Adams, Jennifer, *Little Miss Austen: Pride and Prejudice: A BabyLit Board Book*, Gibbs Smith Books, Layton, 2011

Angelini, Sara, *The Trials of the Honourable F. Darcy*, Sourcebooks, Naperville, Illinois, 2009

Arthur, Sarah, *Dating Mrs Darcy. A Smart Girl's Guide to Sensible Romance*, Tyndale House Publishers, Carol Stream, Illinois, 2005

Austen, Jane, and Grahame-Smith, Seth, *Pride and Prejudice and Zombies*, Quirk Books, Philadelphia, 2009

Austen, Jane, and Raphael, Lev, *Pride and Prejudice: The Jewess and the Gentile*, BookNookbit Digital Editions, 2011

Aylmer, Janet, *Darcy's Story*, Harper, New York, 2006

Bader, Ted and Marilyn, *Desire and Duty*, Revive Publishing, Colorado, 1997

Barrett, Julia, *Presumption*, Michael O'Mara Books, London, 1994

Barrington, E., 'The Darcys of Rosings' in *The Ladies*, The Atlantic Monthly Press, 1922

Bebris, Carrie, *Pride and Prescience: or, A Truth Universally Acknowledged*, Tom Doherty Associates, New York, 2004

Beckford, Grania, *Vice and Virtues*, St Martin's Press, New York, 1981

Birchall, Diana, *Mrs Darcy's Dilemma: A Sequel to Jane Austen's Pride and Prejudice*, Sourcebooks, Naperville, Illinois, 2008

Brinton, Sybil G., *Old Friends and New Fancies: An Imaginary Sequel to the Novels of Jane Austen*, Revive Publishing, Lakewood, 1998

Butler, Nancy (adapter), *Pride and Prejudice (Marvel Illustrated)*, Marvel Books, New York, 2009

Cohen, Paula Marantz, *Jane Austen in Boca*, St Martin's Press, New York, 2002

Connelly, Victoria, *A Weekend with Mr Darcy*, Harper Collins, London, 2010

Dawkins, Jane, *Letters from Pemberley: A Continuation of Jane Austen's Pride and*

Prejudice, Chicken Soup Press, New York, 1999

Eckstut, Arielle, and Ashton, Dennis, *Pride and Promiscuity: The Lost Sex Scenes of Jane Austen*, Simon & Schuster, New York, 2001

Fasman, Marjorie, *The Diary of Henry Fitzwilliam Darcy*, New Leaf Press, Los Angeles, 1997

Fenton, Kate, *Lions and Liquorice*, Michael Joseph, London, 1996

Field, Alex, *Mr Darcy*, New Frontier Publishing, Sydney, 2011

Fielding, Helen, *Bridget Jones's Diary*, Macmillan, London, 1996

Ford, Michael Thomas, *Jane Bites Back*, Ballantine Books, New York, 2010

—, *Jane Goes Batty*, Ballantine Books, New York, 2011

—, *Jane Vows Vengeance*, Ballantine Books, New York, 2012

Fowler, Karen Joy, *The Jane Austen Book Club*, G.P. Putnam's Sons, New York, 2004

Gillespie, Jane, *Deborah*, Robert Hale Ltd., London, 1995

Goodman, Selene, *Roses and Thorns: A Poetic Pride and Prejudice*, Chicken Soup Press, New York, 1999

Grange, Amanda, *Mr Darcy Vampyre*, Sourcebooks, Naperville, Illinois, 2009

Hale, Shannon, *Austenland: A Novel*, Bloomsbury USA, New York, 2007

Hannon, Patrice, *Dear Jane Austen: A Heroine's Guide to Life and Love*, Plume, New York, 2007

Henderson, Lauren, *Jane Austen's Guide to Dating*, Hyperion, New York, 2005

Hurt, D.A. Bonavia, *Pemberley Shades*, Allan Wingate, London, 1949

James, P.D., *Death Comes to Pemberley*, Faber & Faber, London, 2011

Jeffers, Regina, *Vampire Darcy's Desire*, Ulysses Press, Berkeley, 2009

Kiely, Tracy, *Murder at Longbourn: A Mystery*, St Martin's Press, New York, 2009

—, *Murder on the Bride's Side: A Mystery*, St Martin's Press, New York, 2010

Lathan, Sharon, *My Dearest Mr Darcy: An Amazing Journey into Love Everlasting (The Darcy Saga)*, Sourcebooks, Naperville, Illinois, 2010

McCullough, Colleen, *The Independence of Miss Mary Bennet*, Simon and Schuster, New York, 2008

Memoir, *Gambles and Gambols*, Shelter Cove, 1983

Morton, Camilla, *A Year in High Heels: The Girl's Guide from Everything from Jane Austen to the A-List*, Hodder and Stoughton, London, 2007

Nathan, Melissa, *Pride, Prejudice and Jasmin Field*, Piatkus, London, 2000

Newark, Elizabeth, *Consequence, or Whatever*

Became of Charlotte Lucas, New Ark Productions, San Francisco, 1999

Odiwe, Jane, *Mr Darcy's Secret*, Sourcebooks, Naperville, Illinois, 2011

—, *Lydia Bennet's Story: A Sequel to Pride and Prejudice*, Sourcebooks, Naperville, Illinois, 2008

Pierson, C. Allyn, *Mr Darcy's Little Sister (Pride and Prejudice Continues)*, Sourcebooks, Naperville, Illinois, 2010

Pinnock, Jonathan, *Mrs Darcy Versus the Aliens*, Proxima, 2011

Potter, Alexandra, *Me and Mr Darcy*, Hodder and Stoughton, London, 2007

Reynolds, Abigail, *Mr Darcy's Obsession (Pride and Prejudice Continues)*, Sourcebooks, Naperville, Illinois, 2010

—, *A Pemberley Medley: Five Pride and Prejudice Variations*, Intertidal Press, Madison, 2002

Rigler, Laurie Viera, *Confessions of a Jane Austen Addict*, Penguin Books, London, 2007

Roberts, Belinda, *Prawn and Prejudice*, Beetleheart Publishing, UK, 2009

Ross, Josephine, *Jane Austen's Guide to Good Manners: Compliments, Charades and Horrible Blunders*, Bloomsbury, New York, 2006

Russell, Anne and Arthur, *The Wedding at Pemberley (A Play in One Act)*, H.F.W. Deane and Sons Ltd , London, 1949

Scott, Jennifer, *After Jane: A Review of Continuations and Completions of Jane Austen's Novels*, privately published, UK, 1998

Slater, Maya, *The Private Diary of Mr Darcy*, W.W. Norton & Co., New York, 2007

Smith, Lori. *A Walk with Jane Austen: A Journey into Adventure, Love and Faith*, Waterbrook Press, Colorado Springs, 2007

Smith, Naomi Royde, *Jane Fairfax*, Macmillan, London, 1940

Szereto, Mitzi, *Pride and Prejudice: Hidden Lusts*, Cleis Press, Berkeley, 2011

Tavner, Gill (retold by), *Pride and Prejudice (Real Reads)*, Skyview Books, UK, 2008

Tennant, Emma. *An Unequal Marriage: Pride and Prejudice Continued*, Sceptre Books, London, 1994

—, *Pemberley A Sequel to Pride and Prejudice*, Hodder and Stoughton, London, 1993

Wallis, Cedric, *The Heiress of Rosings*, Samuel French Ltd., London, 1956

Waters, Sarah (ed.), *Dancing with Mr Darcy*, Honno Welsh Women's Press, Aberystwyth, 2009

Webster, Emma Campbell, *Being Elizabeth Bennet: Create Your Own Jane Austen Adventure*, Atlantic Books, London, 2007

White, T.H., *Darkness at Pemberley*, Victor Gollancz, London, 1932

Wilson, Enid, *Mr Darcy Vibrates: A Collection of Pride and Prejudice-Inspired Steamy Short Stories*, Steamy D Publishing (digital), 2011

Index

Acknowledgments
'She was grateful . . .'

When I was twelve years old we went on a family holiday to Christchurch and it was there that my mother decided to read me and my sister *Pride and Prejudice*. I remember nothing else of that holiday except lying at the end of the double bed, while Mum knitted and read aloud at the same time. She paused often to laugh, which annoyed me – I just wanted her to get on with the story so I could find out what happened to Elizabeth and Darcy. Now I know exactly why and where she laughed. Later she got my youngest sister to read the novel aloud to her, an experience both of them loved, and so a new generation of women was given the incredible joy of knowing *Pride and Prejudice*. My mother died far too young, but the legacy she left me through that reading changed, and enormously enriched, my life. She could have given me no greater gift and I will forever be grateful to her.

Many Jane Austen experts have contributed to this book. I thank most sincerely Marlene Arditto, Carrie Bebris, Michael Giffin, Hazel Jones, Maureen Kelly, Jennifer Kloester, Maggie Lane, Joanna Penglase, Elsa Solender, Pamela Whalan and Ruth Williamson for the quotations they have added to these pages. Dr Oddvar Holmesland also gave invaluable assistance. Every Jane Austen scholar must pay a debt of gratitude to Deirdre Le Faye: her edition of Jane Austen's letters and her biographies and critical works are superb.

Ann Channon and the fabulous staff at the Jane Austen House Museum in Chawton have been of great assistance with illustrations. I am also extremely grateful to Jennifer Weinbrecht and her daughter Amy of Jane Austen Books in the USA for all their kind assistance with pictures and information.

No book can be written without support and understanding from good friends. I am so lucky that many of my dearest friends belong to the Jane Austen Society of Australia and so are happy to discuss *Pride and Prejudice* with me endlessly. I'd like to thank Catherine Barker, Elizabeth Budge, Sarah Burns, Helen Cook, Peter Cox, Margaret Frey, Teresa Grace, Jenny Grebler, Jenny Harkin, Faye Hope-Allan, Christine Humphreys, Amanda Jones, Judith Jacks, Brigitte Lucey, Helen Malcher, Maryanne Moore, Josephine Newman, Merrilee Parker, Joanna Penglase, Chester and Jean Porter, Anthea Scarlett, Kay Schneider, Debbie Williams and Ruth Williamson. Anthea Scarlett spent many hours web-searching *Pride and Prejudice*-related weird and wonderful merchandise and gave constant and warm encouragement; Judith Jacks found examples of the media's use of the novel's famous first sentence; Helen Malcher and Debbie

Williams assisted yet again with illustrations; Amanda Jones generously lent books and answered queries; Christine Humphreys sent encouraging emails or met me for fabulous lunches – my warmest thanks to all these dear friends. Jennifer Kloester has given greatly valued support by phone, and Gabriele Black has probably heard far too much about this book during our walks in the park and has been incredibly encouraging. My French conversation class assisted by proving how hard it is to translate the first sentence of *Pride and Prejudice* into another language – thanks, Irina, Irma, Marie Judy and Yvette. My dearest friend Jon Spence tragically died in 2011, but many ideas in this book are based on conversations we had during our 'Jane Austen lunches'. I miss him so much and will always be grateful for the privilege of knowing him.

I have been lucky to work with Frances Lincoln Publishers. My warm thanks to Andrew Dunn for having had confidence in my idea for this book, to Anne Askwith for being a dream editor and to Nicki Davis and James Nunn for the expert design of the book and the cover.

Unlike Mr Bennet, I have no library to which I can retire. Much of this book was written at the kitchen bench, in the midst of family life. If my mind has sometimes been far away in the world of Jane Austen, I 'hereby beg leave to apologise' to my family. I thank my husband, Ian, and hope that one day he might discover the joy of re-reading *Pride and Prejudice*, my sons Kenneth and Carrick, who have all the joy of a first reading still to come, and my daughter Elinor, who has delighted me by loving that wonderful novel. I don't know what I'd have done without Carrick's computer expertise and 'fix-it' abilities. Like Elizabeth Bennet, I am one of five siblings, but I am luckier than she in that my brothers and sisters are all wonderful, intelligent people who support me and take an interest in what I write. Thanks so much, Nicholas, Marion, Graham and Rachel. And thanks, Dad, for being an infinitely better father than Mr Bennet.

Most of all, I thank Jane Austen herself, for bringing into my life Elizabeth Bennet and Mr Darcy, for making me laugh at her Mr Collins and Sir William Lucas, for showing me that Lady Catherines exist both in fiction and in the real world. I can honestly say of that first reading of *Pride and Prejudice* that 'until [that] moment I never knew myself'. I first encountered the novel in a place Jane Austen had never heard of (indeed, the city of Christchurch did not then exist), but her genius reached me there and has never ceased to give me joy. I have written other books about her writing, but no book has given me as much pleasure to write as this one. Whenever I told anyone I was working on a book about 200 years of *Pride and Prejudice* they smiled – smiled at the own memories of the novel, at the idea of writing about something so delightful (or perhaps Colin Firth in a wet shirt suddenly came to mind?). I hope this book will make all its readers smile. I hope it will send readers back to *Pride and Prejudice* to discover its power and its glory, and to see just why it has provided 200 years' cause for celebration.

Picture Credits

The Publishers would like to thank those listed below for permission to reproduce the illustrations in this book and for supplying photographs. Every care has been taken to trace copyright holders. Any copyright holders we have been unable to reach are invited to contact the publishers so that a full acknowledgment may be given in subsequent editions.